THE TRIBE

BY

GREGORY TOWNES

Black Print Publishing Inc.
4511 Avenue K
Brooklyn, N.Y. 11234

ISBN 0-9748051-3-0

This and many other titles Published by Black Print Publishing Inc. may be purchased for educational, business, sales or promotional use. For information please write: Marketing Department

Black Print Publishing Inc 4511 Avenue K, Brooklyn, N.Y. 11234

Published in 2004

by Black Print Publishing Inc.4511 Avenue K, Brooklyn, NY 11234

DEDICATION

I dedicate this book to four distinct people.

1)   To everyone who died in the bowels of the awful slave ships during the Middle Passage. Your watery graves go unmarked, but not forgotten.

2)   To everyone who made the journey, subjugated themselves to unimaginable hells so that this generation could breathe free. I honor your courage and vision.

3)   To everyone that escaped the talons of tyranny, and fought with incredible valor to reach the magical place called the Promised Land. Your commitment to the future of our race is the very definition of Bravery.

To this and future generations: Honor thy fathers and thy mothers. Remember the sacrifices of the elders. Continue the fight. Keep your eyes on the prize. Complete the circle...

Acknowledgements

You see me, because I am standing on the shoulders of giants.

First and foremost, I would like to thank God, the answer to all prayers. My mother: Clarice Townes, who taught me that prayer changes things. A lesson I'll never forget. My wife: Cinthai Townes, living proof that love truly conquers all. My children: Cintasia, Shalisse, Lord Shatique, and Jasmine- you make me immortal. You are my Stars. My siblings: Dr. Darryl L. Townes: from GED to PhD-one degree at a time. Tonia Townes: the matriarch of the family. Vincent Townes: There's a new Sheriff in town! Erick Townes: the world will soon know your rap skills-just keep at it, baby! Clarice, Junior and Joshua: family is family. My niece: Chanequa Townes, you were my first designated reader!

My grandmother, Louise Copeland: Women like you make the world go 'round. My aunts, Barbara Hayes and Joyce Nurse: You took us in when our mother passed away. I don't know how to thank you enough. My uncle, Rupert Nurse: The only father I've ever known.

Kevin Ahern and Allan Hynd, your turns are coming soon!

Jackie Pratt and Debra Kosek: you kept telling me I'd do it, so I did it!

My publisher, Black Print Publishing: Together we will do great things!

And last but not least for you, Dear Reader. We are going to get to know each other very intimately in a little while. We are going to take a trip together, just you and I into some very dark and mysterious rooms. I will be your guide throughout this. I thank you for coming with me and I ask that you hold on to this book tightly while you read.
It's the only way I can guarantee you a safe return.

PROLOGUE:

∞

Silver Eyes

The woman screamed from the pains of labor. "Push!" the midwives ordered as they held her. She sat up, swimming through a sea of agony. It felt as if a flame of sharp metal had imbedded itself into her spine, while thick groping snakes coiled around her back and hips threatening to squeeze her in two.

"Push! Push, Kayla!" the midwives shouted. The other mothers in the village had told her what to expect when the pains came. There is no ache like it, they said. It is like the beginning and the end of the world meeting!

She took a deep breath and pushed with all she had. Her bottom felt as hot as stones over an open spit when she felt the child slide into place. "He will arrive soon!" the eldest midwife announced. "I see the crown of his head! Push, Kayla! Push strong and hard!"

He will arrive soon! The words echoed through the pain, grounding her. She sucked in as much air as her diminished lungs would hold and prepared for the final push. She prayed to the gods for a son.

"Now, Kayla! Push now!"

She could not see who spoke. The pain had grown so great it consumed her in its wrath. A searing heat spread up and down her back, hips and thighs in alternating pulsing waves. Her muscles felt like frayed rope. She pushed until the veins and cords in her neck flexed in ridged anger. The pain was now an unyoked steer running amok through her bottom, but she was determined not to succumb to it.

"He will arrive soon!" she spat through clenched teeth. The enormous pressure in her rear stretched her to what she swore was an impossible width. Despite the pain, she was comfortable in knowing all she had felt was expected. The heat in her womb symbolized life and movement. The heat was a cleansing, fluid feeling she knew would not linger a moment longer than necessary. The heat-as mean and unforgiving as it felt, was natural.

Then the cold came.

It was the most alien unwelcome sensation. She instinctively stopped pushing. Something was wrong. What was a torrid fire mere seconds ago was now an ice cold numbing pain. Her first thought was that the child had died in her womb, but she could still feel the infant settling into the birth canal. She watched in amazement as her swollen womb rippled and pulsed. The cold spread throughout her body, numbing her back, arms and legs. There was no pain now, just pressure.

A burst of fluid shot out of her and she was embarrassed she could not control her bodily functions at such an important event.

She looked up to apologize to the women surrounding her, trying to convey her fear when she saw she had splattered the midwives with a thick silver broth that clung to them like painted sweat.

She felt a deliriously overpowering urge to laugh as the child slid effortlessly out of her.

Outside the hut, her husband paced nervously back and forth while the Elders chanted songs asking the gods for a strong man-child who would bring joy, honor and prosperity to the village.

When he heard his beloved Kayla scream a dagger of fear pierced his soul. He had lost two wives in the course of three springs to childbirth. She was his favorite and he prayed she and the child would not die.

She screamed again. The undulating sound of terror swiped at him like unsheathed claws, but this time there was the cry of another. The child was born! He rushed to the hut, stopped by the tribal leader.

"When the time is right, my son," the leader said. "When the time is right."

After what seemed an eternity, the midwives came to him.

"Well? Do not stand there gawking, woman! Is it a son? Is my Kayla all right?" he bellowed.

"Your wife is fine," the eldest mid-wife said. "You have a son, but…"

The woman stood silent, unable to bring herself to utter the words.

"What? What is it?" the man asked, overtaken by a fear that stifled his breathing.

"He has the mark! He has the silver eyes!" the mid-wife gasped. The village became quiet as the woman's words sank in.

"Silver Eyes!" someone grumbled.

"The cursed mark!" from another.

The murmurs grew louder and panic spread throughout the village like wildfire.

"No! It cannot be!" the man sank to his knees, weeping inconsolably. "The gods have damned me! Must I now mourn the birth of my son?"

The tribal leader looked down and felt the man's pain. The child could not remain in the village. The gods would show their anger at such a thing.

"The child must leave," he ordered. The midwives nodded and scurried back into the hut. Kayla suckled the infant, forming the bond between mother and baby.

"You must give him to me...the leader demands-"

"No! He is my son! I will not let you!" she hissed and held the child tight. They would have to pry him from her. The tribal leader entered and sat near her, stroking her head gently. As the head of the village he enjoyed many comforts, but he could not shirk this duty.

"Daughter, he must go. Your love for him shall never die, but he must go. His presence will bring death to the village. Give him to me. I shall see that he is taken to the appointed place."

Kayla bit her lip hard. Hot tears scalded her face. "Let me take him."

"As you wish. A group will take you as far as the mountains. After that you will have to find the forbidden jungle on your own."

The village wept as she left with the child. She looked back at her husband. If her son had been born normal she would have been the top woman in his hut. Now she would forever be known as the woman who birthed the Silver Eyes.

Six warriors walked with her for three days.
They camped at the base of the mountain while she
kept going. They would follow her no further.

With her son strapped to her, Kayla headed
deep into the jungle. She took from the men just
enough food and water to last three days. She figured
it would take her a day and a half to reach the
appointed place and a day and a half to return to the
camp. If she did not return within that time, the men
would leave her.

The infant was fast asleep, cradled to her
breast. She maneuvered through the thick foliage with
ease, listening very carefully for wild animals. The
appointed place was set in the center of the jungle
where the gods demanded the marked children be left.

Her son had the mark on his left shoulder. She
noticed it the first time she suckled him.

It was said these children were the cause of
major droughts, mutated crops and strange ailments
that affected many neighboring villages. These evils
ceased the moment the children were driven away.
Soon word spread throughout the region that any child
born with the strange emblem must be taken away.

Kayla stopped to rest. Her breasts were heavy
with milk and she knew the child was ready to feed.
She stared at him as she fed him. If not for his eyes
and that damned mark he was perfect. His lustrous
locks of hair, as thick and as proud as a lion's mane.
His chin, so regal and strong like his father's. There
was a sense of nobility about him, and why not? His
father was brother to the chieftain. Her son would
have one day inherited the mantle of power if not for

his eyes and the cursed mark.

Kayla looked at the baby through tear soaked eyes. It was not easy to leave him. What if the rest of the marked children did not accept him? How would they feed him? These thoughts haunted her as she gently rocked him.

"I must do what the gods have demanded, little one. Drink long and deep, for I fear this is the only milk you shall taste for a good while."

She was torn between her motherly instinct and her duty to her tribe. The mere presence of the Silver Eyes meant death to the village. She would have to sacrifice her first born for the better good.

She traveled until she was exhausted, then pre-pared a fire and lay down to sleep.

Sunlight littered the forest floor in broken beams. The sounds of wild birds cawing overhead woke her. In the distance, she heard a growl and instantly realized the danger. A cackle of hyenas had her surrounded, enticed by the smell of her just-given birth. She grabbed a branch and lit it, brandishing it at the animals, but they would not be deterred. Hunger had them crazed with anticipation and nothing short of death would stop them. There were six of them, the biggest one the leader. She swung the flaming branch hitting him hard across the head. The hyena yelped in pain as red-hot embers blinded him.

The rest sensing opportunity used the moment to attack. One clamped its teeth around her ankle, dragging her down. Another bit her in the crotch, rip-ping her sore womb to shreds.

Despite the incredible pain, Kayla managed to

cover her baby.

The hyenas ate away at her flesh. Her legs and buttocks were now bloody tendrils of meat. One turned her over and saw the infant strapped to her. He motioned toward the infant and the baby screamed.

The hyenas drew back.

They glanced at each other strangely, howling in a mixture of fear and pain. The child shrieked again and the hyenas jumped up and down. They shook their heads wildly and used their paws to rip at their ears. They ran around in chaotic agony. Some bashed their heads against the trees and rubbed their bloody maws raw in the ground.

None dared venture near the child.

Kayla near death watched all of this in a mixture of wonder and horror. Her last thoughts were an odd fusion of joy and sadness.

Her son would survive the jungle.

But would the jungle survive her son?

∞

The children watched the spectacle from the treetops. They heard the child when he first entered the jungle and secretly followed the mother and infant. They didn't know the child was one of them until the hyenas arrived. Slowly they climbed down toward the baby. The eldest approached him first. He leaned over and inspected the mother. She was dead and from the look of her, death was her best option. He unstrapped the infant and picked him up, examining him for the mark.

"He is one of us!" he exclaimed to the rest of

the group.

"Our circle is complete!" the others chanted in unison.

∞

Twelve Years Later…

Captain Luke Bartholomew Pearson had been in Africa for all of a month and could not wait to get back to the Colonies (now known as the United States). The jungle seemed to breathe with a life and pulse all its own. The night carried a terrifying symphony to which bizarre and exotic creatures danced.

His men were bone tired and soul weary after four days of searching for the elusive forbidden jungle. They followed the crude trails and maps drawn by the natives. Some of the tribes were more than willing to work with him in capturing rival tribesmen, while others had to be persuaded with the business end of a rifle.

Slave trade was a dangerous occupation, wrought with hazards and perfidious traps, but it was men like him who made it possible braving the seas and the treacherous jungles to capture the cargo. His ship, the Good Ship Jesus was docked six days away with the rest of his crew.

"Africans are strong," he told his crew, "but so are apes." It was no large feat capturing them. The fact that they carried firearms helped tremendously. Some of the more superstitious tribesmen viewed the rifles as gifts from the fire-gods.

Although this was his twelfth journey to the Dark Continent, he never felt so afraid or so alone, as he did in this jungle. It was unlike anything he had ever experienced before. Many times he wanted to turn back. The rustling of the wind through the foliage veiled the promise of unspeakable evils to anyone foolhardy enough to venture deeper. The trees were so tall their shadows cast the ground into perpetual darkness. There were parts of the jungle that were darker than the blackest night. Not even the torches they lit could provide more than the slightest illumination.

At times they would see eyes glaring malevolently at them out of the dark, but when they flashed their torches in the direction there would be nothing there. The jungle held terrors that shook the bravest among them.

Captain Pearson learned of the strange tribe on his first visit to Africa. One of the captured tribesmen spoke English, courtesy of the missionaries and told him of a band of children with god-like powers. He offered to show where the tribe hid in exchange for his freedom. Unfortunately, the would-be guide died from dysentery before the captain could complete the mission.

There were twelve of them as the story had it and each possessed a unique gift. Soon word spread throughout the civilized world about the tribe and he was commissioned to capture them.

Captain Pearson became obsessed with the idea of darkies with such powers. He could not retire until he fulfilled this one last assignment. The heads of many nations coveted them. Their bounty would be worth an emperor's ransom. Both the French and the Colonies wanted the strange tribe. Even the Spaniards and the Portuguese wanted to bid for them.

There would be no mistaking them. They were all born with the same defining marks-silver colored eyes and a birthmark, a perfect figure eight, also silver.

It took him twelve visits, but he was finally able to piece together enough pertinent facts to lead a team into the forbidden jungle to find them. It would not be easy. The Tribe was supposed to possess talents that staggered the imagination.

He learned their names, their powers, and their fears. He came to know them through the strange tales. There were the males D`ike (DEE-EYE-KEY), K`embe (KEY-EM-BAY), Molo (MOE-LOW), Jomo (JOE-MOE), and Kwame (CRAW-MAY). Then the females, Nicah (NIGH-KA), D`aim (DEE-YAIM), Iyanni (E-YAWN-E), T`keya (TA-KEY-YA), Meeka (MEEK-KA), and S`ianna (SEE-ANNA).

Strange names. Strange children.

But the strangest of them all was the youngest, Malik. As legend had it, he was the leader of the tribe. Malik meant King in their heathen tongue.

The fact that these darkies were only children did not detract from the danger. The capture of this tribe would take extraordinary character and tremendous strength of spirit.

He had to remain vigilant in this godforsaken jungle. One mistake would spell certain death for him and his crew.

Pearson kept looking above him. He swore they were being tracked. There was always movement high in the treetops. Not the swinging of monkeys or

the flutter of birds, but the sentient silent movement
of man.

He could hear the jungle snickering at him; a
cold calculated laugh that would have forced any sane
man to turn back. He mustn't show a moment's weakness. The jungle senses fear. The jungle preys on fear
and self-doubt. There was great disparity in the information he received about the Silver Eyes, but one
thing all of the reports had in common: the jungle was
like a living thing and the Silver Eyes were its heart.

Gwendolyn, his betrothed, made him promise
this would be his last voyage to the Dark Continent.
Pearson swore to her with the booty earned on this
trip he would retire and build them a house far from
the sea. He would beat his sword into a plowshare and
study war no more.

It pained Gwendolyn to learn he had to take
lives, but it was necessary to complete the mission.
Pearson could never tell Gwendolyn all of the
grotesque things he'd seen the natives do, or of the
horrific things he had to do to them. She would never
understand. Africans were savages, totally immoral
and with no soul. They were a damned and desolate
people. Hewers of stone and drawers of water-just like
the Bible said.

They were meant to be slaves.

It was God's holy word.

And now with the knowledge of such a tribe,
such an anomaly against God and nature he felt compelled to capture them-to discover their secrets. He
would not rest until this mission was complete.

Most of the other tribes he had come across

were heathens worshipping snakes, mountains, the rivers and such. Some tribes were a bit more civilized, having had a Christian education thanks to the missionaries. These tribes helped capture the heathens by acting as interpreters or scouts. They would venture into a village and pose as a wandering stranger looking for a night's lodging. Then they would return and report to the captain the number and ages of the male bucks and potential child bearing wenches, along with the positions of any sentries. The captain would use this information to determine the best method to capture the sturdiest of the tribe with the least amount of bloodshed.

In this way, he assured the interpreters, they were performing an invaluable service because they saved lives and helped to fulfill God's holy plan. And as an added bonus when their work was through, they could return with the captain to the New World and live in splendor.

His soldiers sometimes delighted in the lust of the dark flesh taking a few of the female savages for their fancy, but never him. He viewed it as one step from bestiality. What if he caught some dreaded disease and gave it to his Gwendolyn? Although he frowned upon such fraternizing, he did little to discourage it. Some men needed a physical outlet after being away from loved ones so long. He could hardly bring himself to admit it, but he sometimes enjoyed watching his men as they raped the women. Though they were savages, some of the darkie wenches were very well endowed and did possess a certain sultry, bewitching demeanor. He could plainly see why a man of lesser rank and control could submit to such temptations. A few times he came upon a darkie so alluring, he himself was enticed to lie with her. He resisted such petty carnal wants of course, opting to have the darkies bathe him-slowly.

One of his men tried to take a male once and the captain immediately had both of them shot, then drawn and quartered in front of the rest of the men. Discipline was mandatory at all times. Without it anarchy would reign and they would be no better than the darkies. The Bible dictated the penalty was death for such deviant and abominable behavior.

The wind shrieked through the trees, causing a high-pitched wail that sounded like a medley of the damned. Gossamer vapors rose and caressed the soldiers with its silver and ebon touch. The rustling of the leaves had a strange, melodic rhythm that was much too organized to be coincidental.

The earth was too soft beneath his feet. The sod was like quicksand. This slowed him down considerably, but he and his men did not sink. Somehow, he knew the Silver Eyes were causing all of this. What manner of darkie-or man for that matter could control the ground?

The ground vanished in a shroud of silvery haze. The darkness greedily devoured the light of their torches. The captain put the maps away; they would serve no use in this unholy blackness.

They had arrived in the heart of the jungle.

More eyes blinked in and out of the dark. No matter how swiftly he swung his torch, the eyes would disappear. The men felt a cold breath blow past them, as silent and as invisible as the dark.

"They have no bodies!" his first mate, Mr. Briggs muttered in a clump of fear. "The eyes are floating in space! Let us abandon this quest, Captain! We cannot capture them! They are not human! They are like ghosts and this place is hell!"

"Quiet, fool!" the captain reprimanded. "Be sure to keep the moon to the east of us and gird yourself like a man! They are human enough, Mr. Briggs...they are human enough."

Were they?

Pearson held the crucifix Gwendolyn had given him and kissed it, mumbling The Lord's Prayer. Mr. Briggs merely nodded and motioned the others to continue. Though the foliage was so thick the sky was blocked, every few hundred feet or so they could make out the slimmest rays of moonlight. By Briggs' best estimation they were to the east of the moon, though he hardly knew why that was important. This mission seemed simple at first, but now he wished to Christ he was in a tavern with a few pints under his belt. Although Briggs was terrified, he wouldn't show it. He was Pearson's enforcer, ensuring the men maintained discipline at all times. Disobedience to one's superior was mutiny. And the penalty for mutiny was death by the plank if at sea, or by the pistol if on land.

∞

Malik was the first to notice the strangers had entered the jungle. He counted about three dozen of them. He looked on in amusement at this strange tribe with skin like milk and hair the color of sand. They carried strange spears with openings in the tips instead of sharp ends.

He watched them from the treetops, easily keeping pace with them. He wondered what the odd looking tribe wanted in his jungle. When he had his fill of watching the strange creatures, he left to inform the rest of his tribe about the interlopers.

Nicah and D`ike tracked the group into the heart of the jungle. Malik enjoyed the sport of hunting. There was something about this group of foreigners that worried S`ianna. Iyanni was terrified of the white skinned strangers, but Malik assured them this group was no different from any other wayfarers who trespassed into their realm.

T`keya gracefully skipped from branch to branch, circling the group. She felt as at home in the tops of trees as most people felt on the ground. It was an exhilarating feeling living so close to the sky. The jungle was theirs and they would teach all intruders the price of admission.

"T`keya!" Molo whispered, "Be careful! That branch is not sturdy!" T`keya felt the branch threaten to give way beneath her feet. She flipped and glided through the air with silent ease, landing safely on a neighboring branch.

"Have a care, my love! You will alert our guests before we are ready for them!" T`keya said, smiling gently. Just then, there was a rumble of thunder. The Tribe looked to the sky, but there were no clouds, no evidence of a storm coming. T`keya felt herself slip off the branch. There was no pain, only a tremendous punch in her stomach that forced her back. She fell silently, her arms thrashing and flailing.

"T`keya!" Molo screamed, leaping to catch her. He saw the look in her eyes, a mixture of disbelief and outrage. There was a puff of smoke from below. That's where the thunder came from, he thought as he tried to match her speed. Her abdomen was a red open flower of bloody tissue. He gasped when she hit the ground with a dull thud.

Malik silently motioned everyone down. He saw one of the men below point the spear-like object at T`keya and the smoke that came out sounded like thunder. They were all on the jungle floor now, looking eye to eye with the men who had tried to take the life of one of their own.

"Hold your fire!" Captain Pearson ordered. The men stood in shock looking at the strange group. Their eyes glowed in the twinkling light. Their skin was as black as onyx with the luster of marble. The captain quickly counted all twelve, marveling at the physique of the children. The oldest male was barely in the full bloom of manhood, yet his sinews were as thick as logs. The girls were beautiful-their features as soft as the raven-colored tresses that cloaked their breasts. He would've never thought darkie slatterns could be so comely-yet so strong looking.

They are magnificent, the captain thought to himself. Superb!

They fell from the sky like rain, gliding silently across the branches and foliage. They each seemed to land in a pre-arranged spot creating a V around the wounded girl. Captain Pearson searched the Tribe for Malik and found him at the apex of the formation.

Their eyes met briefly and the captain knew then why Malik was called king. Scarcely on the fringe of adolescence, the boy radiated with authority. He stood from the captain's guess about six feet tall-clearly the shortest male of the group, but his diminutive stature in no way belittled his worth.

Malik was the leader.

The legends are true! They are real!

Although he had heard in great detail what to expect, his mind was momentarily overwhelmed at the sheer beauty of the Tribe. He had seen many strange and exotic things in Africa-from beast to bark, but he never expected anything like this.

"Don't look in their eyes! No one fires unless I give the order! Cover yourselves well! Don't let any of them touch your skin!" Pearson shouted. He could see the fear in his men's eyes. They would sooner shoot this strange lot and be done with it. Still, they slowly lowered their weapons and covered themselves with the padding they brought.

The Tribe surrounded T`keya. Malik gave the order to attack. D`ike ran at Captain Pearson with the speed and strength of a rhinoceros. The rest of the Tribe reacted with the precision and discipline of a well-trained military unit. Captain Pearson readied himself. This was the moment in which he would win, or lose it all.

And as the sun rose, the jungle screamed, welcoming the new day.

CHAPTER I:

∞

THE DEAD KNOW...

It was hot, that much no one could argue. Hot, like an oven on Thanksgiving. Like steamy sidewalks and no shade. Hot, like the basement of hell.

Heat waves in the inner city were known to be notoriously brutal and this one was proving to be the worst. The National Weather Service issued a heat advisory for all residents in the five boroughs of New York City. Those who did not have the luxury of air conditioners were warned to avoid alcohol, strenuous work, and most of all the sun. That life-giving orb of light and heat seemed to be everyone's enemy now.

Two days ago, the temperature shot up from fifty-five to over one hundred and six-degrees Fahrenheit. Con-Edison did its best to supply the extra power needed, but everyone was worried about another full-blown blackout.

I didn't mind avoiding the strenuous work part. It was too hot to do anything that resembled work and I've never been much of a sun worshipper, but I grew up in Brooklyn. Cold beer went with the heat like fireworks went with the Fourth of July. Still, seeing so many people being carried into the emergency room from heat exhaustion on the Eyewitness News Report, I decided to take it easy.

Heat waves in New York City weren't uncommon, but it was only March and no matter how logically the weatherman explained it, it just didn't seem natural. They reported over seventy deaths from the heat in the past forty-eight hours and now inhaling the fiery fumes I was convinced that hell held no chamber as hot as downtown Brooklyn. The streets became wavy from the heat. In some places the asphalt totally gave way from the weight of traffic and the heat expanding it.

I promised my eight-year-old daughter, Star I would take her to get the new FUBU sneakers today. It was her reward for scoring a ninth grade reading level and now I could've kicked myself for not picking a cooler day to go shopping.

Even though Sharon, Star's mother and I were separated, I prided myself on being there for my daughter. No one-especially those bloodsucking bastards at child support would be able to say I neglected my fatherly duties. I hired a lawyer to ensure the money I gave Sharon was going to Star's upkeep and purchased all of her clothes, keeping receipts in case I was ever audited.

Financially I can't complain. I'd just received a hefty raise from my company. I'm a Credit Risk Analyst, fancy title meaning I decide the likelihood of companies paying their bills on time. It's boring work, but at $85,000 a year, I'm not complaining.

The air conditioning broke down on the bus. The driver said we could get off and wait on the next

one or just tough it out. Some peo<del>ple</del>
and ranting. I decided to stay on. <del>The</del>
was going to stand outside waiting
was just too hot.

Two teenage kids sitting i<del>n front of</del>
me started talking loud. I winced at the language.
There were old people and little children on the bus
and these two had no regard for censoring themselves.

"Yo, son! Dat's my word, son! I buss dat
nigga's ass, son! Dat nigga waz trynta fuck wit my
girl, son!" one shouted to the other. I tried my best to
ignore the conversation wishing I had a pair of head-
phones as a distraction.

The bus driver, a huge middle-aged white
man, snickered and mumbled something under his
breath. I knew the two kids had no idea how ignorant
they sounded.

Finally we got off the sweltering bus. My
clothes stuck to me like a slimy second skin.
Everyone looked as if they were about to either collapse or go crazy from the heat. A group of scantily
clad girls were all wearing halter-tops, low-rider
daisy-dukes with the same colored thong. The shorts
were so tight you could literally see the outline of
their private parts.

Across the street, I saw a tall man dressed in
what looked like a suit made of sackcloth with a sandwich board around his neck. This had to be the blackest man I had ever seen. His skin was coal-black.
Black as a starless sky. His hair was matted to his
scalp and sweat dripped off his face like a faucet. I
looked at him and wondered how anyone could stand

heat dressed like that. I thought the man was azy, but he didn't look it. In fact he looked quite sane-eccentric and a little odd, but quite sane. He reminded me of the man from that old movie, The Invasion of the Body Snatchers. The one who knew aliens had invaded us, but had a hard time convincing the world of the truth. The sandwich board read:

THE DEAD KNOW WHAT THE LIVING ARE DOING!

The man steadily screamed words of doom trying to convince anyone who passed that the end was coming. Someone yelled that Jesus might come back in the winter, because it was too hot now for even the Lord to appear. This made several people chuckle and then one of the kids from the bus threw a rock at the sandwich board man and called him a nut. He ignored the rock. His eyes followed us like early travelers followed the North Star.

He looked at me as if he knew me. There was a connection for a moment-the eye contact yielded an invisible bond. I felt that not only was the man sane, but he was probably well-educated.

"Let's hurry to the mall! I'm dying out here!" Star said, trying to fan as much air as possible in front of her face. The bus pulled away from its stop letting out black, hot exhaust. The driver shot Star a quick glance and winked at her. There was something about his smirk I found unsettling. I made a mental note to report him to the transit authority.

The fumes from the bus made me lightheaded. I grabbed Star's hand and pulled her toward the mall. "We'll be in the cold in a few minutes! Just think of all that ice-cold air blowing on you! You'll get goose bumps!" I said, trying to imagine it myself.

The streets were unusually crowded. I figured everyone had the same idea-bum rush the malls and stores where it was cool. I managed to maneuver around a lot of people without having to slow down. There was an obese woman dripping globs of sweat mixed with make-up and heavy perfume blocking my path. She looked to be in her late sixties, dressed in an African robe with entirely too much jewelry on. She looked like she was about to faint.

"Miss? Are you okay?" I asked. We were jammed so close together that if the big woman fell she would have crushed us both.

"She looks sick, Daddy! Call a doctor!" Star exclaimed and she was right. The woman was disoriented, stepping as if she were drunk. She reached out, her arms flailing in a semiconscious effort to grab anything to keep her up. I managed to catch her. The sweat off her body made her slippery. Another man came over and soon there was a crowd around the fat woman in my thin arms.

"Give her room! Somebody call an ambulance!" I said. I had the presence of mind to keep Star close to me. Good Samaritan or no-this was still Brooklyn.

The woman's eyes fluttered wildly. Star reached down to help her. It was innocent enough, but I instinctively reached to pull her away. The woman grabbed Star's arm and pulled her desperately close to her bosom. As if Star was her child, and she was trying to protect her from me.

"Hey, lady let her go! That's my kid!" I yelled, gently but firmly prying the woman's arms from around Star's back. The sunlight glistened off the jewels on the old lady's hands and the woman whispered something to Star. Something that changed her expression in an instant from a child's innocent smile to the hard stare that only comes with the pain of adulthood. Star's eyes narrowed to two sharp balls of steel. A chill went through me seeing her like that. I snatched Star away from the woman and the moment I did her expression softened back to normal.

"Star, are you okay? Did she scratch you or something?" I asked, inspecting her arms. The old woman was probably having some sort of seizure.

"I'm okay, Daddy! She needs a doctor!"

The crowd moved back when the EMS workers arrived. People gave them just enough room to get to the woman, but stayed close enough to see what was happening.

"What happened?" the paramedic asked.

"This nigga's grandma got shot!" the same kid from the bus yelled. This caused more people to gather and everyone gawked at me. I shook my head in disgust. Was it some kind of perverse nature that people always had to slow down to stare at car wrecks and accidents?

By now hot dog vendors had pushed their carts toward the throng and ice cream trucks made U-turns to own the street. I thought of how each would go back and tell their version of what happened. Exaggerating how the heat had people dropping like flies all around them, or how a gang of thugs just opened fire downtown and killed an old lady. One or two would even claim they saw the gunmen-

This nigga's grandma got shot, and guess who did it! Little Raheim from Bushwick! I saw the whole shit! He blasted her back out wit' the sawed off!

The paramedic chuckled and motioned his partner to bring the gurney.

"Do you know this woman?" he asked me.

"No. I saw her fall. I was walking-"

He didn't stop to listen. They had the woman on the gurney and were pushing her toward the ambulance. An oxygen mask was placed over her mouth and nose and the man lifted her head to place the elastic strap around the back of her neck.

"Looks like another heat stroke, Jerry," one paramedic said to the other. I got a real good look at the woman's jewels as they hoisted her up through the ambulance doors. They couldn't be real, I thought. They're too large. No one wears jewelry like that but drug dealers. I figured it was more than likely costume jewelry.

I saw the man in the sandwich board behind the crowd across the street, mouthing something. His eyes pierced the crowd and focused only on me. I turned my attention back to Star. All I needed was for her to go back and tell Sharon about this. Any excuse to wreck my visitation rights.

I could just see her and her slimy, shark shyster lawyer telling the judge I exposed my daughter to dangerous influences.

Sharon and I had been separated for eight months and with the exception of not being able to see Star everyday, it has been the happiest eight months of my life.

"C'mon, Star! Let's get those sneakers and get home. The game'll be on in a little while," I said, trying to take my mind off what just happened. The crowd slowly dispersed after watching the ambulance drive off. I took Star into Lil' Sneaks, a store that specialized in children's sneakers.

There were two men in the store, one in front of the sneaker racks and the other behind the counter. The man in front of the sneakers was a Rastafarian with dreadlocks that hung down to his waist. The man behind the counter was a gray and balding white man. He was reading a magazine and looked just as bored as it was hot. I pushed the door open and felt the welcome blast of the air conditioner hit me.

"Thank God!" I mumbled, wiping sweat off Star's brow.

"Wha' 'appun, mon?" the Rasta asked, staring out the window. He was a fierce looking man, six feet five and at least two hundred and eighty pounds rock solid. He could probably bench press a Cadillac, but he had very kind eyes-eyes that displayed a gentleness that belied his physical stature.

"Old lady got sick!" Star reported, fanning her face and smiling. I saw then that she had seen the same thing in this man's eyes I had. I say this, because after the bus driver's weird wink, the sandwich board man's strange stare and then seeing the old fat lady pass out and bear hug Star, I was a bit spooked and kind eyes were just what I needed to see.

"The heat. An old lady passed out from the

heat," I replied. I picked up a display of the sneaker style Star wanted and held it out to the store clerk. "You got this in a size three?" I hoped he wouldn't ask any more questions about the old lady. The more it came up the more I knew Star would remember it, and it would be the only thing she would be able to talk about for a long time.

"Yeah, mon; be right back!" The Rasta turned and disappeared behind a curtain. The sneaker store was small, but well stocked and very clean. The sandwich board man followed us to the store pressing his face against the window, trying to get my attention again.

"What the hell does that nut want?" I mumbled a little louder than intended. The balding cashier came from behind the counter.

"Another a those bastards back again? Dexter! Dexter, get up here! We got company!" He pulled a two-by-four from behind the counter. My first reaction was to grab Star. Dexter tore out of the stockroom with a shoebox in one hand and a lead pipe in the other. He rushed past me with such speed that if Dexter was coming for me, I wouldn't have had much time to do anything but get hit and judging from the size of Dexter's arms-fall down very quickly.

Dexter ripped out the store with the look of a madman. "Yo! Whut me tell you, mon? Me done tole you bums don't fuck round dis' bumbaclot store! Me no fuck wit' you bums no more, mon! Me done talk!"

The heavy glass door closed before I could hear what the sandwich board man said. Dexter swung the pipe at him, close enough to let him know

26

he meant business, but far enough to give the man a chance to retreat. The sandwich board man stared at him coldly without flinching from the swing and then turned and walked away. Whatever prophecies of doom he wanted to preach at Lil' Sneaks would have to wait.

"Dat mon mad! 'im come here wit' dat madness!" Dexter said, giving the bald man the pipe. He stretched the word mad, so that it came out maaad. The bald man went back to his magazine. The incident wore off him as quickly as it grew.

"Me sorry to act vex in front of you little girl, mon! Let me try de sneaker on 'er, me gwan get 'im to give you good price! Irie?" Dexter said.

"Irie," I said, smiling uneasily. This was supposed to be a simple trip to reward my daughter for doing so well in school and now my nerves were shattered. I couldn't wait to get to the safety and comfort of home.

Star would undoubtedly blab all of this to her mother. No amount of bribery would buy her silence. Not even McDonald's and Baskin Robbins together would keep this a secret. She sat on the bench and Dexter pulled the sneakers out of the box. They were the same style I had asked for, but they were silver.

"I didn't know they came in this color," I said looking at the sneakers. The color was so polished and glossy I thought the material was satin instead of leather.

"Yeah, mon! Dey makes evy-ting silver now. Makes it look like dey future!" Dexter tried one of them on her. "Walk for me, darlin'. Me need know 'ow dem fit."

"They feel good. What was that man saying to you? Why you wanted to hurt him?" Star asked, walking around in the sneaker. Her eyes were pinned to the outside glass, looking for the sandwich board man.

"Me no 'urt no mon, me just scare 'em way from 'ere. 'Em cause trouble cause em mad."

"Mad at who?" Star imitated Dexter's accent, not convinced with his answer. I shushed her-looking at Dexter with eyes that read, never get into it with an eight-year-old. You can't win!

"You such a smart child. You do good in school?" Dexter asked her.

"I got a ninth grade reading level! That's why I'm getting the new FUBU sneakers! I'm the smartest in my class and my daddy is sending me to a private school next year! I'm going to own my own company one day!"

"Lord, why did you get her started?" I blushed. Star was bright and very talkative and when she got a roll going, she could roll for days. It was a gift-a combination of her mother and me. She had my brains and Sharon's outgoing attitude.

"Mon! She bright, mon! Brain-box dis one! Hey, wha' you name, mon?" He extended his hand. There was a smell of incense pouring off the man that I oddly equated with a smell of safeness.

"David," I said shaking his hand. "David Peters."

"Me once know a Peters from Trinidad, mon. You from de islands?"

"No," I smiled. "I'm from Brooklyn."

"Oh! A Yankee, heh? Well no matter, me brother! De boat made many stops! Me name Dexter, mon. Me gwan make sure you get a good price!" He turned and walked over to the counter.

"Mon! You hear dis kid, mon?" Dexter motioned to the cashier, who briefly lifted his head and smiled. Having done that, he promptly went back to his magazine.

Dexter winked at me and put the box on the counter. "Look, mon; dis me goddaughter, she got forty dollar 'ear? Let 'er get dis for me. Me make it up on de next customer!"

"Fifty," the cashier mumbled without looking up.

"Forty-five. No tax," Dexter answered back, as if rehearsed.

The cashier grunted, huffed, shuffled from foot to foot and finally relented. I fished in my pocket for the money. I had separated the bills by denomination and pocket. My left front held twenties; right front held the fifties. I peeled one fifty off without taking all the bills out of my pocket.

"You wan' wear 'em 'ome, little pumpkin?" Dexter asked Star.

"No! They'll get dirty. Too hot out- I'll wear them later," Star replied, taking the bag off the counter. I pushed the door open and the heat entered like a furnace. Hot, thick sticky air rushed in.

"Come on, Star. Let me get you home. We're going to catch a cab and it better be air conditioned!" The heat seemed even more stifling than when we stepped off the bus. In the distance I heard sirens blaring, more ambulances no doubt. The heat would probably kill more people this year than bullets.

I stood on the corner of Fulton and hailed a cab. Yellow cabs are a rarity in Brooklyn, so that meant a gypsy cab. Usually it was a guy just out trying to make a couple of extra bucks with no insurance, but in this sweltering sauna I would have settled for the back of a goat if its ass came with a fan.

"Taxi!" I screamed, with my arm extended as if bidding on something at an auction. A Lincoln town car turned the corner with a Livery sign in the windshield. The car pulled over almost instantly, the driver no doubt seeing me with Star. These are the rides they look for-the ninety-nine percent safe rides: the families, or someone traveling with a small child.

Odds are they won't get robbed.

The driver was a young East Indian man with armpits that screamed funky. He looked at me and smiled, then he pressed a button that unlocked the back door.

"Yo, how much to Nostrand and Vernon?" I asked. Star climbed into the back seat.

"How much you usually pay?" the driver asked. His accent was sing-songy.

"Eight dollars," I said flatly. I usually paid ten.

"Give me nine."

"Yeah, okay. Just keep the AC up!"

The car was luxuriously cool. The air conditioner had the interior nice and frosty, even cooler than the shoe store. The driver cut on the radio and a rap song blared out. Star sung along with the words. I thought some of them were a bit too strong for an eight-year old, but after all the day's events I was too exhausted to argue. I sat back, feeling the cool touch of the Corinthian leather surrounding me. Star was busy trying to snap her fingers-she hadn't quite gotten the hang of it yet-and swaying to the beat. We were stuck in traffic, but I didn't mind. As soon as I dropped Star off I would go home, shower, watch the game and take one hell of a nap.

My eyelids became heavy. I started dozing off and soon the beat became too far away to hear. I was snoring lightly and enjoying the break from the heat when the screech of the car's brakes being mashed threw me forward, snapping me awake. Star flew out of her seat. I barely grabbed her in time to keep her from being thrown over the front seat. The impact was so sudden and fierce she would have probably been thrown through the windshield.

"What the fu-" was all I managed to scream.

"That damned guy came out of nowhere! He ran right into me!" the driver screamed. "Are you guys okay?" He looked back to check on us, just as he exited the cab.

Star was okay. A little shook up, but no worse for the wear. I kissed her and got out of the car to see, thinking it was true. People have to slow down to see car wrecks and accidents. "You stay here! Let daddy see what happened!"

Again I found myself in the midst of a grow-ing crowd of people with awed and ghastly looks on their faces. I fought through them to get to the front of the car. I looked back every few seconds to make sure Star was still in the back seat. I saw the glare of horror and shame in the driver's face. I looked down at the figure in front of the car. I understood why.

"The man with the sandwich board!" I gasped.

His right arm was broke at the elbow, held together by a sliver of skin. His chest was so crushed it almost looked flat. His face was a contorted blood soaked mask of pain. Every breath was an obvious prayer for death. His sandwich board was shattered, the message soaked in blood. The sackcloth was torn to shreds, as if a wild animal had attacked him. It was a miracle he was still alive.

"Somebody call an ambulance! Hurry!" I screamed. The driver had his cell phone to his ear. "I just saw this guy on Fulton!" I blurted to the driver. Seeing the old lady was one thing, but this guy was something out of the old horror movie, Faces of Death. "I had to help an old lady that passed out from the heat, the paramedics-"

Just then, the man said something barely audible-slightly above a whisper. But from the look on his face I figured it took all of his strength to say it. I bent over to hear him, it was the man's eyes you see-his eyes didn't reflect the pain and obvious horror of the moment. His eyes looked more like a man told his prison sentence was up. Later I would think this was a stupid thing to do, leaning over that close to him and all. The man was bleeding badly and could very well have had AIDS or any other disease. But after seeing this man three times in the last hour, two of which he was trying to tell me something, my curiosity was a bit more than piqued.

"They were not paramedics," the man whispered and then his eyes closed. I stood as goose pimples danced up my spine. I suddenly wanted to get far away from downtown Brooklyn. Things were just a little too crazy today.

I went to the back seat to retrieve Star, anxious to get home to a cold beer and the game. The crowd covered the car like ants on sugar. I had to force my way to her. I was really getting worried now.

"C'mon, Star! We're getting out of here!"

I picked her up, trying to shield her from the mangled pile of flesh that used to be the sandwich board man, but she saw anyway. "Eeeel, Daddy-that's the same man the shoe guy was going to beat up! Did he kill him?"

"No, precious. The car hit the man. He ran in the street. Don't look."

I maneuvered through the crowd jaywalking across the four-lane street, trying to catch another cab. "Taxi!" I screamed. My throat was raw from the dust and heat. Another Livery signed car pulled over and I poured Star into the back seat. This one wasn't air conditioned, but I didn't complain. I gave the driver the address and didn't even bother to haggle over the price. The strange man's words kept playing repeatedly in my mind.

They were not paramedics...

I thought about the way he said it. His diction was perfect, educated. Not the way you would expect a derelict to sound. Was that the message he kept trying to give me? Was that what the man was screaming from across the street when he was waving his arms trying to get my attention? Was that what he was mouthing when Dexter threatened to brain him with a lead pipe?

They were not paramedics...

There was something else about the man-his body odor. He didn't have one. The cab driver smelled like the reason Right Guard was invented and I had more than expected when I bent down for the man to reek of the dry stink-that pungent sour smell that is synonymous with bums, but no such smell came off the man. No smell came off him at all.

Even in this heat.

"Daddy, you all right?" Star asked. The look on my face must have given away my thoughts.

"Yeah, baby. Daddy's just tired. The heat. Hey! Do you like your new sneakers?"

"Yes. I'll be the only girl in my class with the silver ones!"

"That's not what's important, baby. You can't worry about what other people have. You just worry about what you have. Okay?"

"Okay, Daddy. Thank you for the sneakers."

"You're very welcome, precious. Give daddy a kiss."

She pecked my cheek and I put my arm around her. Never too hot to hold my baby. Never going to be that hot.

"Did you know the man and the lady, Daddy?"

"No. I didn't know them, but I feel bad for them...both of them. Let's not tell mommy about this, okay? She'll just get all upset and start yelling."

"But it wasn't your fault! You didn't do any-thing!"

"I know that, and you know that, but your mother won't see it that way."

"Okay, I won't say anything. Do you think they went to heaven, Daddy?"

"I...I don't know. I don't know what kind of people they were. I didn't know them. Did that woman hurt you when she grabbed you?"

"No, Daddy. She said something weird though."

"What did she say?" My stomach churned just remembering the look on Star's face.

"She said the dead know what the living are doing. She must've read the message off that man's board. Right, Daddy?"

"Yes, baby. Let's not think about it, okay?"

The car pulled in front of the brownstone Star called home. Her mother was out in the yard, along with her Aunt Tara and grandmother. They were drinking beer and playing cards on a fold out table. It didn't look right for ladies to be out with forty ounce bottles like that, but I guess it was just too hot to be inside.

"Hi, Mommy!" Star yelled, running to the house. I chuckled. The way she ran to her mother you'd think that I had her for a few years instead of a few hours. I paid the cab driver and turned to hear the usual inane babble from my almost-could've-been-never will be- mother-in-law.

"What's up," I said, trying not to look at any-one directly.

"Hey, David! How's things going?" Tara answered. Tara was Sharon's older sister.

"Just trying to stay cool in this heat."

"Tell me about it! You want something to drink?"

"Yeah, but you know I don't drink malt liquor."

"Neither do I! I was referring to a glass of lemonade!" She held up her glass to show me she wasn't sharing the forty on the card table.

"I'm sorry!" I was about to take Tara up on her offer when Sharon quickly interrupted. "Listen," she said, taking a long drag off a cigarette letting it dangle from her mouth as she shuffled a deck of cards. "I'm going to a party tonight, so if you want to keep Star for the rest of the weekend it's okay."

Sharon cut her eyes at Tara, who lowered her gaze back to the cards. If I wanted something to drink I'd have to buy it, or wait till I got home. She did that out of spite. It was obvious I was thirsty.

She didn't even ask to see the sneakers I bought Star.

I struggled to hold my tongue. I could feel my blood boiling and not just from the heat. Sharon knew how to press my buttons, get me riled up to the point where I would say something I knew I would later regret. The nation had gotten tough on domestic violence and it was just too hot to deal with her calling the cops. The last thing I needed was to be sitting up in Central Booking in this heat.

This was typical Sharon-I'm going to a party tonight! No consideration for my feelings or for Star's feelings. She would shuffle Star off to anybody if there was a party and every party was the party. The one she couldn't miss, the one that warranted a new outfit and shoes.

"Pick her up whenever you're ready." I fought to check my temper. "What if I wanted to go to a party, you couldn't give me no more notice than this?" that slipped out. I didn't mean to say it, but I did and once it was out, it was out.

"Look!" she shrieked, stubbing out her cigarette. "If you don't want to keep her then say so. Don't come over here with the bullshit 'cause it's hot but it can be a helluva lot hotter!" She jumped up from the table with her hands on her hips, ready to whup some ass, as she was known to put it.

Bitch! I thought, but this time I didn't say it. I just didn't have the energy to deal with her after everything that occurred. Besides, Star did not need to see us arguing.

"Let's go, Star!" I grabbed her hand a lot rougher than I meant to, pulling her out of the yard. I swallowed hard, trying my best to ignore Sharon. This type of behavior was an everyday thing with her. It was one of the main reasons we broke up. Sharon acted as if she always had something to prove to everyone. She had a natural chip on her shoulder. She swore she could whip everyone although she was all of a hundred and ten pounds soaking wet with a brick in her hand.

She was the biggest pain in my ass since hemorrhoids.

"Ain't you gonna get her clothes?" Sharon's mother asked snottily. I could truly say this woman won the first runner-up award as the biggest pain in my ass. I could see why Sharon turned out the way she did. Her mother was one of those backward women who could never keep a man of her own, but could tell everyone else how to keep theirs.

"Why? Most of them are at my house already," I replied, making sure my voice dripped with sarcasm. I turned my back and didn't bother to turn around. Fuck them, I thought. Star would never grow up like them.

I would die first.

"Don't call yourself dissin' my mother either! I'll whip your ass, David!" Sharon barked, threatening to run out of her yard. Her sister and mother held her back. They knew their roles well in this little melodrama. Hell, we had played this little scenario out before: Sharon screaming at the top of her lungs about how bad she would whip me and me walking away to the snickers and laughs of the neighbors.

I continued up the block, ignoring Sharon's taunts and raves. I didn't want Star to see me argue with her mother, but I didn't want her growing up thinking it was okay to jump in a man's face either.

"Why Mommy so mean to you, Daddy?" Star asked, hurt. I knew it was hard on her not seeing us together, but she seemed to have an understanding-a grownup perspective on things.

Because my dear precious, Star, I wanted to say so badly. Your mother is a loud mouth, no good, slutty bitch!

"It's just her way that's all. Sometimes she wants to show off, but that's not right and I don't ever want to see you behave like that...okay?" is what I did say and a sense of pride filled me. Just for acting like I had home training. Just for keeping my cool in the heat. I was better than they were, and so was Star.

"You won't, Daddy. I'm going to make you very proud of me."

"I'm already very proud of you. You're the best thing in my life. Don't ever forget that. Now let's get to my house where it's nice and cool."

"Daddy?"

"Yes, Star."

"I'm glad I'm staying with you tonight. Aunt Tara had me play a game I didn't like."

"What kind of game?" I asked nonchalantly. I figured Tara had probably tried to put make-up on her, or something like that.

"Just a game. I just didn't like it."

I didn't press it further. My main concern was to get out of the heat. I figured if it were something important, Star would have told me. She knew she could always come to me. She could come and tell me anything.

Star is my only real family. My parents were killed in a fire when I was an infant. I have no other known relatives other than a foster sister named Gina. I grew up in different foster homes with different foster children. Gina is the only one I stayed in contact with. The rest are either dead, in jail or on drugs.

As soon as I opened the door the phone rang. It was Gina.

"Hey, girl! How is it?"

"I'm okay. I just called to check up on you. You didn't melt from the heat did you?"

"Damned near! I got Star with me now. She's gonna stay the night. Sharon the wicked witch has a party to go to."

"Must be a full moon out tonight. Witches always gather at the full moon," she quipped. She didn't care much for Sharon-never did.

"Yeah! The bitches of Bushwick must be having their annual Eye-of-Newt award ceremony!" I joked. I turned and saw Star listening. She frowned about the way I spoke about her mother. I mouthed the words, I'm sorry and she gave me a weak smile.

"I gotta go, Gina. Star overheard me. I had a really rough day with her today. I don't know how you women love shopping! For me it was like a nightmare and all I got was one pair of sneakers!"

"Well, I'll leave you while you're in Daddy mode. Just called to say hi. I...I dreamt about you."

"Hope I had money and a few fine women in your dream!"

"No, but you...are you okay?" she asked, her voice strangely hesitant.

"Yeah, why-what's wrong?"

"Nothing, just make sure you're careful in all this heat."

"I will," I answered, not really knowing why I was starting to feel nervous.

"And David?"

"Yeah?"

"Stay away from the beach."

She hung up and I tried not to pay too much attention to the call. Gina was one of those superstitious people who believed everything and anything was an omen. She's two years younger than me, but she was always brighter. When we were growing up, she would entertain me with stories since we never had toys. She and Star got along great. They both shared a very lively imagination.

"I'm sorry for saying those things about mommy, Star." I bent down and stared into her eyes, holding both hands in mine. "I was mad at the way she spoke to me, but that didn't excuse what I did. It's not good to talk about people behind their backs and I was wrong."

"I know, Daddy. Mommy says some pretty bad things about you, too. Except she doesn't say sorry." She held me by both ears and stared long and deep into my eyes. She kissed my forehead and said, "You had a rough day, didn't you?"

"Nah, it was a piece of cake!" I joked and we both laughed.

"Do you think I'm a good dad?" I asked her.

"Nope!" she replied smiling.

"Nope?" I feigned a frown.

"Nope. I know you're a good dad!" I hugged her tight and tickled her. Moments like these made me so thankful for Star. She is without a doubt the most important person in my life.

It took a few minutes for the air conditioner to fully chill the house the way I liked and when it did I sat back with a six pack of ice cold Budweiser and tried to forget the weird and stressful events of the day.

Star sat next to me. I put my arm around her and tuned on the TV on. The basketball game was on channel four. NBC had just finished its pre-game report and I looked forward to seeing the Knicks match up with the Nets. The house was quiet except for the TV.

"Chips...dip...beer," I said out loud, going over the checklist-the basketball ritual. "Fresh batteries in the remote control, and the air conditioner's working! Thank you, Lord!"

"Thank you, Lord!" Star repeated and we both laughed. The stress of the day had begun to fade like a bad dream. Star soon fell asleep in my arms and I laid her down in her bed. I had converted the spare bedroom for her room in hopes that one day I'd gain full custody.

There was a news interruption about the weather. A spokesman from the Health and Hospital Corporation urged everyone to get anywhere that was air conditioned to avoid the heat. The temperature was now a hundred and eight degrees. The death toll had now exceeded six hundred people.

There was also something about giant malaria carrying mosquitoes found in the marshlands around the Brooklyn-Queens Expressway. The reporter showed one of the bloodsuckers in a jar. This thing looked like a small bird. I couldn't imagine getting stung by an insect that big. I would need a blood transfusion. I had to remember to get some bug repellant the next time I went to the store.

The CDC was preparing to spray the area. They flashed the symptoms of malaria on the screen. They were predicting the worst heatwave in history. I listened half-heartedly, wishing they would get on with the game.

The game finally started. The announcers came on with their usual rhetoric of how the Knicks and Nets were too evenly matched to call. They droned on with the stats about this player and that player, and one of them even predicted this game was a preview of the Eastern Conference Finals.

"It's about time!" I screamed back at the TV. "New York's gonna win it all this year!" This was the moment I'd been waiting for all day, the cool and safe feeling of my apartment with a cold beer in one hand, remote control in the other and the two best point guards in the league taking each other to school.

Tip off began and New York managed to intercept a pass and score, sending Madison Square Garden into a tizzy. In that moment, I felt all was right with the world.

The phone rang at half time. It was Shakim, calling to talk about the game. "Man did you see the way my man stuffed that thing?" he barked. "We gonna win this one by at least twenty points!"

I laughed, enjoying his enthusiasm. Normally he'd be with me watching the game and we'd be whooping and hollering like two madmen, but I had Star today and nothing and no one would interfere with our time together.

"Yo! I'll bet you we smoke them like a pack of Newports!" I quipped. We laughed and joked about the last time we met on the basketball court and he slam-dunked on me. I called him a no drawers wearing punk. He retaliated by saying I was the ill nourished son of a woman that sucked every dick in the C

Building in Rikers Island. And since I was born out of the ass instead of the pussy, I should inquire as to what jobs were available for a man of my special talents. He further suggested web sites I could log on to, to meet people of similar circumstance.

We went back and forth like that-two grown men acting like children, trying to see who could come up with the best rank. After a while, I told him about my day. I left out the part about the sandwich board man's weird eye contact with me and for some reason I also left out what he told me before he-

Died?

No! Don't think about that!

The Knicks won the game by seventeen points. Star was still asleep in her room and I was feeling the effects of the six-pack. I took a long hot shower and went to bed.

That night I dreamt I was in a jungle standing by a mighty waterfall watching the water roll off the cliff. The trees were as tall as buildings and beautiful, colorful exotic birds painted the air with their wings. The crisp cool mist of the cascade was soothing and I felt my body gently swaying to the musical roll of the water crashing against the rocks.

The dream seemed so real, but I knew I was dreaming. I could feel the sand beneath my bare feet. I could see incredible detail in everything. It was like the dream was in high definition. I could feel the swipe of the breeze against my cheek. I could easily distinguish the different sound of each bird's cawing.

Star was busy playing with the birds and I marveled at the size and expanse of the waterfall. The

man in the sandwich board and the heavy-set woman draped in jewels were behind me. They were healthy and I somehow realized this jungle was their home.

The waves danced and frothy silver colored spume splashed over my feet. The man in the sandwich board was telling me something, but it was in a language I couldn't understand. I ignored him, reading the message on the sandwich board.

"The dead know what the living are doing…"

I read this, repeating it over and over. I woke up hearing it echoed throughout my small apartment. It took me a minute to gain my bearings. The echo came from Star's room.

"The dead know…what the living…are doing. The…dead…know…what…the living are doing…"

The voice was eerie. It was Star's and yet it was not hers. It was thick with a French accent. I got up walking way too slowly, but my legs threatened to buckle from under me if I moved any faster. I was so scared-scared beyond anything I ever felt before. A blind, nerve numbing fear.

The doorknob was ice-cold. My hand stuck to it. I looked down and saw the knob had frosted into a thick milky sheath, like ice cubes left in the freezer too long. The sound wafted and danced through the apartment. I could feel the vibration of Star's voice rumbling in the walls and floors. I gasped in horror. My breath formed bitter wisps of vapor in the air.

I opened the door to her room. I tried to call out to her, but the sound was stuck in my throat. A low guttural whine escaped.

Star sat on the floor, her silver sneakers laced

tightly on her feet. In her hand she held a silver magic marker, violently scribbling a large figure eight as if some unseen hand forced her. Her eyes were turned up in her head, only the whites were visible. I tried to take a step toward her but my legs were petrified, rooted to the floor. Finally, I found my voice and called out to her.

"Star!" I screamed, hoping to snap her out of her trance. She turned her head and her eyes seemed to glow. A slender thread of drool hung from her bottom lip.

"Daaaad...deeee!" she cried and I picked her up and held her tight. She fell asleep in my arms. The room went back to its normal temperature and I stood there wondering what in the hell had just happened.

Star has always been a very special child. Gina would tease her, saying she was an old woman in a little girl's body. I often referred to her as my diva. From the time she learned to talk, she developed an opinion on everything-people included. If Sharon or I brought some one home as a guest and Star didn't like them they never got invited again. It was like she was born already set in her ways.

Once, when Star was three I was out of work. The phone company threatened to cut our service. I had just gone on a successful interview and I was expecting a call back. The telephone was my only contact with the outside world.

The only way to keep the phone on was to immediately pay one-hundred-six dollars and forty-eight cents. I paced the floor arguing with the woman on the other end who told me I had all of twelve hours to pay the bill at a check cashing place, then call her back with something called a Z number or I could kiss my service goodbye.

Star came to me with three numeral flash cards and asked, "Daddy, what's these numbers?" I tried to send her to Sharon while I contemplated selling blood to raise the money-at the phone company's customer service specialist's suggestion, but Star insisted I put the phone down and listen to her. When I did, she showed me the cards and insisted that I read the numbers to her.

"Seven-four-nine! Okay, Star! Now go play and let daddy take care of important business!" I snapped.

"Okay, Daddy!" she answered with a smile that touched her eyes. "I'm going to go play seven-four-nine."

Later that day I was in a bodega with Shakim and on a hunch I played seven-four-nine for fifty cents. It came out straight in the state lottery and I collected two-hundred and fifty dollars. I called the phone company back with their Z number with specific instructions on where they could deposit it.

When Star was four I bought Alex Haley's Roots on DVD. Star watched it and had nightmares for days. She kept dreaming she was sold and taken away from her mother and me. It took many hours of conversation to convince her nothing like that could ever happen again.

"How, Daddy? How do you know it will never happen again?" she asked me.

"Because Blacks would never allow it to happen again!" I trusted I was telling her the truth, but with statistics saying one out of every four black men are in some stage of the judicial process I couldn't swear it.

I bought an entire multimedia package for children on black heroes and heroines to show her how far Blacks have come since that terrible time. The books and CD's were the only thing that really calmed her down. Star always took to the stories about Harriet Tubman and Sojourner Truth.

"Strong black women," she would say after reading their stories. "One day I'm going to grow up and be a strong black woman. Just like them!"

It was during this time she developed an imaginary playmate. A little boy she claimed would come and see her whenever she was sad. Her teachers told me this was a natural adaptation to being the only child. It had been years since she mentioned him and I really thought it was something she had grown out of. But that moment in her room, I wondered.

I laid Star in my bed and sat next to her hoping this was all some kind of bad dream.

Star slept soundly throughout the night, while I was scared shitless for the duration of the evening. I carefully went over everything that had occurred and tried to make sense of it. As an analyst I tend to assess things in a sensible and pragmatic fashion.

Okay, so I saw an old lady passed out from the heat. So did a lot of people. And the weird guy with the sandwich board, it was quite possible and very probable that he was a nut. Making that business with the car just a tragic coincidence.

If that hypothesis flew then the weird thing with Star's room also had a logical explanation. Perhaps the air conditioner was out of whack, blowing out freezing air instead of just cool air.

It was possible.

The strange dream I had was just my mind's way of dealing with the stressful events of the day. And then Star's catatonic episode could have been combination of the day's events and the room being too cold. The psyche of an eight-year-old is a very fragile thing. Children need plenty of love and order in their world. Seeing the old woman pass out and the man get hit probably really shook her up. That nasty argument I had with her mother didn't help matters either.

This became the acceptable version of what happened. It was a matter of convincing myself there was nothing supernatural about the day's events. It was all just a weird coincidence.

The sun came up and announced to the world Saturday had officially arrived. Star woke up around seven, ready for the morning cartoons. The X-Men were interrupted by a news brief. The heat was killing the animals in the Brooklyn Zoo.

The zoo's newborn elephant died of heat exhaustion and they were transferring special cooling equipment from the Bronx Zoo for the rest of the animals' safety. Star was heartbroken. I'd planned to take her to see the baby elephant as soon as the heatwave broke.

I made breakfast; cheese omelets and beef sausages, but all Star wanted was a bowl of cereal. I took the opportunity to clean her room while she slept in my bed, removing all traces of what had occurred. I promised myself I'd have the super look at the air conditioner.

"What are we going to do today, Daddy?" Star asked. I thought about taking her out, but with the heat and all of the deaths resulting from it, along with yesterday's occurrences, not to mention last night's eerie episode in Star's room maybe a day at home wasn't a bad idea.

"I don't know, baby. What would you like to do?"

She shrugged her shoulders and went back to her cereal. "We have to get ready for the funeral," she said, staring into the bowl. That cold hard look was back in her face. The same look she had when that fat lady grabbed her. It stunned me for a second seeing it so clearly. Star somehow seemed so much older to me.

Something is happening right now. Something I can't quite get my arms around...

She raised her head and looked me in the eyes. A chill went through me. Star seemed as if she had aged sixty years in an instant. It wasn't that her hair grayed or she developed deep lines or wrinkles. No-it was something much more subtle, yet glaringly unmistakable.

It was her eyes.

She suddenly had the eyes of an old woman.

When I was fourteen, Shakim and I cut school and went to Manhattan to hang out. We wandered around the garment district looking for something to do. I saw an elderly black woman sitting on a bench. She looked to be in her late seventies. She was wearing a white uniform with MIKE'S BUILDING CLEANERS stenciled in bold block letters across the back.

I watched this elderly slip of a woman-she couldn't have weighed more than ninety pounds, rubbing her calloused and bruised hands. Hands that looked as if they spent a lifetime scrubbing and scraping against the rough shell of the world just to etch out the most meager level of existence. After a few minutes, a white guy (who didn't look a day over eighteen) carrying a clipboard yelled at her to get back to work. Her eyes met mine. They were the eyes of a woman who had seen all the bad the world had to offer and none of the good. They were empty orbs of sorrow that somehow reached out and stunned me like an electric shock.

"I'm so tired of working," she mumbled as she got up to follow the man with the clipboard. "I'm so tired."

I never cut school again. The look in that woman's eyes haunted me something terrible. I could not see myself growing old and that tired. I could not see my hands that cracked and gnarled from years of spine bending mindless labor. I could not see that look of utter hopelessness-that glare of total defeat in my eyes.

But that same dead stare was in Star's eyes now. These were not the eyes of an eight-year-old who was excited over getting a new pair of sneakers.

"Whose funeral, Star?" I asked softly holding

her hands. I stared into her eyes, trying to reach her-trying to breach that cold dead sheath that reminded me of that poor old lady. "Baby, listen-I know how hard it must've been seeing that old lady and old man like that and I know you're sad about the baby elephant, but try not to think about it, okay?"

I wanted to take her over to my sister's house. She lived in an apartment building that had a bunch of kids and maybe Star needed the company of children her age to take her mind off things.

Anything to get her to smile, anything to get that damned look out of her eyes...

"You wanna go see Aunt Gina? Wanna show her your new sneakers?" I asked, wondering why kids didn't come with instruction manuals. They were almost as hard to figure out as women were.

"I'm not talking about them. I'm not talking about the elephant and I'm not talking about the old man and the old lady," she said coldly and then her eyes twinkled as if glints of light were caught in them. They sparkled like the facets of a diamond and I instantly thought of the jewels the old lady wore. The gleam grew larger, as if her eyes were penlights. I could see the pupils dilating, but instead of dark openings, the pupils glared with a bright light that made me flinch.

I started to say something, but the words caught in my throat like a lump of hot coal. The expression on Star's face could have cut stone. I shut my eyes tight and opened them. Star's eyes were normal again. Her facial features softened. What just happened, I thought to myself. Did I just see that? Did

I really just see that?

She ran out of the kitchen to her room.

The doorbell rang. I was torn between running behind her and answering the door. I decided I would tell whomever it was to come back later, and then I would take Star to Gina's. I would treat everybody to the movies or anyplace that was air-conditioned.

I could hear Star's sobs as I went to open the door. I looked through the peephole and saw it was the police. There were two of them, one White, one Black.

"May I help you?" I asked, feeling every nerve in my body jump like live wires.

"Mr. David Peters?" the white cop asked me. He looked about my age-mid thirties and from the expression on his face, he wasn't bringing good news.

Did they ever?

"Yes, how may I help you?" I asked, still not opening the door. "This really isn't a good time. I have my daughter-"

"May we come in, sir? It's...well it's about your girlfriend."

"My girl-Who? Sharon?"

Oh Lord, what did that damned chick go and do now? Cut somebody?

I opened the door and stood looking at the officers. I guess I was a bit relieved when I heard it was about Sharon. She had been locked up for fighting before. It was only overnight, but it served her right. Besides, it helped me tremendously with the visitation rights. When my lawyer got through with her, the judge thought she was suffering from a chemical imbalance and ordered a psychiatric evaluation.

I giggled like hell over that one.

"Sir, we don't quite know how to tell you this," the black cop said. His head lowered, staring at his shoes. A chill went up my spine, since when did they send a black cop and a white cop and why did they keep calling me sir?

"Wha-what happened?" I asked. The smile slowly evaporated as I realized something was horribly wrong.

"She's dead, sir. She was killed in a car accident last night on her way home from a party. An ambulance struck her car. She died instantly."

My mind went blank. If at that moment someone told me to recite the alphabet, I wouldn't have been able to remember how it started. For a second it was as if I could actually feel every thought fall out of my head, leaving it as empty as a dry bowl.

The officers helped me to the table and I saw Star. That hard gleam in her eyes was replaced by an arcane sympathy. She looked so sad standing there, but for some reason I got the impression she was sadder for me than herself.

We have to get ready for the funeral...

She knew! She knew her mother died! It was Sharon she was talking about! I sat at the kitchen table numb. The white officer turned the stove off for me. The black one poured me a glass of water. Star hugged me and I felt her little lips wet with tears.

"We're going to be okay, Daddy. I'll take care of you."

"I'm really sorry, sir. She's at Kings County

Hospital. Someone will have to go and make a positive identification. Did she live here?" the White cop asked.

"No," Star said. "My mommy and daddy were separated." She said this carefully pronouncing each syllable, as if she had rehearsed saying that line a thousand times.

"Does her mother know?" I asked. I felt as if all the wind had been knocked out of me. I felt confused and bewildered. I didn't know what to think.

"No, sir. We found a picture of you three in her purse, along with an address book. Your name was listed as the contact in case of emergency. I am sorry, sir. Here is the information on where she is and my number if you have any questions. We're still doing an investigation, but at this point, I'm confident it was just an accident. I don't know if that makes it easier."

I thought of how many times I wished Sharon dead. Not meaning it, but wishing it just as well. Now she was gone. Gone! I thought of how many times Shakim teased me saying Sharon and I would get back together and how many times I secretly believed it. If we had somehow worked things out would she still be alive? Was it my fault?

The officers left. The White one smiled at Star and touched her hand. He must be new to the force, I thought. The Black one looked as if he'd seen and heard this type of thing a million times before.

I picked up the phone and dialed Sharon's house. Her mother answered and I searched for the strength to tell her what happened. I told her, listening to her scream with rage and grief. I would meet her at

Kings County Hospital, at the morgue.

Star stared at the photo the police left. It was the last picture the three of us had taken together. We were at Coney Island last summer, walking along the beach and enjoying the day. A man came along with a Polaroid camera and asked if we would like our picture taken. I agreed and offered to pay him, but he refused. He left us with the picture. Sharon kept it, saying how pretty she looked in it. Looking at it I realized she was right.

Overwhelmed with grief and confusion I tried to figure out what made Sharon so insecure about our relationship. There was a hard shell about her. A protective covering that shielded out everything and everyone-friend and foe alike. She was deathly afraid of becoming too attached to anyone.

Even me.

On the surface Sharon would appear bright, confident and assured. But just beneath the skin she was afraid, unsure and wrought with issues. I encouraged counseling, but she mocked me for suggesting it. Her rationale was that only very weak, frigid sexually inhibited women needed counseling to save their relationship.

And we had no problems in the bedroom-just every other room.

She was the type of woman who would defend me to the bitter end in front of company whether I was right or wrong, but she would viciously rip me to shreds when we got home.

In private she would berate and put me down, telling me that no woman would put up with me and that I was so lucky to be with her. She'd parade a list of old boyfriends, reminding me of how much so and so was making and how much they paid for their house.

In public she'd brag about everything I did-my profession, my education and so on. But alone she was brutally critical. Nothing I did satisfied her. The harder I tried the more miserable the failure.

And yet deep inside I knew she loved me. She would constantly tell me how I was not fulfilling my potential. How I could achieve and accomplish so much more than I was reaching for.

I thought of Star's reaction to the police. How she said we were separated. It was her deepest wish Sharon and I reconcile and be a family again.

I sat at my table holding her picture, confused over the past. Star wet a washcloth and put it on my head. I held her tightly. She was the only constant joy I had in life.

I mumbled a simple prayer asking for strength to get through this. I had to be strong for Star. I don't consider myself an overly religious man, but I do believe that a higher power in the universe guides and balances our way, a universal scale of sorts.

And the events of the past day went totally against that scale.

Star sat in her chair with a blank expression on her face, tears streaming out of her eyes. The hard look was gone, but there was something else now. She sat quietly, but not the way a child would sit. She sat with an adult-like aura. I stared at her wondering how she knew what had happened.

"Star, I have to ask you a few questions. I know this is a hard time for both of us...but, I need to know how you knew mommy passed away." I wiped away both of our tears.

"The old lady told me, Daddy." Star didn't look at me as she spoke. She stared off into space as if she was seeing something I couldn't. "We were by the water and she said the bad times are coming, but not to be afraid. She said, 'the dead know what the living are doing.'"

The blood froze in my veins.

"When did she tell you this, baby?" I asked. The words came out in a wheeze.

"Last night in the dream. The old man was there too, but he wasn't hurt this time. Do you think they are bad people, Daddy?"

"I don't know, baby...I don't know."

How could we have dreamt the same thing in the same night? Fear crept through me. Not a fear of what had happened, but a fear of what was going to happen. I suddenly had an overwhelming premonition of doom.

The bad times are coming...

I dropped Star off at Gina's then I called Shakim and he met me at Kings County Hospital. The morgue was in the sub-basement. Sharon's people had beaten me there. They were crying hysterically and I knew then they had identified the body.

As I walked the hall, I remembered when I first met Sharon. It's funny how a thing like that came to mind during that walk. Sharon was my first blind date. I was just coming off a bad relationship and I really wasn't ready to meet anyone, but Shakim swore to me I would like this girl.

We met at Peter Luger's Steak House. Shakim brought whatever girl he was seeing that week. I was pleasantly surprised at Sharon's intelligence. During dinner she conducted herself like a perfect lady and was well-versed on a myriad amount of subjects. After dinner we went dancing at Bentley's and we club hopped over to the Silver Shadow and the Tunnel. We danced, drank and laughed. I remember the look of pride Shakim had that night for introducing us. He finally did something right.

We left Manhattan and went to Shakim's place. We played music and I kissed her while the Isley Brothers' sang Don't Say Goodnight. I never wanted the evening to end. Shakim took his date to his room and Sharon and I went and sat on the stoop all night. We held each other and talked.

By the time the sun had risen, I was in love.

I proposed six weeks later, sure I had met my soul mate. Shakim kept teasing me saying if Sharon ever caught me cheating on her, she would whip me black and blue. We stayed engaged for a while, postponed the wedding three times and I don't know how many times we broke up and got back together. It went on like that, until the arguing just got to be a bit too much.

Our first big quarrel started over a can of fruit cocktail. We were in the supermarket shopping and I suggested we pick some up. It was a spur of the moment thing. I enjoyed it as a child and thought it would be nice to have in the house. Well, I didn't know there was a beautiful girl in the canned goods aisle...

"So! That's why all of a sudden your ass wants fruit cocktail! You must think I'm stupid! Just go live with that bitch!" Sharon blubbered, throwing a can of fruit cocktail at me. It skimmed my head and hit the girl in the arm. I never felt so embarrassed in my life. She stood there with her hands on her hips and proceeded to curse that poor girl out, chasing her out the supermarket. I didn't even know the girl!

To make matters worse after everything calmed down about a week later-who shows up at my job for an interview while Sharon came to visit? The fruit-cocktail girl! Needless to say, I've changed companies. Fruit cocktail never found its way to my house and to this day, I don't eat it.

It went on like that for years. Little things would send her off the deep end. I found myself walking on eggshells around her. I felt like an abused husband. It wasn't all bad. When it was good, it was good. But when it was bad, it was very bad.

Sharon loved altercations and drama. It was like she got off on it. She would pick a fight with me and later she'd want to make love all night. I loved her, but she was detrimental to my mental health. Shakim said Sharon was the type of woman that needed a real strong man, the type who respected a man who'd beat her.

I could never get into that type of relationship and so I planned to leave.

Then she became pregnant with Star.

I really tried hard to make it work. I'm not saying I'm a pleasure to live with, but Sharon was just impossible to please.

The apartment was too small. The furniture was never right. The TV wasn't the right size. We never went to the chic parties. I didn't dress right. I didn't hang out with the right type of crowd and I damned sure didn't earn enough.

Everything I did was wrong.

Some time after Star's seventh birthday I just got tired of jumping through hoops and I packed up and walked. Funny enough, Star helped me make up my mind about leaving. She had drawn a picture of the three of us and she drew me with a frown. When I asked why, she said I always looked sad and that I couldn't call our house home unless I was happy there.

Out of the mouth of babes and sucklings...

I found a two-bedroom apartment in a renovated building and I left. Sharon's mother cursed me out, called me a no-good nigger and a deadbeat dad. But Star was there for me and that was all that mattered. At first I felt Sharon and I would get back together, but the longer we stayed apart the more I saw we really didn't have anything in common. We just weren't compatible outside of the bedroom.

And then it got so we weren't even compatible there.

I walked down the hall to see her body on a slab. The halls leading to the morgue were quite appropriate; gray and as gloomy as a rainy October Sunday. Tears welled up in my eyes. This was going to be a lot harder than I thought.

Although they had already identified her, I had to see for myself it was really Sharon lying on that slab. We were taken into a partitioned room separated by a wall of curtained glass. An attendant asked if we wanted to sit. I declined, but Shakim sat. Finally they wheeled a gurney into the other room and opened the curtain. I closed my eyes and mumbled a last minute prayer for a miracle, but it was really Sharon.

Her face was a ghastly gray color. The hue of death, I thought to myself. Just like the walls. The bland depressingly empty color reserved for the dead. The coroner's report read death by massive trauma to the torso. Her chest was crushed from the impact of the accident. It was hard seeing a woman who held such fire and life reduced to something so cold and dead like that. I swooned looking at her lifeless husk, thinking of how ridiculously fragile life is. We work so hard and plan so much, but in the end we all wind up on a cold slab. Black, White, rich or poor. Man or woman-it doesn't matter. In the end we are all the same. Reduced to meat for the ground.

Tara came into the room and hugged me. Her face was wet with tears, leaving my cheeks moist. She was the only one out of Sharon's family who bothered to even acknowledge my presence.

"It's gonna be all right, David. I'm going to help you through this. Me and Star will take care of you," she whispered in my ear. I released her, staring into her eyes. There was a softness-a quiet gentleness about Tara. It was as if I saw her for the first time.

Over the next few days Tara and I became inseparable. She really helped me with Star and just handling the grief. I had come to enjoy and rely on Tara's company. She would be the first person I'd contact in the morning and with the exception of Star, she would be the last person I'd speak to before going to bed. We'd stay on the phone for hours if we were away from each other and never ran out of things to talk about.

She suggested a small funeral home in the area. She claimed the funeral director came highly recommended. I don't know what type of person recommends funeral directors. Like most people I find death terribly morbid and anyone associated with death as an occupation to be more than a bit odd, but I was in no shape to disagree with her.

She dragged me in to meet the funeral director. I kept reminding her it wasn't a wedding we were going to attend. We didn't need to practice. Anyway, I never realized until then how detailed a funeral really is. How much is involved in putting someone away with some modicum of decency.

The director was a peculiar looking fellow by the name of Cleophus Gilly. Upon meeting and hearing him say his name I instantly thought this man was the stereotypical idea of a mortician. He looked as if he was born to be a funeral director. His face wore a constant blank expression.

He had the ultimate poker face.

"Please sit down," he said as we entered his sparse but very clean office. "And tell me how may I assist you, in this very trying time of the spirit." He said this as if he had said it a thousand times before, with as much sincerity as saying good morning to a total stranger. I regarded it as no more than idle chatter, his way of being polite. Cleophus stood about six feet even and weighed all of about a hundred and thirty pounds. His beer belly seemed to account for about sixty percent of his weight. I listened to him drone on with the rehearsed rhetoric of how his funeral home was sensitive to the needs of the community. I tried to picture him laughing, hanging out with the boys and having a good time.

It took a lot of imagination.

He looked as if he'd never smiled. One of his hands was much larger than the other, the same with one of his feet. I had to force myself not to stare. I pictured Cleophus as a child, being teased and ridiculed because of his birth defects. Ridicule that didn't stop as a child, but continued even into adulthood. I thought he looked like the saddest man in the world.

I imagined how I would feel if I saw death and grief all day and made a profit from it, especially in Brooklyn where the customers were getting younger and younger.

Tara did all of the talking. I tried to keep my mind off what was behind the double doors in the rear of his office. Sharon will be back there soon, I thought to myself. They'll cut her open and remove all her insides.

I shuddered as a chill went through me. We'll all have to go through this! Even Star! One day we're all going to die! Suddenly I couldn't sit still in that office. I felt as if all the air had been sucked out of the room. Tara put a hand on my shoulder and I calmed down a bit. She and Cleophus kept talking as if nothing were wrong.

We picked out the casket (I had no idea those damned things were so expensive!) and made all the arrangements.

"How long have you known that guy?" I asked while we were heading back to Tara's car.

"About five months. I met him in class."

"Oh yeah, which class was that? Weird one-oh-one?"

"No...I took a class on ancient African civilizations. He was in my class. Why?"

"He's just spooky that's all...I mean even for an undertaker. I think he likes you, though."

"He's a nice man, David. Not everyone is as handsome or as bright as you are," she said plainly.

I never thought of myself as handsome. Bright-yes, but not handsome. I look all-right I guess and I consider myself to be well-groomed, but for someone as attractive as Tara to think of me as handsome...kind of...made me blush.

"So...tell me about this class you took," I said, trying to make idle chatter. I'd obviously hit a sore nerve talking about Cleophus. We got into her car and the heat was unbearable. I prayed the air-conditioning wouldn't take too long to kick in.

"It was just a class...we studied African folklore and religions. You know how we're always being depicted in the media as being savage cannibals. Well it wasn't like that at all! We were the gods and goddesses of this world long before Europeans came out of the caves. A lot of the biblical characters were black and there is a rich history in ancient Africa, but do they teach us that? No! They teach us that Abraham Lincoln freed the slaves, but go back and read the Emancipation Proclamation! Abe didn't hardly free anyone! He had absolutely no love for black people, and he damned sure didn't see us as equals!"

I had never heard such raw passion and aggression from Tara. It just seemed so unlike her. She was usually so easy going-so reserved in her opinions. The exact opposite of Sharon who was always ready to give you a piece of her mind, whether she could spare it or not.

"Don't tell me you're going to grow dreads and change your last name to ex!" I joked. Tara didn't think it was funny.

"I'm sorry, Tara. I didn't mean to offend you."

"You didn't. It's just that…well-"

"Well what?"

"Do you believe in God, David?" she asked flatly.

"Yeah…of course I do!" I answered, suddenly feeling uncomfortable and squirming in my seat.

"Do you believe that God is black or white?"

"Wha-what kind of question is that? He's not a color! He's…a spirit…right?" I didn't understand what she was getting at.

"When you picture angels, or any of the biblical prophets…are they black or are they white?" she pressed.

"I guess they're white," I answered, reluctantly.

"That's because from the time you were a child that's what you were taught. All Bibles have pictures

of white heroes and white heroines. How can a child
of color identify with white angels?"

I thought of Star. She was always painting and
drawing pictures of strange things, unicorns and dol-
phins-things like that. Once, while Tara was babysit-
ting her she drew a picture of a black angel.

"So you were the one that had Star draw that
picture! Okay...I think it is healthy for a child to think
of angels that look the way they do. That goes for
blacks, whites, Asians or anyone!"

"Star is very special...she's going to do very
big things." Her voice trailed off, as if she was lost in
thought. I sat there wondering how the conversation
suddenly took this turn when she said:

"There's just so much more to the world than
Brooklyn, you know. When I was growing up, they
called me egotistical and said I was trying to act like I
was white. All because I wanted something better."

"You remind me a lot of your father the way
you talk sometimes," I said. "He was always talking
about black power and owning our own. I wish
Sharon would've-"

"You knew Sharon and I had different dads,
didn't you?"

"No," I replied shocked. "I damned sure did-
n't!"

"Jim Levy is my daddy. Momma never admit-
ted who Sharon's dad is, but daddy never treated
Sharon any different. It's funny, but you've always
reminded me of my daddy."

"Really?" I asked, impressed. It was no secret
Tara loved her father and stood by his side throughout

her parents' separation. Just as Sharon took her mother's side. "How?"

"You two have the same quiet strength. I know all of the things that you've put up with to try to keep your family together. Just like daddy did. Sharon and I would argue about the way she treated you. I just think it's wrong for a woman to say there are no good men and then turn around and dog the first good man they find."

The silence lingered a bit longer than what was comfortable "How is Mr. Levy?" I asked.

"He's…he has his good and bad days. When was the last time you saw him?"

"Man, it's been a while! I think about maybe two months ago." I remembered arguing with Sharon the entire trip there and back, but I didn't mention that.

"Let's go see him now. I went the other day, but it was one of his bad days. He doesn't know Sharon passed on."

I really didn't want to go. Mr. Levy was in a long-term treatment facility. He suffered from senility. It wasn't that I didn't like him-I did. It was just that it was very hard seeing a man who I grew up respecting and looking up to reduced to a feeble minded child.

"Okay," I mumbled, not knowing how to get out of it. Especially after Tara gave me such a compliment.

As we drove to Staten Island I found myself intrigued by Tara. Prior to Sharon's death, I thought of all Levy women as instigating, immature troublemakers and that was no reflection on Mr. Levy. Now sitting in the car beside her I saw a mysterious and beautiful black woman. We spoke about everything from politics to literature, to her awakening of black culture. And I was more than surprised that we shared many of the same views.

"When did this happen, Tara? I mean the sudden renaissance with you and black pride?"

"I've always been fascinated by African history; since I was a little girl about Star's age. My daddy used to tell me stories about Egyptian mythology and ancient African kings and queens. I especially loved the stories about Hannibal, how he took the elephants over the mountains to fight the Romans. Now you ask a kid who Hannibal is and they're liable to tell you about Hannibal Lecter."

That made me think of the two kids on the bus that day downtown. Which made me think of the weird driver, which brought back the man in the sandwich board, which brought back Sharon and I arguing, which brought back her death.

Which reminded me of why I was sitting next to Tara in the first place. I rushed these thoughts out of my mind.

"So," I asked, clearing my throat. "You seeing anybody?"

"No, I'm waiting for the ice cream truck." She giggled. I stared at her curiously.

"When I was about thirteen, just hitting puberty, all of my friends had boyfriends but me. My dad sat me down and taught me about the ice cream truck."

"Okay. Is this a private story? Because you got

me interested now!"

"Well, he asked me what my favorite flavor ice cream was and I told him butter pecan. Then he told me to imagine a blistering hot day-much like this one and he told me to picture a big beautiful sundae of butter pecan ice cream, complete with cherries and whipped cream and chocolate fudge. He made me close my eyes and envision it. I could see the cherry-the most perfectly formed cherry that God ever made, sitting atop two massive scoops of butter pecan ice cream. Arrayed with whipped cream and dripping with hot chocolate fudge. He made me smell the chocolate fudge melting the ice cream. I could almost taste it, David. Daddy had a way of making you see what he was saying. Well, after listening to him I wanted that sundae real bad. Real bad. Then he told me the sundae was just down the block on its way to me and only me-that the sundae was on an ice cream truck that was coming just for me and no one else. "

"Okay."

"He then said to picture someone coming up to me with a half emptied container of butter pecan ice cream, with a dirty spoon stuck in it. A spoon that everyone had licked on."

Her voice lowered as she spoke. "He asked me to decide which one I'd prefer. I told him I'd want the one off the ice cream truck and he told me that was good. He told me to wait on the ice cream truck. He told me never to settle for anything less than that wonderfully special sundae. A sundae that was spe-cially prepared for me and only me."

"I don't think I'll ever look at ice cream the

same way again. As a matter of fact every time I hear an ice cream truck coming I'll need to take a cold shower!" She laughed and my heart fluttered. I wanted to say something else witty, something to make her laugh like that again. But instead I said, "I have to remember to tell Star that when the time comes. Mr. Levy is a very wise man."

"I couldn't have asked for a better father."

There was an uncomfortable moment of silence. Tara's eyes saddened and I struggled to find something to say to alleviate the tension. I hoped that Star would one day refer to me in such an august manner.

"Well, what about you?" she asked.

"Excuse me?"

"Are you seeing anyone?"

"I was. It didn't work out."

"What happened?"

"Well, she wanted me to spend more time with her and less with Star. Besides, Star didn't really care for her and I don't think I was too gung-ho on getting serious then. So now I just stick to the occasional lap-dance."

"Just make sure you keep your pants on! You don't know what some of these girls have in their laps!"

"Well like the man said, it ain't hard to tell. Especially now with the way the girls are wearing these candy thongs-and I can't believe I just told you that!" I said embarrassed.

We both laughed and it felt good. I touched her hand, squeezing it gently.

"You know we probably should've brought Shakim," I said. Shakim was the only one who could beat Mr. Levy in checkers. "He'd love to see Mr. Levy!"

"I don't know about Shakim," Tara said smirking. "The brother is a good man, but he has issues."

"Like?"

"Well, don't take this wrong. I know he's your best friend and all, but…"

"Yeah, go ahead."

"Sha needs to read a book! I mean I had a conversation with him and he's just clueless! I mean, David-he thinks the IRS is the richest man in the world! He wanted to argue with me that Tupac and Biggie are alive and working for the Indian government!"

I howled with laughter. Shakim was notorious for his bizarre conspiracy theories. It was his main way of keeping his edge in the streets. People really thought he was crazy and so they left him alone. I could have told her stories about Shakim that would've made her head spin.

We arrived at the facility, signed our names and got visitor's passes. Mr. Levy was in a room on the sixth floor. Tara squeezed my hand on the elevator and I blushed like a schoolgirl.

What is happening to me! I've never felt this way! Not even about Sharon!

The walls in this place all had the same dull gray color. The floors were checkered with black and white tiles. Along the walls of the hallway were paintings of landscapes. There were old people milling aimlessly about. One elderly gentleman walked up to Tara us and dropped his pants.

"Have you seen my daughter?" he asked her.

"No, sir. But I'm sure she'll be here soon and you don't want her to catch you undressed now do you?"

The man vigorously shook his head and pulled his pants back up. The orderlies apologized and rushed him back into his room. Tara took it all in stride.

"Daddy's up the hall in the last room on the left."

We continued walking and many of the patients stopped and said hello to Tara, hugging and kissing her affectionately. Some of them were so old and sickly they looked as if their next breath would be their last. Tara greeted each of them as if she had come to specially visit them. One elderly woman motioned to me and commented on what a lovely couple we made.

"A couple of what?" Tara asked jokingly. The old woman laughed and in that instant her eyes lit up. Tara's visit however brief would be the highlight of their day. She brought sunshine into a gloomy room.

Why didn't I see this about her before?

She continued up the hall, her head held high and proud, walking with balance and grace. We entered Mr. Levy's room. He sat in a wheelchair, looking out of the window.

"Daddy? It's me, Tara. Look who I brought to see you!"

He turned and looked at her strangely. He had

become even frailer than the last time I saw him. His once thick curly locks of hair were now thin wispy strands of gray threads. His hands shook badly and his eyes were glassy and unfocused.

"Who dat? Star? Is dat my Star?"

"No, Daddy! It's David! Star's father!" Tara said, kneeling by him. He stared at me with a puzzled look on his face.

"Sharon's dead ain't she?" he said sadly.

"Yes, Daddy. How did you know?" Tara asked, obviously as shocked as I was.

"It'll be okay, baby. Ya'll hafta look after Star now. Boffa you. David, you gonna go through some pretty rough times, but just keep faith in God and it will be okay."

"You okay up here, Mr. Levy? I mean you want us to bring you to the funeral-" I caught myself after the words left my lips. I never know what to say in moments like this.

"No, David. I…can't go. Dis rum and dis view and Tara, you an Star is all I got now. Sharon know I love her. You two take care ah Star, you hear! Don't let nuthin happen to dat chile! Da Lawd work through her! You'll know what I'm talkin' bout soon enuff! David, come here and let me tell you somethin' for your ears only…"

I bent down and put my ear close to his lips. He smelled as if he hadn't been properly bathed in days. He put his hand on the back of my neck and drew me closer to him and whispered.

"The dead know what the living are doing, David."

My breath caught in my throat like a dry gritty pebble. I could feel the blood drain from my face. My body became numb. I stood slowly, not taking my eyes off him.

"What did you say, Mr. Levy?

"He said the bed here is ruined," Tara answered. She walked over and touched my forehead as if checking for a fever. "Are you all right, David? You look a bit flushed. Is it the heat?"

"Yeah...I'm okay. It's just that...you sure that's what he said?"

"Yes, David. He's having one of his bad moments again."

I looked down and saw Mr. Levy mumbling incoherently rocking back and forth. Drool hung from his lips and his nose ran like a faucet. A nurse came in and told us visiting hours were over. Tara kissed her dad on the forehead and walked silently out of the room.

I was impressed with the poise and elegance she showed. She carried herself with the grace of royalty without any egotistical arrogance.

A strong black woman, I thought to myself. I could see where Star took much of her influence. I must have embarrassed Tara when I questioned Mr. Levy. Why did I hear, the dead know what the living are doing? What made me think he had anything to do with the derelict who got killed? I was so ashamed at the way I acted. We got out into the parking lot and I had to tell her.

"Tara, I want to say sorry for anything I may have said or done that upset you. I know I didn't act right in there and I am really sorry. I've had a lot on my mind lately and I guess-"

"You have nothing to apologize for, David. I know seeing Daddy in this type of place is a bit disconcerting. I know it's hard seeing so many elderly people looking like something out of a horror movie, but I think it's important that we take care of our aged and infirm-the only link we have to yesterday is our seniors! These people have fought on the front lines of freedom and the only reward for their labor is to be labeled senile and shoved into a facility where they're just waiting to die! This, David speaks volumes on our lack of respect for history. We are the only race of people who tend to forget what our forefathers sacrificed! We-"

I grabbed and held her tight, pulling her face close against me. She cried burying her head in my chest. Maybe it was the mixture of the heat and her scent, but I suddenly felt lightheaded and a bit giddy. I could feel her heartbeat pulsing in rhythm with my own. The parking lot disappeared. The only thing that existed was the two of us and the sound of our hearts furiously hammering within our chests. The heat intensified the tighter I held her and suddenly all I wanted to do was burn in her arms...

She pulled back from me. The lack of contact snapped me back to my senses. I released her and we both got back into the car without saying a word. I had a hard time catching my breath the entire ride back.

We drove back to her apartment, which was in the same brownstone as the rest of her family. Mr.

Levy bought the house years ago; one of the first blacks to own his own home in this neighborhood.

"You want to come up for a little while? I could use the company. I'm always a bit sad after seeing daddy."

"Sure," I said smiling. "I guess it's hard being superwoman, huhn?"

"Especially when my cape is in the cleaners!" she said without missing a beat. I followed her into the building.

"Da-hell you two been?" her mother asked, poking her head in the hallway. "Why he goin' up the stairs with you? The damned body ain't even cold yet and you ruttin like a bitch in heat!" she slurred from drinking heavily. Her eyes were swollen and circled with thick black rings from where her mascara ran and smeared from crying.

"You okay, Mrs. Levy? You look like you should be lying down." I started down the stairs to her and she shrunk back from me as if I was a leper.

"Don't come near me, nigga!" she seethed. "What? You gone try ta fuck me, too?"

I stood shocked. Mrs. Levy and I never really got along, but I certainly didn't think she hated me. The snarling look on her face scared me.

"Mama, go inside and lie down. I will not have you disrespect David or Sharon's memory like this! That foolishness passed with her! David is the father of your granddaughter, and you should treat him with more respect! And for God's sake stop drinking!" Tara shot back and I was amazed. Not only at what she said, but that she genuinely meant it. I wasn't use to anyone in Sharon's family taking up for me.

"Don't think yo ass is all high and mighty 'round here, bitch! You ain't getting' a dime a' that insurance money!"

"That money is in Star's name and it'll be held in trust until she turns eighteen! Besides, I can't believe you're actually talking about that measly insurance fund! What is fifty thousand dollars going to do in this day and age? By the time Star gets ready for it, she'll be lucky if it covers one year of college!"

"You and that nigga got plans for that money! Ain't while to act like you don't! You thinkin you gone fuck that nigga an get the money and leave me out! I'm fennin to put yo ass outta here, bitch! Sharon would bust yo ass if she was alive! You always did think you was better than us! Just cause you went to college! Well we ain't went and we came up just fine! Just fine!"

"Momma, please stop drinking! That's why daddy left-"

"Don't never mention that bastard's name to me again! Fuck that mutha-fucka!"

Her mother slurred badly now. Her wig sat on the side of her head like a Kangol. The scene was so comical I almost laughed, but the anguish in Tara's face caused any trace of jocularity to vanish.

"Daddy is a good man! When was the last time you went to see him? He left because you chased him away!"

"That bastard left me with two daughters and no money! I took care of you! Me and me al-"

"Liar! Daddy gave you this house! He sent money every week for us! But you lied and told us he never gave you a dime! He wanted to see us, but you wouldn't let him! You raised us to hate him, but I know the truth! I saw all the receipts from the bank deposits. You put my daddy in that hell and you drank and partied that money away! Sharon and I never saw a dime of it! And now with her death you have the nerve to accuse me of trying to get her insurance money! You should be ashamed of yourself!"

"Any money that nigga gave me is mine and no concern of yours! Never you mind what I got! I'm the one who kept quiet through all his girlfriends and his foolin' around!"

"And I for one say God bless daddy for that! I don't know how he put up with you as long as he did! And what about your foolin' around! What about the TV repairman and all the mysterious cousins that traipsed through here while daddy was at work? Which one of them ever helped with the bills?"

There was a look of white shock that appeared across her mother's face. Tara struck the deathblow.

"What do you know about it? If that nigga was taking care of shit at home I wouldn't have had-"

"And who ruts like a bitch in heat?"

Defeated, her mother slowly retreated inside. Tara ushered me up the stairs and slammed the door to her apartment. I didn't know if I should comment or just leave it alone.

"I'm sorry about Momma. I never meant to pull out dirty skeletons. I just don't like seeing any woman putting a black man down. Especially good ones…like you and my daddy."

I stared at her, vaguely aware that my mouth hung open. I had never seen anyone speak to Sharon's mother that way. Judging from the way Tara exploded it was something that had been building up for quite some time.

"Damn, it's hot!" she mumbled fanning her blouse. I couldn't help but notice the blush of her cheeks. Heat rose off her like a radiator. "I'm soaked already! I have to take a shower. Relax a minute, put some music on. I'll be out in a second."

I could hear the shower running. I went over to her music collection and tried to find something to take my mind off the thoughts I was threatening to think.

Let's see, we have Johnny Gill. No, too sexy. Okay, here's Sade. No, too sensual. Here! Here's Luther Vandross…don't even think about it! Shit! By now, my underarms were dripping with sweat and not just from the heat. I couldn't believe how nervous I was, just trying to pick out the right music!

Marvin Gaye, Stevie Wonder, Al Greene, too old school. That'll set the wrong mood. Lauryn Hill, Gladys Knight, maybe…R. Kelly…way too seductive!

"David! I don't hear any music! Is the system okay?" Tara shouted from the bathroom.

"Um, I- uh…can't figure out what to play!"

"Just cut the radio on!"

Just cut the radio on! Now why didn't I think of that! What in the hell was going on in my mind a moment ago? This is Tara!

I cut on the radio and Stephanie Mills warbled about what she would do to me if I were her man. From the shower, I could hear Tara singing along with her.

If I were your woman...

And you were my man...

I stood there, enchanted by Tara's voice. The powerful, smooth richness of it. Her voice oozed and dripped with passion. I was amazed at the things I'd learned about Tara. Amazed and a bit confused why I never noticed these things before.

She entered the living room and her sundress clung to her, showing off a perfectly formed physique. She crossed the room with the fluid motion of wine being poured into a glass.

"You want something to drink?" she asked. I nodded yes. The air conditioner kicked in and cooled the room. She returned with a tray and I sat back with an ice-cold glass of lemonade. My eyes searched the room in a vain attempt to find something to keep them off her body. There were beautiful paintings adorning her walls. I commented on one of them.

"I see you're really into this African thing, I love the paintings. Where did you find them?"

"I didn't find them, David. I painted them."

"Well excuse me!" I said, putting my hands on my hips playfully. "I didn't know you had skills like this, girl!" One painting in particular caught my eye. It was a picture of a waterfall, surrounded by a thick dense jungle. The colors and detail were so vibrant and rich that the painting looked as if it were still wet.

"How long did it take you to do this one?" I

asked, marveling at the texture of it. There was a 3D effect to the painting. I could almost see the water rushing off the cliff.

"That's one of my favorites. It took me a month to work on it, two to three hours a day."

"What made you paint this?" I asked, staring at the painting remembering that strange dream I had the morning I found out Sharon died. Was it a coincidence, or something more? I never figured out how Star and I had the same dream that night and this picture looked an awful lot like the waterfall in my dream.

"I dreamt it," she muttered. I almost dropped my glass.

"I don't know quite how to tell you this, you're gonna think I'm a nut, but...I dreamt this too!" I proceeded to tell her everything that happened to me that day downtown. Then I told her about the dream and Star's weird episode and finally the message that I could have sworn her dad repeated. Her eyes never left mine as I spoke, but there was an odd look of nonchalance on her face.

"I wouldn't think too much of it, David. We all probably saw a picture of this waterfall in a book somewhere. I would've never guessed you'd be so easily spooked. I always thought of you as the cynical one!" she chided.

"Yeah, me too. Just that some pretty weird shit has happened in the last few days." Like how I all of a sudden feel about you! I thought to myself.

"David, really! I know it's been hot, but if you think you're seeing and hearing things you probably should see a doctor," she said and I couldn't tell if she was serious or teasing me.

I finished my lemonade and noticed all the books and magazines on ancient African empires. There were posters of the continent and exotic African masks and sculptures around the room. Tara was serious about this.

"I think it's beautiful the way you're learning our history. Maybe you could teach Star some of this," I said, changing the subject. Tara was right; whatever happened there was a logical explanation for it.

"Yes, I think it's important Star knows a lot of these things. David...did you love Sharon?"

"Yes," I replied, looking at her oddly. "Why did you ask me that?"

"I mean, were you...in love with her?"

I knew what she meant. I loved Sharon because she gave me Star, and because of all we had been through together, but the magic had left a long time ago.

"No, Tara. I loved her, but Sharon and I were on two different wavelengths. I don't mean to speak ill about the dead, but you know she was a bit-"

"High strung!" Tara broke in chuckling. "People change, David. I mean...I'm not the same woman you knew when you and Sharon were together."

"Yeah, I've noticed."

We stood about a foot apart from each other, the smiles on our faces lingering a moment too long. Our eyes glued to each other. Something passed between us-something unseen, but as powerful as the wind. I was aware of an all-consuming urge to hold her again, but I fought it because I knew if I held her, I would go too far.

"Sharon and I never got along as kids, but she was still my sister. I loved her," Tara said. Her voice was low, sultry.

"There's no doubt about that. I mean...well...sometimes two people get together and even though...even though they're wrong for each other...sometimes, something good comes out of it. That's why Star is here," I said. I could feel my pulse pounding in my throat.

"I believe that, and I believe we sometimes get a second chance to make things right." She moved closer to me, maybe an inch or two. Her breathing became heavy and labored and I was mesmerized watching her breasts heave up and down. She reached out and touched my face and I quivered from her touch.

"We'd better be going," she said, withdrawing her hand from my face as if from a hot oven. "Certain things are better left unsaid."

We moved an inch closer to each other when her mother banged on the door.

"Ain't it time fo' yo comp'ny t' be leavin?" she snickered. Her voice drenched with venom and sarcasm. She was really drunk now. The slurring had become more pronounced.

"Time ta go, nigga! Time ta GO!!!"

I could see the veins moving in Tara's head from anger. She bit her lip and opened the door. Mrs. Levy stood in the doorway, her blouse opened to her torso. She was braless, her sagging breasts swung like pendulum sticks. Her skirt was opened and twisted so that the zipper was in front. Her panties were visible. Her wig was struggling to stay on top of her head, held by one lone bobby pin. In her left hand, she held a half empty forty-ounce bottle of Old English 800.

This is Star's grandmother, I thought to myself. She's just lost a child and it's not my place to comment or to judge how people deal with their grief. I turned my head out of respect.

"Momma, I'm only going to say this once!" Tara ordered. "Go downstairs and lie down! Try to get some rest and stop drinking!"

"I ain't goin' nowhere! Long as that no good nigga is up here! Don't bring him here no more! He ain't never done right by Sharon!"

"What did he ever do to Sharon?" Tara asked incredulously. Even I was anxious to hear this one.

"You know what he done! He left me wit a baby! Never sent me a dime a support! He-"

"Mom, I think you really need to lay down. You're getting David mixed up with your hallucinatory version of daddy!"

She stood there, slob dribbling out of her mouth, swaying back and forth. The beer sloshed around in the bottle making foam that threatened to spill over. I felt so embarrassed for Tara.

"Maybe it's best that I just leave," I whispered. The situation had become too uncomfortable. I didn't want to wind up in a fight with Tara's mother. It was common knowledge that Tara's father left because of his wife's infidelity. Mr. Jim Levy was one of the finest men in the neighborhood, until his wife's nagging and cheating drove him to drink. I-like so many other young men in the neighborhood watched as this bitter woman damned near drove that poor man crazy.

As I watched her lean on the wall for support, barely able to stand because she was so drunk, and listened to the hate and poison spew from her mouth, it was easy to see where Sharon got it.

Thank God Tara took after her father's side of the family.

"I'll call you later!" Tara shouted over her mother's drunken tirade.

"I'm looking forward to it!"

"I'm really sorry, David...for everything!"

"Don't blame yourself! It's not your fault!"

I could still hear her mother's ranting as I left the house.

CHAPTER II:

∞

The Wake

There's a part of the funeral process called the wake. This usually occurs a night or two before the actual service where loved ones come and view the body, sit and grieve and sign a little book saying they came. I never understood this part. To me it was like a dry run of the real thing and who the hell needs that?

Cleophus Gilly was there. I shook his hand and felt a bit uncomfortable when I realized I shook the large one. My hand was dwarfed in his huge palm. "Stay strong, young man," he said squeezing my hand and staring at me coldly. "Hold on to Gawd's unchanging hand."

"Thank you," I said, trying to politely get away from him. The man gave me the creeps. Sharon's body was at the front of the funeral parlor, but I dared not go near her. I wasn't ready to see her. Not just yet.

I kept thinking about her being in the room behind Cleophus's office, naked and turned inside out. I hadn't realized how badly spooked I was until that moment. People walked around crying and holding each other.

I inadvertently bumped into Sharon's mother. The silence between us was thorny and piercing. "Hello, Mrs. Levy," I said, trying to be as courteous as possible.

"Hello to you, too, Mr. Peters," she answered, just as snotty as ever. She still reeked of malt liquor. "I see you and Tara have gotten mighty friendly lately."

"Yes, Tara has been a tremendous comfort to Star and me throughout all of this. She has conducted herself with class and aplomb during this very tragic time."

"She conducted herself wit class an a plum, hunh?" she mocked, twisting her wrist, trying to insinuate that I was gay. "Too uppity to talk regular-hunh, nigga?" She poked me hard in my chest with her forefinger.

"I don't like the way you two hang out. And I damned sure don't like the way you look at me!" She turned and slapped her hips in what I believe she thought was a seductive manner.

"You are kidding, aren't you? I mean I know you've been under a tremendous strain, but you can't be serious!"

"I'm bout serious as a heart attack. I always thought of you as a little sissyish, David. You seem to me like your boat floats both ways. That's pro'bly why Sharon left yo punk ass. Now you wanna dig in Tara's stuck up ass an it won't surprise me none if you try ta come at me next!"

"You know," I sighed, ready to really let her

have it. "I know this is your daughter's wake and you're probably not in your right mind, bereavement and all. But that does not excuse you from at least try-ing to remain civil and somewhat decent. Whichever way my boat floats-and it floats one way, I assure you-is of no concern of yours. And I can set your mind at rest that I have never and I will never look at you in anyway that can be described as anything other than pity and grateful that Tara inherited her beauty and grace from her father."

"You got a smart mouth, boy. But your turn'll be soon! I know that's right! Your turn will be real soon! You punk-ass mutha-fucka!" she mumbled under her breath, thinking I didn't hear.

"You know if I didn't know better, I'd swear you were almost sober!"

"Don't think I won't lay yo' ass out right here, nigga! Don't think I won't put you in that casket right wit' Sharon!"

"Oh, I know you wouldn't hesitate to kill me. I've seen what you did to your husband."

"An' if you wanna join him, I'll be more than happy to send yo' ass into the same hell he in!"

"No thank you, Mrs. Levy. By the way, my attorney is going to schedule a custody hearing. Given your alcoholism, ignorance and overall abusive atti-tude, I don't think I'll have a hard time getting full custody of Star...and believe me," I leaned in toward her and said softly, "That insurance money will remain in trust for her."

"I ain't above knockin' the shit outta you right here and now, you know! When you get to hell with a broken ass bone, and ole Scratch axe you how yo' ass got tore outta the frame like it did, you be sure to tell him you was fuckin with Wilhelmina Levy!"

"Oh, he might not know you by that name," I said. "I'll just tell him it was his first wife-Fat-Back Willie from the group home! And please, Mrs. Levy-be careful. You remember what happened the last time you got upset while you were semi-sober, your tongue ring got caught in your dentures!"

She puffed and walked away from me. I felt bad for speaking to her like that, allowing her to bring me down to her level-especially at her daughter's wake. Later, I saw her hugging Cleophus. I chuckled at what a cute couple they made, remembering Tara's comment earlier-a couple of what!

I left early. Star was with Gina during the wake. Bad enough I would have to deal with her at the funeral; I didn't see any reason to put her through both.

The heat still had not let up and although the weatherman mercifully predicted rain in a few days, no one really believed it. I took a long walk and tried to get my head together. Mrs. Levy was right about one thing; Tara and I were getting very close-maybe a little too close. The more I tried to tell myself I didn't have certain feelings for her, the stronger the feelings became. And I was sure Tara felt the same way about me. I knew I was hurling head first into disaster, but I couldn't help myself.

I needed to speak to someone about this. Preferably a woman, so I chose my sister, Gina.

"We have to be very careful who we say we're

falling in love with, David. A pretty face and soft hands isn't reason enough," Gina told me.

"I don't need you condescending to me, Gina. I'm not a fourteen-year-old schoolboy pining over a pretty girl! I mean…it's different when I'm with her, you know? I really enjoy her company. She's so smart and pretty and she always smells good! I mean you should hear some of the things I can talk to her about! I think I'm…really falling in love with her."

"Okay. I'm glad you explained it like that. I mean, you're right. It's not like you're some fourteen-year-old. So, let's see…she's smart and pretty and she smells good. Well, David, you have certainly raised your standards! This sounds like true love! Hell, from the way you described her I'm surprised every man from here to Westchester isn't lining up for her! I mean, she really smells good?"

"Okay, so that came out stupid-but I'm serious, Gina! I don't know what to do!"

"Then let me ask you this, do you think Sharon would want you two together? I mean it would be a helluva lot easier if you didn't have Star, but-"

"I know! It's all complicated. When Sharon and I first got together, I guess it was infatuation at first. I mean, you know…Sharon was fine as hell. But after a while, I noticed we were moving in two different directions, you know. With Tara, it's different. I feel like I know her. Like, I really know her."

"Maybe this is just a by-product of the grief. You know Sharon's family has always been nasty to you. Tara is the only one that even so much as spoke civil to you!"

"No, Gina. It's more than that-much more. It's really hard to describe. I feel like, well I know this is going to sound corny, but I feel like I've met my soul mate. It's like when I'm with her…I feel complete. I mean when I held her outside of her dad's hospital, our hearts were beating together!" I felt foolish standing there saying that, but it was true. I had never felt this way about anyone and it wasn't grief.

It was love.

"Yeah, and she smells good."

"…Yes. She smells good."

"Okay, David. If you're happy, I'm happy for you." She didn't mean a word of it. She just didn't want to discuss it any further. She has always been the type of woman who could cut you to ribbons with just a look.

"Hey, what was up with that weird phone call from you a few days ago? You back playing with them tarot cards?" I asked, trying to change the subject to something lighter. What in the world possessed me to talk to Gina about this? I would have been better off sticking a wet safety pin into an electric socket.

"I just wish you would leave that crazy ass family alone!" she blurted and I knew what was coming next. "I'm sorry Sharon's gone, but you know how I felt about her. And her mother is no better. I just can't see Tara being much different! Why can't you meet a nice girl on your job or something? Why Sharon's sister? It's not right, David! No matter what you say, I can't see it as being right. Why the sister?"

"I don't know! It's not like I planned this you know! It just happened! The more I try to fight it, the stronger the feelings are! Besides, they're only half sisters. I just found that out the other day."

"Well, that makes a whole world of difference! Call her up and set the date! And tell her to make sure she smells good, cause you guys bout to jump the broom!"

"I'm serious here, Gina! I do love her and I have been trying to fight it thinking exactly what you just said-that it would be wrong. But says who? Sharon and I weren't married and we were separated for damned near a year before she passed away. I love Tara and I really enjoy her company. And I am letting you know first, as my sister that I am in love!"

That got to her. Her expression softened and she let loose a deep sigh that I read as defeat.

"God doesn't make mistakes, David. If you two are meant to be together, you will be. I'm...I'm happy for you, David. Just be careful, I don't want to see you hurt and I damned sure don't want to see Star hurt!"

"I won't get hurt, Aunt Gina!" Star said smiling, standing in the doorway listening to us.

"How long were you there?" I asked embarrassed. I hoped she didn't hear me say I was in love with her Aunt Tara.

"Long enough to hear you say you loved Aunt Tara!" she laughed.

"Well," I squirmed. "Go get ready for us to go home!"

Star turned and left. Gina looked at me coldly.

"She is very, very special, David. Don't let anything happen to Star. Ever."

I was taken back by how solemnly she said that. Didn't Mr. Levy say something about Star? Why all the sudden ominous warnings?

We have to get ready for the funeral.

I started to tell Gina about the incident the night before I found out Sharon passed, but I thought better of it. Just remembering it made my flesh crawl with goose bumps. Besides, it had to be a figment of my imagination-just my mind's way of hiccupping the stress.

Gina called a cab and Star and I left. On the way out of the building Star stopped and said in my ear, "Mommy doesn't mind you loving Aunt Tara, Daddy. She wants you to be happy. She's sorry for all of the bad things she did to you."

"Well, that's a nice thing to think," I said, remembering Mrs. Levy's comment about Sharon busting Tara's ass. "I'm glad you feel that way, baby."

"I don't think that, Daddy. I know that." That look was back in Star's eyes. That strange gleam that made me think of...

Starlight?

"How-how do you know that, baby?"

"The old woman told me."

The dead know...

CHAPTER III:

∞

Let the Dead bury the Dead.

Sharon's funeral was beautiful-I mean as funerals go hers was done very well. I've been to some funerals-unfortunately way too many in Brooklyn-where the casket looked like cardboard and the organist couldn't play worth a damn. Cleophus did a fantastic job taking that ugly death hue out of her cheeks. Tara was right. Despite his strange look, the man knew his stuff. Tara picked out the dress, and the hairstylist managed to get that damned blonde weave out of Sharon's hair and fix it in a more respectable style.

A lot of Sharon's high school friends attended. Her coworkers from the Department of Motor Vehicles and her family came up from as far as Virginia. People I had not seen since bellbottoms were in style showed up. This was one of the yardsticks that the old people measured good funerals by: how many people showed up, how good the music and singing were, and how pretty the casket.

I noticed Mrs. Levy standing outside. She was trying to light a cigarette, but her hand was shaking so badly she couldn't. She looked so sad. Her face looked as if it had aged ten years because of this.

"You should leave those alone, Mrs. Levy," I said quietly. "Those things are no good for you."

"I know, David," she sighed deeply. " Hot as it is, I don't even have to light it." Her lip quivered and I could tell she was about to break down crying. I went to her.

"Let's get out of this sun, Mrs. Levy." I offered her my hand. She hesitated and then took it. We walked into the funeral home together and then split up, sitting in separate sections. That was the closest we came to apologizing to each other.

I never saw her again.

The pastor preached on about how we all loved Sharon, but God loved her best. Hymns were sung and before long, the choir had the entire church bawling with their rendition of Nearer My God to Thee. I held Star tightly and tried to stem the tears that flowed from my eyes.

Shakim sat next to me and kept telling me everything was going to be all right. He and I grew up together, somehow surviving the streets of Bedford Stuyvesant, the crack wars and the cops. In other words, the rites of passage for black men in New York City. He was the type of guy I could depend on. Whenever my back was against the wall Shakim was the one I wanted at my side. Guys like me who actually finished school and wear white shirts to work have a penchant to be regarded as either bourgie, or soft ergo a prime candidate for every wannabe gangster to step to. Shakim made sure I was safe on the street. If something happened, he was the one I called. The fact that he wasn't wrapped too tight meant I had to be careful when to involve him.

Once, I asked Shakim to speak to a drug dealer who was hanging a little too close to Star's school. The guy was selling Ecstasy about three blocks from the playground and as the president of the PTA I promised the other parents I would have it taken care of. I stressed the point to Shakim I only wanted the fellow spoken to. No violence. Shakim without saying a word walked up to the guy in broad daylight and shot him three times in the ass. To make matters worse he pinned a "Just Say No" button through one of the wounds.

That was Shakim.

He was tough and very street wise, but he wasn't street. He'd done time for gun possession, but that didn't make him a criminal; at least not to me. In my neighborhood, there aren't too many options for black men and unfortunately, Shakim chose the wrong one. He constantly carried a gun as an insurance policy. If questioned, he was quick to tell you it was better to be tried by twelve than to be carried by six. I disagreed with his thinking on a lot of issues, but whenever I needed him, he was there.

I was expected to say a few words at the funeral. I spent the evening trying to come up with something poignant and appropriate, but my mind kept drawing blanks. I finally settled on speaking from the heart. I was not going to be a hypocrite and say things I didn't mean. There was a lot of good water under Sharon's bridge, but there was a lot of bad water under there also. Whatever came out of my mouth at that moment-so be it.

The pastor called on me and my legs got wobbly. I've always felt uncomfortable speaking in front of a large group of people. Even at work I was passed over for certain positions because I lacked the finesse to give a good presentation. Sharon on the other hand was the exact opposite. She could speak very eloquently when she chose to. Which unfortunately, wasn't often.

I slowly walked to the front of the funeral parlor, feeling everyone's eyes on me. I looked back at Sharon's body in the casket behind me. I moved closer to her. I closed my eyes, opened my mouth and said what was in my heart.

"Sharon loved life. She was the most passionate person I've ever met. She had a fierce love and loyalty for all those she held dear…and woe be unto any and all who messed with her." A light chuckle arose when I said that. I let myself relax a little. Suddenly the words were there in abundance. "She loved hard, she fought hard…if she called you friend there was nothing she wouldn't give you. If she called you enemy-move out of town!" Again, more chuckles and a few, Yes Lawds. "I loved her…and although we were not together, I will always have her memory in my heart. Rest Sharon; your trip is over. Watch over the rest of us…until we see you again."

I walked back to my seat and held Star. Shakim smiled at me, wiping away tears. My entire body shook with relief; it was over and I had gotten through it. An old lady in the pew behind me patted my shoulders and said God would bless me. I smiled and thanked her. The choir went into another song.

Star fell asleep in my lap, right before the viewing of the body. I gently passed her to Shakim and rose to join the line. This part of the funeral service was very important to me. It aids the grieving process. Seeing your loved one in a casket is a very sobering experience. It is what I call the penultimate part of the service. The actual burial is the end. Seeing the body lowered into the ground drives home the finality of death like a spike in the railroad track.

I know how people say the dead look as if they were only asleep, but Sharon really looked like that. Even in death, she was beautiful. Beautiful. That was the only word that could begin to describe her. She had her hands folded and she looked so peaceful. I was riveted to her casket, mesmerized by her remains.

"Rest in peace, Sharon. I have Star, she's going to be okay," I said. My tears fell on her cheeks in large drops and stayed there like microscopic swimming pools. An ache filled my heart as I realized I would never see her eyes or hear the fire in her voice again.

I felt Tara's hand on my shoulders gently pulling me away. Her face was wet with tears and the funeral parlor filled with the wails and moans of grief.

"Let's go. They're ready to take her to her final resting-place. I'm right here with you," she said. Her grip on my shoulders was strong and reassuring. By now my eyes were swollen from crying and Star was awake. She walked over and saw her mother in the casket as they were closing the lid.

"NO! My mommy's in there! She won't be able to breathe!" Star cried. Her voice burst with panic. She tore at the man trying to close the lid. I felt my heart drop. What kind of damage would this do to her? I ran and grabbed her. She struggled in my arms like a fish caught in a net.

"No, baby!" I said. "She doesn't need to breathe. She's in heaven-remember?"

"No, Daddy! She's in that box!"

"No, baby. Only her body is in the box...her soul is in heaven! Remember? We spoke about this! We-"

"She's in that box! Let me go!"

I carried her out of the funeral home, passing the screaming old ladies who would talk about this funeral for many years to come. Star felt heavy in my arms, as if I was carrying a great weight. Tara was right behind me, her hand still on my shoulder. My legs felt like cement blocks. Every step was an exertion of energy. Star thrashed and kicked wildly, steadily screaming that her mother would not be able to breathe if I allowed them to close the casket lid.

Tara and I left the funeral. I motioned to the limousine driver to open the car door, while Star struggled in my arms. Tara got in the car with us. She told the driver to pull off and we left the crowd standing on the curb.

What a fucking day.

Tara took Star out of my arms and rocked her to sleep. The limousine driver closed the partition and I searched for the strength to get through the moment.

"I'm very proud of you," Tara said to me. Her voice was thick with emotion, her eyes misty. I could only imagine how hard this was on her, but here she was being a pillar of strength to me.

"Why?" I asked. The heat had my vision blurry and I could feel another headache coming on.

"You're dealing with all of this like a real man. I saw the look on your face when Star ran to the casket. I know how badly this must be tearing you up. Let me help you with her. I-I feel Sharon would want me to."

I nodded yes, keeping my eyes closed. I felt like someone was stabbing me in the brain with a hot sword. What was it that Star told me? Sharon wants me to be happy. My mind was one large flame, burning any reasonable thought to a cinder. The driver pulled in front of my building. Star was fast asleep in Tara's arms.

"I'll take her."

"I'm coming up with you, David. I don't want to be alone, and I don't think you do either."

I had to admit she was right. Tara would be nice company at a time like this. She carried Star to her room and put her to bed. I went and fixed myself a drink. Lord knows after the day I had, I needed one.

"We should be at the burial! I'll call my sister to stay with Star. I should have never taken her; it was a mistake! We can get a cab back to the funeral." I gulped the scotch like it was Kool-Aid, trying to get real drunk, real quick.

"Bullshit! We'll stay here with her. Right now Star needs you to be here when she wakes up. Let the dead bury the dead. That's what the Bible says isn't it? Let the dead bury the dead? You have to go on living…for Star. Sharon would want you to be here when she woke up. Mom and the rest will see to Sharon."

"You sound as if you don't even care," I mumbled.

"Of course I care! But Sharon is dead, David! Her spirit has left her body! We are still alive and we owe it to her memory to keep living! Star is going to need a lot of counseling now and…I want to be here…for the both of you."

I wanted that also. I would need someone to help me when Star woke up- someone like Tara.

A strong black woman.

She poured herself a drink and we began to talk about Sharon. About the times Sharon and I argued and fought. About the times we got caught making love. About Sharon's pregnancy and Star's birth.

"You know," Tara said smiling, "Star was named after Sharon and I. Ess for Sharon and Tar for Tara."

"That's bullshit!" I grinned. "Sharon and I named her Star because that night we made love under the stars was the night she was conceived."

We went on like that for hours, putting one hell of a dent in the bottle of Johnnie Walker Black. We sat on the couch and held each other. More affectionate than physical. We'd both lost someone dear to us. I guess there was a need to walk down memory lane, sort of like a mental spring-cleaning.

Tara got up and made another drink. As she walked toward the bar, I couldn't help but notice how beautiful she was. She sat down, my arms around her. Her head resting on my chest. I consciously willed myself not to become excited or aroused, but it was so hard. The combination of her light and airy perfume and the liquor had every nerve ending in my body tingling. This moment had been building between us for days and in some ways perhaps longer. The way she fit in my arms, so comfortable-so right.

"I love you, David, but I guess you've known that for quite some time now."

There was a tinge of sadness in her voice. I was overcome with emotion. An ache filled my heart and my loins. It had been so long since I had a woman. I don't mean just a piece of ass-I mean a woman. There is a difference. Contrary to what most women think, men do know that much. We didn't speak. We both sensed words would only ruin the moment.

She nestled her head deeper in my chest. I held her hand. My fingertips traced her palm like a feather floating on the wind. A soft, barely audible moan escaped her lips.

I was so blind with desire I'd completely forgotten about everything. I shifted my body so I was directly between her legs. My hardness pressed against her. I could feel the heat of carnal need rising from within her. I slipped my hand beneath her dress and massaged the soft wet mound of her womanhood. Her breath was small urging gasps in my ear.

"My ice cream truck has come," she whispered.

I looked deep into her eyes and watched her breasts heave up and down. Her skin was so flushed she went from cocoa brown to a reddish bronze. I feverishly undressed her. She lay naked, as beautiful as moonlight.

"I love you, too, Tara. I have been trying to find a way to tell you that for a while now."

"Don't tell me, David. Show me."

I was possessed with a craving so strong my soul trembled. I entered her and felt our spirits mesh and intertwine. We were one being. One heartbeat. One breath. With each thrust I seemed to awaken pleasure centers I never knew existed. Every pore awoke with a vengeance. She quivered everywhere I touched her. Her body was a liquid flame I wanted to immerse myself within. She wrapped her legs around my waist and lunged with the strength of a wild storm. The couch hit the wall in a violent barrage of rhythm.

It wasn't just love we were making. It was lust. We were feeding a violent hunger, fierce and angry. The dark fleshy side of nature that begs release. I could feel her heartbeat against my chest thundering like a jackhammer as I lunged and pounded her with boundless energy.

My libido seemed to know no end. As her body hungrily searched for the ends of my virility, I summoned more strength. We thrashed and flailed with unchecked passion. Our bodies contorted and writhed into several positions before reaching the apex of fulfillment. I exploded within her, shaking from waves of the most awesome climax imaginable. We collapsed into each others arms physically sated, spiritually invigorated and utterly satisfied.

And for the first time, my soul felt complete.

∞

I woke up the next morning in the middle of the livingroom floor with a size fifteen hangover. Sunlight blasted through my window like a shotgun through tissue paper, causing a sensation that felt like sharp needles were being roughly inserted into my brain.

I couldn't open my eyes. They wouldn't adjust to the light. I felt detached from my body, as if I was just a passenger and my body was a bus. I was just along for the ride.

I stumbled around the house in nothing but my boxers. My arms stretched in front of me like Frankenstein's monster. I wasn't quite yet convinced I was awake, but I knew something was wrong. Dreadfully wrong. Images flipped and flashed in my mind like a strobe light as I attempted to blink my way back to sight. My aquarium was shattered. My tropical fish lay dead on the carpet. The screen of my TV was busted. All of the food lay in the floor with the kitchen cabinets empty and the refrigerator turned over.

Had I been robbed while I slept?

I kept rubbing my eyes, trying to get them to focus. While I stumbled through the apartment bits and pieces of pictures fluttered in and out like a photograph that wasn't developed properly. My head throbbed. One vein in my scalp created a line of thick pain from my forehead to the back of my neck.

I managed to make it to the bathroom, feeling my way along the walls. I washed my face in the bathroom sink, flushing my eyes. My senses still weren't anywhere near one hundred percent. I came to realize I was in a great degree of bodily pain.

The cold water served its purpose. Bit-by-bit my sight became clearer, my head also. The pain was no less, but my awareness was back. I looked at myself. I was covered in blood. Had Tara gotten her period during the night? For that matter where was Tara? I didn't remember seeing her when I woke up.

In that instant, reality threatened to send me over the edge. In my heart, I knew something terrible had happened. How terrible was all that was left to be determined. I ran through the apartment viewing the destruction. The clothes hamper had been torn from the wall. The toilet was shattered. There were massive holes in the walls as if someone took a sledgehammer and tried to hammer their way...

Out?

In?

Star's room was a complete mess. All of her clothes were ripped to shreds, and the furniture hacked to pieces. The mattress was shredded and the air conditioner was torn open.

"What the fuck? Star! Star, where are you?" I screamed. I searched the closets and under the bed. She was gone. I ran to my bedroom and I saw-

I saw-

"Tara!"

Beautiful Tara lay dead in my bed, ripped from vagina to throat. Her body spread open as if someone performed an autopsy. Her face was a bloodied mask of tangled tissue. She died in pain, I thought. They cut her while she was awake. I was covered in her blood. My mouth filled with water, the only warning I was about to throw up. I stood there pissing, shitting and puking all over the place.

My mind was ablaze with a thousand questions, but none of them made any sense. Where was my baby? Who killed Tara? Who tore my place up? Did I do this? Where is Star?

Don't let anything happen to her...

I collapsed at the foot of the bed as the reality of the situation impaled what was left of my sanity. I slowly understood the trouble I was in. Everyone would think I killed Tara. Judging from the destruction of my place, I was sure there had been a lot of noise. My neighbors would no doubt say they heard a terrific struggle. No matter how I analyzed it, I was fucked.

Think! Think!

I tried to rationalize what had happened, but all I could think about was Star. Where was she? Where was my baby!

A steady banging sound grew louder and more pronounced. There were voices now. The radio of my mind was finally tuning in to the signals. By the time I was able to figure out there was someone knocking on the door and screaming, the door damned near flew off the hinges.

"Freeze, mutha fucka!"

It was the cops. I was suddenly surrounded by a half dozen police officers in what looked like space age riot gear. One of them made a comment about me stinking. They were wearing plastic gloves and instead of handcuffs, they put these little plastic wires around my wrists. They reminded me of garbage bag ties.

At that moment, the closest thing to a cogent thought popped isolated in the soon to be chaotic bedlam formally known as my mind. Not even Johnnie Cochran could get me out of this one. There I was wearing nothing but my boxers, covered in blood with a mutilated body on my bed, surrounded by cops.

"You have the right to remain silent. If you wish to give up the right to remain silent, anything you say can and will be used against you in a court of law. You have the right to an attorney, if you cannot afford an attorney one will be provided for you by the state free of charge. Do you understand these rights?" one cop asked, very coldly.

"Yes," was all I could answer. I was numb with shock. Surely, this was just a dream. A very bad dream. I think it was then I passed out.

I woke up handcuffed to a hospital bed by those little plastic garbage bag ties. An IV was hooked up to my arm and I strained to see what I was being injected with. My entire body was sore. My skin felt as if it could fall off in one clumped piece. I quickly scanned the room. A privacy curtain surrounded my bed. There were various monitors beeping in a monotone cadence. The bed sheets were stenciled with blue lettering that read, PROPERTY OF KINGS COUNTY HOSPITAL.

"I'm glad you're awake, Mr. Peters. How are you feeling? Do you know where you are?" a beautiful female doctor asked me, parting the curtains. Her I.D. tag read Jasmine Walters, M.D.

"I'm assuming the G building," I answered, a bit surprised at how calm and rational my voice sounded. The G building was the psychiatric wing of the hospital. "Where's my daughter?"

"I'm Dr. Walters," she answered, ignoring my question. "I am here to evaluate you. To see if you are mentally able to answer for the things that has happened. I am not here to judge your guilt or innocence, only to assess your mental acuity. Will you speak with me?"

"Yes, doctor, but could we start by your answering my question? Where is my daughter?"

"We were hoping you could tell us that," she answered flatly.

"I don't know where she is. I woke up and found the place wrecked and Tara murdered! I didn't do it! I didn't do it!" I stammered like a mumbling idiot. I was naked except for the blue stenciled sheet that covered me. At least someone had the decency to clean the blood off me. No doubt after photographing and taking samples.

Taking samples?

"I've been arrested. Shouldn't I have my lawyer present for any questioning?

"You don't need a lawyer with me, Mr. Peters.

I'm your friend." Her tone was so condescending and insulting that I became angry. Who did she think she was dealing with?

"I am not your usual Saturday night crack fiend, Dr. Walters. Something terrible happened, yes. I'll accede that, but I am a victim in this! Obviously, while I was unconscious someone took the liberty of undressing me and cleaning me up. Well, if anything discovered while I was out is incriminating it won't be allowed in court! This violates my rights! I demand to see a lawyer! Your smug attitude doesn't fool me one bit! I demand to know where my daughter is!"

"You do not demand anything. You have been in a virtual state of catatonia since you've been arrested. The court remanded you here for a preliminary evaluation. You don't need and you will not receive a lawyer here. You'll need one in court-and judging from the charges-a very good one."

She never raised her voice. Not even to emphasize her point. An air of malevolence surrounded this woman. She adjusted the mechanism that controlled the drip flow on my IV.

"What's in that? What are you giving me?"

"Something for my special patients, Mr. Peters. My more educated patients." She wheeled a cart holding a TV/VCR combo. She inserted a videocassette and pressed play. The picture flickered until the auto-tracking adjusted. I saw myself, struggling against the plastic straps. There was a crazed, detached look on my face. I looked like a drug addicted derelict. My eyes had turned up in my head so that only the whites were visible. Spittle flew from my mouth in foamy streams.

"Do you speak French?"

"No," I answered, confused. What in the hell did French have to with anything?

"You were speaking French while you were out, a very thick patois. I just thought it was a bit strange." Dr. Walters turned up the volume. I heard this alien, thick and husky voice come out my mouth. It sounded like-

Like that old lady in my dream...

"What am I saying? Do you know what it means?" I asked, feeling a bit lightheaded. I started sweating profusely, although all of the spit in my mouth dried up.

"We had it translated. Roughly, it means-the dead know what the living are doing. Do you believe that, Mr. Peters? Do you believe that the dead know what the living are doing? Do you sometimes hear voices?"

I screamed and kept screaming until they injected my IV with a very strong sedative. I felt as if the glue in my world had finally come apart. I entertained the thought that maybe I really did kill Tara.

Maybe I really was crazy...

CHAPTER IV:

The Difference Between Men and Worms...

When I finally came to, I was sitting in a wheelchair on the ward for the criminally insane. My head felt as if butterflies were swarming around in it. Everything was disjointed, fuzzy. I had drooled on myself and it took every effort to get my hand to wipe it away. Whatever medicine I was on, it had dulled my senses considerably.

All of the doors were controlled electronically. There were no locks to pick, no keys to steal. Security cameras covered everything-including the showers. All of the orderlies were at least three hundred pounds and they carried stun guns and Mace.

This place was the Fort Knox of all nut houses.

Two men were playing cards at a table. One would shuffle and then throw all fifty-two cards in the other man's face. I sat there watching this, slightly amused. There was an air of insanity about this place. One glimpse of it was all you needed to know you were in the loony bin.

An extremely large man that smelled like an unholy fusion of shit, piss, ball sweat and bad breath walked over to me and said, "Yo! If L.L Cool J. and Clarence Thomas had a battle who would win?"

I swallowed hard and slurred, "Clarence Thomas would smoke that nigga!"

There was weak applause. The large man hugged me tightly. Someone placed a paper hat on my head and kissed me on the cheek. Another person placed a chain of dried spray painted macaroni around my neck. I was one of them now.

"Yo, my name is Troy. This is my crew! You can be down with us now," the large man said smiling. His teeth were missing except for a few on the bottom and he liked to talk using his hands to accentuate words like punches.

The air was filled with elevator music and I was wheeled into the bay area. There was a TV suspended on a platform above us in a wire box. Everyone on the screen looked like they were in jail. The TV only showed the cartoon channel, so little things like the news and weather were denied us-but I could recite every episode of the Flintstones that ever aired.

Time had no purpose in this place. One moment was indistinguishable from the next. The only time that did matter was when the medicine came. A bell would go off and everyone would drop what they were doing and run to the line. The response reminded me of Pavlov's dogs, running for food whenever the bell rang.

I learned the stories of the other inmates. Some were very close to sane, while others were as far from reality as the Brooklyn Bridge is from the

Panama Canal. Troy was one of those individuals that was diagnosed as criminally insane-and rightfully so.

If asked, Troy would tell you he was locked up because Don King knew he was the true world's heavyweight boxing champion. According to him, he met Evander Holyfield one night in a gym in Brownsville, and while closing the place, challenged him to a fight and knocked him out. He further claims Don King witnessed the fight and now owes him sixty Kazillion dollars-his number, not mine.

The fact that he was caught on the number two train dressed in boxing shorts, a multi-colored afro wig and high heels, punching passengers in the face with two bricks taped to his hands is just another trick of the white man to oppress him.

As bad as Troy was, he was nothing in comparison to Skippy. Skippy was a psychologist's worst nightmare. This nut actually thought he invented the plastic bag, chewing gum and the lubricated condom. His room was filled with these items. Although no one ever asked him what the condoms were lubricated with, we all had a pretty good idea.

Skippy was arrested for raping elderly women and suffocating them with plastic bags. He claims all of his victims were related to government agents who were trying to keep him from getting the royalties he deserved for his inventions.

Then there was Jamie, who claimed to be man, woman and child in the same body. This guy was actually a successful preacher in a storefront church before he was committed. His crime? Well, besides being a pedophile he was also into necrophilia.

Jamie liked having sex with dead children.

Even Skippy and Troy avoided this guy.

There were a few others, but none were as interesting as Jamie, Skippy and Troy. Whom I came to affectionately call, The Three Stooges.

I was scheduled to meet with Dr. Walters for refusing to take any more medication. Two huge orderlies accompanied me. Her office was really a treatment room with a desk and lounge chair placed on one side. There was a rather uncomfortable looking steel table placed in the middle of the room, surrounded by machines with LED displays and gadgets that looked as if they belonged in Cleophus Gilly's line of work. The sterile white walls and stainless steel utensils gave the room an inhuman feeling of intimidation. The wall behind her desk was blanketed with all of her degrees, certificates and accreditations. If Cleophus looked like the stereotypical undertaker, then Jasmine Walters was the atypical psychiatrist. Her frosty aloof manner and hard piercing eyes seemed better suited to a sadistic school matron.

"Have a seat, Mr. Peters. I trust this session will yield a better fruit than our last." I sat with the orderlies standing staunch at my sides like robotic drones. Their snow-white uniforms added to the room's depressing persona.

"The orderlies have told me you've been quite uncooperative, not taking your medicine. That's always disturbing to hear. It's so much easier when the patient is willing to help the doctor. Don't you agree?"

"Yes," I mumbled. I found Jasmine Walters unnerving with her ice-cold demeanor and her puncturing hazel eyes. Her diction was immaculate, her voice monotone and even. Not the slightest bit of inflection or accent. She spoke so calmly that it was disarming in a threatening way. I immediately pictured her as the type of person who could never be taken by surprise. Calculating. Didactic. I started to tell her that she missed her calling; she'd make an excellent dominatrix, but I thought better of it.

She fit in perfectly with this room, cold and unfeeling. No empathy for anything. I knew she was well trained in human behavior as a psychiatrist. I'd taken a few Psychology classes in college and I had a rough idea what to expect.

"They also tell me you have been demanding telephone privileges and visits. Is this true?" she asked in such a nonchalant tone I thought she was being rhetorical.

"Yes, doctor. At the very least, I am entitled to make a phone call to let someone know where I am. I-"

"What you are entitled to, Mr. Peters is whatever I decide to give you. I and I alone will determine when, where and what you are entitled to." There was no anger, passion, or malice in her voice as she said this. But there was no mistaking her conviction. I imagined she could slit someone's throat with the same smooth stolid manner.

"Place him on the table."

The orderlies roughly grabbed and strapped me down to that cold table. My hospital gown was removed and I lay there naked. I struggled furiously against the restraints, but they wouldn't budge. "Let me go! This is illegal and you know it! I know my rights! I'll have all of you fired!" I thrashed and kicked but the leather straps held firm.

"Bind his head," she ordered. They placed a thick leather strap around my forehead and chin. This I was not prepared for. I imagined more of a counseling session where she would probe and ask questions about my childhood, sexual fantasies, that sort of thing. What started as a small bubble of unease quickly blossomed into a huge balloon of fear. I tried to twist my way out of the restraints to no avail. I only succeeded in chafing my skin until it burned. The orderlies snickered and Dr. Walters glared at them. They instantly fell silent, looking down at their feet away from her icy frown.

"Just let me go!" I pleaded. Thoughts of electric shock went through my mind. Shakim had told me about a guy he knew who had gotten caught in a southern town with a kilo of cocaine. The guy refused to give up his buyer in town. The sheriff tortured him by soaking his testicles in rubbing alcohol and then taping a low voltage wire to his scrotum. "Let me go! I can cause a lot of trouble for you, bitch!"

"To cause trouble you have to have power. You're not empowered to cause trouble, Mr. Peters. This is all a part of your evaluation and treatment."

Dr. Walters slowly walked over to me. I was really scared now. I had no idea what she had planned, but I knew it would be something bad-maybe not as painful as a live wire on my nuts, but something equally horrifying. The room grew cold. My skin crawled with thick goose pimples. I shivered in icy fear.

"You can leave us now. I'll call you when I am done."

"Yes, doctor," the orderlies murmured and left. The panic knob in my mind just turned up. Why would she send the orderlies out of the room?

So there'll be no witnesses...

"Mr. Peters we are going to start by a sort of cleansing." She pressed a button and a group a bright lights flashed overhead. "Keep looking at the lights, Mr. Peters. It will make things a little easier if you cooperate. It is of paramount importance you understand your place in the grand scheme of things, Mr. Peters."

Her voice droned on in my ears, creating a soporific effect. The lights flashed in quick random patterns and combinations-blue, red and green. "Mr. Peters, there are men and there are worms. The two species were not meant to intertwine..."

Suddenly I could feel worms writhing all over me. My skin was covered with them. I wanted to scream but the sound was too heavy for my lungs to expel. The worms slithered and slimed all over my legs and privates. I could feel them slipping into my ears and nose, choking me. I could not move a single muscle, not even to blink my eyes. Each worm split creating another worm. Their numbers doubled and then tripled.

Every nerve ending in my body exploded in unfettered terror. My heart pounded in dry thumps. I have always had a tremendous fear of worms. Once when I was a child, my foster parents let Gina and I spend a summer in a camp sponsored by the Fresh Air Fund. The counselors took us out to teach us how to fish. They brought a package of worms that were supposed to be guaranteed to lure fish. I grabbed a worm out of the package and tried to get the squirmy thing on my hook. Holding it between my thumb and forefinger the worm shot from my fingers as if propelled out of a cannon into my nose. Before I realized what was happening the worm had lodged so deep into my nostril I could feel the thing in my throat. I hacked and coughed in a blind furious panic, desperately trying to dislodge the worm before it decided to make my snot box its permanent residence. The counselors tried to pull it out, but they only managed to snatch it in pieces. The other children teased me, called me worm boy and worm booger the entire summer. Gina and I agreed that summer was the worst of our childhood; a lofty and extremely competitive distinction.

I had nightmares for months about that worm. I kept dreaming it climbed up my nose and into my brain. The worm would find rooms filled with special memories in my brain and eat them.

"But when a man does not perform as instructed," Dr. Walters continued, "or he blatantly refuses to obey his superiors he is then reduced to the station of a worm."

More worms now, thousands and thousands of them splitting and multiplying like an insane infinite Hydra. I could hear them moving like dirty water down a sluggish drain. The weight of them threatened to crush me. They filled my mouth, sliding down my throat like thick strands of live spaghetti. I couldn't breathe. My head pounded in rhythm with my pulse. They mashed my chest, squashing all of the air out of me. I felt as if I would implode. My eyes felt as if they would shoot out of their sockets. The weight of the worms created a great heat. My skin welted and blistered from their noxious slime leaving sickly white patches and streaks. My insides felt like a preheated oven, like a boiler that had too much pressure built up.

"But the unique thing about man," her voice droned on, "is that he can always become a man again. While a worm remains a worm."

The worms disappeared without a trace. The weight and pressure were gone and so were the heat and blisters. My skin regained its normal color. It took a while for me to gain my bearings. The sudden shift in perception was unsettling. I was finally able to take a deep breath. I gasped, sucking in as much precious air as my lungs could hold.

"Are you a worm, or a man, Mr. Peters?" Still the same flat monotone. No emotion. How had she known of my deep-rooted fear of worms?

"Fuck you, Nurse Ratched! It's going to take a lot more than your little parlor tricks to get me to fly over the cuckoo's nest!" I screamed, determined not to let her break me. "You can rest assured I'll be reporting your narrow, reticulated ass to the American Medical Association! I have friends in the State Congress, bitch!"

"That was just your first treatment, Mr. Peters. I think your condition requires more intense therapy. Sometimes a parent has to try radical things to get a wayward child back on the right path."

Daddy!

That's Star's voice! She's here!

"Star? Star! I'm here, baby! Where are you?" I squirmed and twisted furiously. The chinstrap held my head immobile. Dr. Walters ignored me and kept speaking in the same dry flat voice.

"I feel compelled to inform you that any unpleasantness you experience now is unavoidable, Mr. Peters. Just as sometimes a parent has to hurt a child for the greater good."

Daddy, come get me! They're hurting me, Daddy!

I could hear Star clearly. As if she stood right next to me. I could hear the raw panic and burning fear in her voice. She sounded like she was running from something.

And it had just caught her.

"Star, I'm right here, baby! I can't see you! Can you see me?"

Daddy they're hurting me! They're doing bad things to me, Daddy! Please come and get me!

"It is never easy, Mr. Peters. But I have come to accept the good with the bad. I cannot heal everyone who comes to me, but I try with all the skill I have."

Daddy! Please, Daddy! They're hurting me! It hurts so much, Daddy! Please come and get me! I promise I'll be good!

"God in heaven, please help her! I don't care what happens to me, just help her! Please help Star!" I was hysterical. How could Star be here? Who was trying to hurt her? What did she mean, they're doing bad things to me?

Dr. Walters grabbed my face roughly and stared hard into my eyes. Her face was devoid of expression. "Your God is no longer in heaven, Mr. Peters. He is in the pills that I have required you to take. You can view me as God's caretaker, Mr. Peters. I am obligated by a Hippocratic oath to see that you take your medicine."

"What have you done with my daughter? I hear her! I know she's here! Where is she?"

Dr. Walters turned the knob on a machine and the lights violently swirled and flickered. I shut my eyes and desperately tried to remember that this was just a mind trick, some sort of hypnotic suggestion. Star was not in the room with me. She couldn't be.

Daddy, please! Please don't let them hurt me anymore!

It's not real. It's a trick! A simple mind game and I won't fall for it!

Daddy, they're touching me! They're touching me…down there!

No! No, it's a trick! A trick!

Daddy, please help me! Please, Daddy! I'm so scared! You said you'd never let anything hurt me! Daddy! You said I was your princess, Daddy! Daaaadeeeee, pleeeaase!

I screamed in rage and fear. This couldn't be happening to me. Not to me. I obeyed all of the rules. I went to school. I worked and studied hard. I didn't smoke, use drugs or drink excessively. I didn't use my childhood as a reason for failure. This sort of thing didn't happen to guys like me. This happened to the other guy. The guy you read about in the newspaper or heard about on the eyewitness news report. Not to me. Not me. I didn't deserve this.

Star's voice echoed in my mind, pounding away at my resolve, eating away at my sanity. What man could stand to hear his child crying like this? What father could ignore his daughter's pleas for help?

Daddy, it hurts so bad! Daddy, please come get me!

"It's not real!" I shrieked, trying to hold back tears of impotent frustration. Desperately trying to cling to some semblance of the man I once was. Star's screams tore at me, ripping my reason to shreds. I wanted to die, to disappear into a deep black hole and never come out.

Daddy! Daddy, pleeeeeeeease!

It's not real! Not real! Not real! I cried uncontrollably, trying to wring her voice out of my head. I was a failure. As a man. As a father. As a person. A failure. My education, my hard work meant nothing here. Her screams echoed throughout my soul, scorching and searing until all that was left was burnt ash and dust. Star is my life. Without her, I am nothing. Without her...

There are men and there are worms, Mr. Peters.

...I am a worm.

"I can make all of this go away, Mr. Peters. Peace is yours for the asking."

"Yes," I whimpered, broken and defeated. I

couldn't stand to hear anymore. I couldn't take hearing her scream knowing there was nothing I could do about it. "Please make it go away."

"Make it go away, who?"

"Make it go away...doctor."

"And you agree not to ask anymore about visits or phone calls?"

"Yes."

"Yes, who?"

"Yes," I swallowed hard; forcing what was left of that thing called dignity down into the abyss of my soul. "Yes, doctor."

"You agree not to agitate the other patients with such nonsense as the Patient's Bill of Rights?"

"Yes, doctor."

"That's so much better. I knew you would see things my way. Such fuss over something so trivial as sanity. After all, who is to judge what is real and what is not."

I felt a pinprick in my arm, and then a burning sensation through my veins. My eyesight became blurry and Star's voice faded deep into the background.

The moist velvet hand of unconsciousness beckoned and I willingly followed.

I slept a dreamless sleep that blurred the line between reality and illusion. Nothing mattered. I sat in a wheelchair satisfied to watch the other patients. Sometimes I'd sit and think about the strange twist my life had taken and I would scream and throw a tantrum until one of the orderlies would give me my medication. Then I'd settle back into my chair and feel content.

I tried to concentrate, to focus my thinking, but the medicine seemed to anticipate this move. Thinking only made my thoughts fuzzier. I would try to think of Star and my mind would see the word instead of her face. It was as if the information was there, but it was just out of reach. Teasing me.

I don't know which torture was more insidious, hearing Star's screams of panic and pain, or not being able to remember her face, her voice. But deep down inside I knew she was alive. Star was alive and although I didn't know where she was or what was happening to her, that had to suffice.

I felt that I would somehow jinx Star if I tried to think about her too much. She was alive, but if I made waves or tried to think too hard, Dr. Walters might get angry and she might make Star scream again.

I was assigned to a room with an older guy named Justice. Justice stood about six feet six and weighed about two hundred and seventy pounds. Cock Diesel. He was a fierce looking man with salt and pepper dreadlocks who always smelled like incense.

I lay on my bunk and stared aimlessly at the ceiling. My thoughts were as disheveled as I was. Justice sat on his bunk and stared at me, without saying a word. I regarded him impassively. Nothing mattered.

"She really did some job on you," he said.

"Wha? What you mean?" I slurred.

"That doctor. Walters she calls herself. She did

some job on you. You came in roaring like a lion and now you're as meek as a lamb. You don't know the difference between being a man and being a worm, do you?"

There are men and there are worms, Mr. Peters...

"I don't know what you talkin about."

"You are not a worm, David. You are a man. Come out of the hole before it's too late."

I sucked my teeth and turned on my bunk, enjoying my medicinal stupor.

The next morning in line for breakfast, Jamie snatched an orange off my tray. The entire cafeteria seemed to stop moving when this happened. Everyone waited to see my reaction. If I didn't stand up to this nut I would be regarded as soft and more than likely I would have severe problems getting any respect.

"Unless you're tired of breathing, I suggest you give him back that orange and sit your crazy ass down," Justice said sternly.

Oh great! I thought to myself. Now everyone will think I'm his bitch!

"That's okay, Justice," I said, pushing him back. "I can handle this idiot and any other one of these bitch-ass, punk mutha-fuckas!" I hoped I sounded a lot tougher than I felt. At least tough enough to make Jamie back down.

Jamie looked at me coldly and then stared at Justice. He hesitated and then put the orange back on my tray.

"Here, man. I didn't really want it," he murmured. The crowd went back to their usual inane chatter.

"Thanks, Justice!" I said, relieved.

"No need. I knew you could handle him. People like that only try guys that won't fight back. You show them any resistance and they back down. Besides, it proves you're a man and not a worm. A worm would've cowered back into a hole."

I had no problems after that incident.

Justice was the only man on the ward that Troy, Jamie and Skippy didn't mess with. He was very quiet, but when he spoke, everyone listened. Our particular ward was nothing more than a holding bay. From here, Dr. Walters would determine if we were fit to stand trial. If we were declared legally sane by the courts, we would be sent to a place that made this shit hole look like heaven.

Justice showed me how to survive the nightmare. He saved my life and oddly enough my sanity. He constantly seemed to follow me around, sprouting cliches of what it means to be a man. At first he irritated me to no end, but soon I began to realize his presence was forcing me to dance closer to the edge of sobriety.

I discovered that Justice was an extremely intelligent man, well versed in a large number of subjects. Even through the medicinally induced haze, he intrigued me. We discussed things like chess, politics, and history at length.

We were sitting in our room one night right before lights out when he trusted me with a secret.

"I'm going to show you something, but you must promise never to tell anybody!" he said, as he pulled back his mattress. He kept his back blocking the security camera. I squinted and tried to focus on what he was showing me. There were at least three-dozen pills secreted in a pouch he had cut into his bunk. At first, I didn't know what to think and then it dawned on me.

Justice wasn't taking his medicine.

"So…how much you want for it?" I asked groggily. Justice slapped me so hard I thought my head had left my body. The sound of his hand hitting my face sounded like the recoil of a high-powered rifle. My ears rung and I had to steady myself to keep from passing out.

"Nigga! Is you crazy!" I grumbled. I didn't want to fight Justice, but I didn't want him thinking I was a punk either. After all, we were on the mental ward. He could have been having some kind of Vietnam flashback or something.

"I did that to wake you up. You don't belong here! Stop taking that damned medicine. I know what that bitch did to you! I know how she broke you! You are not a worm, David. You are a man. A good man! I was downstairs when they brought you in here. You were covered in blood and one of the nurses said you killed your sister in law and they don't know what you did with your daughter. But I looked at you and I knew. I knew something was wrong! It takes a special kind of crazy to do shit like that. And boy, you ain't that crazy."

He got back in his bunk. I just stared at him, the side of my face still stinging. His words penetrated me like a hot knife. I was innocent. Innocent! And someone knew it!

I wasn't crazy.

You are not a worm, David...

"Can you help me? I asked crying. "I want to be a man, Justice. I don't want to be a worm that hides in a hole. I want my life back. I want my daughter back!" It was then that Star's face came back to me. My angel. My beautiful, precious angel. Where was she? Who had her?

Help me, Daddy! Help me!

My head throbbed as if someone had a recoilless hammer slamming away inside of it. Justice helped me to the bunk. I sat weeping.

"Tell me what happened," Justice said, and I found myself telling him everything. Everything, from the weird heatwave downtown Brooklyn, to how I slept with Tara and woke up covered in her blood. I told him about the dreams, I told him about Gina's call. I told him how Star knew Sharon had passed before the cops came to the door. He listened without saying anything. When I was finished, he just stared at me for a long time. Finally he spoke.

"There's a lot of things you said don't make sense and I'm not just talking about the weird dreams or the noise your baby was making."

"What do you mean?" I asked, exhausted from talking.

"Well let's look at this from the beginning. The man in the sandwich board as you put it, told you after being hit by a car that you were a passenger in, that the men you saw put an old woman in an ambulance, were not paramedics-right?"

"Right."

"Then your daughter's mother tells you to watch her while she goes to a party. She is struck and killed by an ambulance. This is told to you by two cops, after they bring a picture of the three of you that was taken last year in Coney Island-right?"

"Right...so?"

"Stay with me here. I don't know how well you were thinking, but it doesn't take Sherlock Holmes to figure out those weren't real cops. You yourself said your in-laws met you at the hospital-"

"Yeah, I called her mother-"

"Remember what you said, man! How did the cops know she was your girlfriend? Remember? You could have been her brother, or a neighbor! Anybody! There was nothing written on the back of the picture was there?"

"No," I gasped. Justice was making more sense than I wanted to admit.

"The hospital would have called you and said they had her and that would've been much later. Why did the cops ask you if she lived there?"

I answered that I didn't know.

"Well let's add it up. Two guys dressed like cops come to your house and tell you that your baby's mother is dead. How did they know she had just left a party? They asked a lot of questions that real cops wouldn't ask. Less than a week later, your sister in law is dead and your daughter missing and you're framed for it. Makes sense so far?"

"Why would anybody want to frame me?" I asked.

"You sure you grew up in Brooklyn?" he replied sarcastically. "The part I don't understand is why they killed her. Was she into drugs? Numbers? Anything?"

I thought about his words before I answered. Why they killed her.

We're still doing an investigation, but at this point, I'm confident it was just an accident...

All of this time I accepted, or rejected Sharon's death as just that-an accident. I never put the ambulance thing together with the so-called paramedics from downtown. Now, it all made sense.

Well, not yet...

"No, Sharon was as straight as six o' clock. She talked a tough game but she was scared to death of shit like that. It doesn't make sense, Justice! It doesn't make sense!"

I got up and washed my face in the basin, shivering from fright. Every nerve in my body was on edge. I wanted so badly to tell Justice to give me a few of those pills. This was the most lucid I'd been since I had arrived. Somehow, it seemed telling my story cancelled out the effect of the drugs. "It doesn't make any damned sense!" I said again, this time loud enough to cause the inmates in the other rooms to stir.

"Yes it does. I think there are some real evil forces working against you. Things that seem to defy logic."

"Justice, I have to get out of here! I mean it, man. There's some weird shit happening! I have to find my little girl! She's in trouble. I know it!" Justice stared at me. His eyes were hard and seemed to burn right through me.

"Stop taking the medicine. I might be crazy, but I think you have some very powerful enemies. Enemies that kill."

I looked at him. His eyes seemed sure and calm. There was something very sane about Justice. I thought about the sandwich board man. Of how I first thought that he wasn't crazy-just misunderstood. Justice had that same look about him. Something told me I would need Justice. He would become an important ally.

"Why are you here, Justice? You don't seem crazy at all!"

"I'm here to help you find the enemy," he said calmly.

∞

It wasn't easy to stop taking the medicine for two reasons. First, I was addicted to it. My body would crave those pills and I would get sick when I missed my dosage. I'm talking diarrhea, vomiting, and chills. The shit men usually stay home from work for.

This is where Justice came in. He was with me every step of the way. Constantly reminding that Star was out there somewhere, that there was a conspiracy to take my baby and my freedom away from me. He would remind me that men rose to meet adversity, where worms slithered and hid into deep dark holes. He would say this to me and I would grit my teeth and bear it.

The second reason was the staff checked us thoroughly to make sure we took our medicine. This meant I had to come up with creative ways to hide the fact I was clear-headed. We were given urine tests twice a week to ensure we were taking our medication. Justice suggested I trade Skippy my medicine for condoms filled with his urine. Justice would constantly remind me not to appear too sober in front of the staff.

My wit returned to me after awhile. I would mentally practice complex math exercises, or verbally play chess with Justice. My reasoning sharpened. It was then that I was able to assess my surroundings and try to formulate some type of plan to escape.

That was until I was told my court hearing was coming up. This meant there was a strong chance I would be sent to Rikers Island if the judge didn't buy the crazy bit. I was on the verge of panicking. The night before the court date and my gut feeling was I was doomed. The entire ward knew and they avoided me like the plague. According to the rules of the ward, I was bad luck. I've often heard it said that the sane are locked up and the crazies walk the street. Well, with the exception of Troy, Jamie and Skippy I can say that's true.

The night before my hearing I couldn't sleep. I kept pacing the floor of my small room. Justice lay on his bunk looking at me walk back and forth with the rhythm of a pendulum.

"What if I told you there was a way out of here? Would you believe me?" He asked stoically. There was something about the look in his eye that night. As if he held some knowledge no one else had.

"Yeah, I'd believe you. Shit, you were the one

that got my head back right. If you got a way out of here, tell me. I'll do anything!"

I was more prepared for a knock down, drag out, snatch the guards and fight our way out type of plan. Instead, Justice said one word. One strangely, beautiful word. A word that changed-no saved my life.

"Faith," he said. And it wasn't just what he said-it was how he said it. Calm, arrogant, assured. It was take two of these and call me in the morning. It was as simple as it was complex. It was, and I knew even then, the perfect answer.

"Yes," I answered. "That's what I need."

And I did.

The miracle occurred somewhere between three-fourteen and three-twenty in the morning. One moment I was stretched out on my cot wondering what would become of me, if my daughter was still alive and what motive the bastards who set me up have. The next moment everything was pitch black. A wailing, pulsing siren blasted through the ward.

The lights flickered. There was a violent electrical hum and then everything went dead. The first thing that hit me was the constant purring of the air conditioner had stopped and the only light now shone through the window, courtesy of the moon.

"I'll be damned! It's another blackout!" I shrieked. All around me were the screams and commands of turmoil and madness. The orderlies were running about trying to maintain order, while the patients howled at the darkness like lunatics.

"C'mon! Before the emergency lights kick in!" Justice said. Through the little light that shone through the window, I saw the wide-eyed look of awe in his eyes. This was the miracle-the emergency generators did not kick in. There was the possibility however slight I could escape.

Justice and I maneuvered through the rush of guards and orderlies. We were able to get off the ward since all the doors were now open. Once off the wards the security was a bit more lax. Not much, but enough.

"They'll have all the exits blocked by now. We gotta get uniforms and get cleaned up. C'mon, I know this place like the back of my hand!" Justice gasped, excited. He moved through the darkened halls like a cat. We ducked and dodged the beams of the guards' flashlights. We climbed into the ventilation ducts, shimmying through the narrow aluminum pipes above everyone else. I could hear guards rushing patients back into their rooms. It was confusion on a massive scale and my heart pounded so hard I thought it would explode.

"Follow me, I know the way!" Justice said. He guided me through those ducts in total darkness. The heat was incredible. I was drenched with sweat. It made the floor of the ducts slippery. Every few yards there was a vent opening and I could see the criss-crossing beams of flashlights sweep the corridors below us. The commotion became more organized. The guards were successful in restoring order.

Whatever we were going to do, it would have to be quick.

Justice sensed the same thing. He paused in the ducts, motioning me to be quiet. We no longer had the noise below us to mask our movements. We moved slower, more cautious. I thought the ducts would never end, but Justice seemed to know exactly where we were going. I don't remember how many left and right turns we took, but after a while we came to a treatment room.

"We're here! This is it!" Justice said, kicking out the grate. The room was pitch black. Justice reached into his pocket and lit a match, which gave off just enough light that I could see my hand in front of my face.

"Look around, find a pair of scrubs that fit you! Look for a pair of scissors! We gotta cut these bands off!" Justice said looking through drawers and closets. The match went out and he lit another.

I was scared now and not just scared that we might get caught. I guess I sort of expected that. Oddly enough, I was scared that we would get away. I joined Justice in his search. One closet had lab jackets and blue scrubs that were the attire of most hospital personnel. It was easy to find a set that fit. The pants came with a drawstring.

I found a flashlight in one of the closets. Justice found a small pair of clippers and we cut the bands off our wrists and ankles. I had been given a shave and haircut the night before. They wanted me to look presentable for my court appearance. Looking at myself in the mirror I could easily pass for a doctor-Justice an orderly.

"Looking good!" Justice said, as if reading my mind.

"What's our next move?" I asked him. Before

he could answer, the lights began to flicker again. The emergency generator was trying its best to come on.

"I figure the only way is for us to try to walk out of here. Blend with the crowd and try to get to the street," he said.

Just then the doorknob turned. Someone was coming!

"Hide!" I whispered. Justice ducked behind one of the machines and I hid in the kneehole of the desk. I hadn't noticed it until then, but we were in Dr. Walters' office!

A few people walked in. I could tell by the different footsteps. Flashlight beams danced on the wall behind me. Dr. Walters sat at her desk, her legs mere inches from my face. I held my breath in shock, praying she wouldn't stretch her legs and kick me.

"Make sure all of the important files are secure!" she ordered. "I don't want my little worms crawling out of their holes." For the first time I heard anger in her voice. She crossed her legs and I barely moved in time to keep from being grazed. I was so close I could smell her. A mixture of the hospital and fruit scented soap. I heard a desk drawer open and slam shut. I had to bite my lip to keep from yelping in fear.

There are men and there are worms...

From the large cones of flashlight's beams on the wall I saw the silhouette of Dr. Walters with a pistol in her hand. A large revolver. The sound of file cabinets being opened and slammed shut masked my heavy breathing. My heart thumped so loud I could hear it over the chaos in the halls. My palms became slick with sweat. My stomach roiled, and turned threatening to give me away by passing gas. I sat motionless, praying that we wouldn't get caught.

"I want every patient accounted for and I want to see my special worms in the recreation room in less than fifteen minutes. Have I made myself clear?"

"Yes, doctor," a few voices grumbled in unison. I was worried about Justice. They were sure to find him if they kept walking around the room. What would they do to him? Would he betray me? Would I let him get captured alone?

"Hey, doctor! I think I found something!" one of the orderlies said. Justice! They found Justice! Dr. Walters rose from her seat, the pistol firm in her left hand. "What did you find?" she asked.

Shit!

There are men…

I swallowed hard and prepared to give myself up. Maybe I could give Justice a chance to escape, maybe I'd get us both killed. But I-

…and there are worms.

-couldn't sit in a hole and do nothing. I braced myself. If she caught me in her office, she would be angry. She might make me hear Star's screams again. She might-

"The file we were looking for! The one you thought you lost!"

"Good! Grab them and let's go."

I breathed a sigh of relief. They hadn't found Justice! There was still a chance! I heard the door open and a few seconds of the hall's screams and shouts bled into the room. Then the door slammed shut and silence reigned.

I sat under the desk, terrified to move. Suppose it was a trick? A ruse of Dr. Walters' to get me to expose myself? "Worms stay in holes, men stand straight." I whispered, climbing out from under the desk.

"Justice? Justice, you still here?"

No answer. Panic bubbled within me like hot bile. What if they caught Justice and he didn't give me up? What if he was the missing file the orderly was talking about?

"Justice?" I called, jumping at how loud my voice sounded.

"Yeah," a voiced whispered back. The thin slats of moonlight through the venetian blinds allowed the barest trace of sight. I saw Justice stand up from behind a machine too small to cover a man his size.

"Thank God! How did you hide from them?"

"Just lucky. They never looked down my way. Best way to hide is in plain sight. You wanna split up now?"

"No!" I said. "We stick together!" I knew the only way I was going to see this thing out to the end was with Justice at my side. He nodded yes. I took a moment to get myself together, looking at the steel table in the middle of the room. Remembering the sound of Star's screams. God, please let that had been a hallucination! Of all the offices in the hospital, why did we stumble into hers?

Now came the hard part.

We opened the door to the treatment room and joined the crowd in the hall. There were doctors, nurses, police and security guards rushing about. Flashlights were everywhere. "Where in the hell are the lights?" Justice screamed. I looked at him as if he was crazy, but then, thinking about it his reaction made perfect sense.

"What's happening?" I asked someone in the crowd, trying to meld and blend in with the exiting throng.

"They got the generator running in the other buildings of the hospital, we're waiting for ours to kick in," a nurse informed us. People regarded us impassively. I kept a sharp eye out for Dr. Walters. We joined the crowd moving toward the stairway, with the hospital police leading us.

"Figures! Any word on how far this thing has spread?" Justice asked again. He was playing his part well. I meekly followed behind him, listening as he drew the woman into casual conversation. I overheard the woman say the blackout had affected all five boroughs. Justice mentioned that Con-Edison needed a good ass whipping for this one.

We were soon in the lobby and had no problem getting out of the building. The streets were even more chaotic than the ward. With the lamp posts and street lights out, the only light came from the moon and the high beams of cars. It gave Brooklyn a gothic, spooky look.

The air was hot and stale, but I took a long deep whiff of it as if it were the scent of roses. In the time I spent on that ward, I really thought I'd never see the street again. Funny how you take little things like freedom for granted, until you don't have it any longer.

My reverie about being free came to a quick and abrupt halt once I took a good look around. Chaos held sway as people suddenly seemed to be infused with some sort of madness. The streets wailed with a cacophony of shattered glass and people screaming in horror. The noise of sirens and alarms blaring coupled with the earsplitting peals of insanity. If evil could be defined by a sound, then this was certainly its concert.

It seemed like the end of the world.

"No time to stand here gawking, man! We gotta go!"

I quietly followed him, awestruck at what I saw. It seemed the dark brought out the rabid animal in some people.

Black smoke billowed overhead and covered the streets like a malevolent storm cloud. Fires raged out of control as people ran around in pandemonium. Ash covered the streets like a fine blanket of gray soot.

An old man stumbled into me, clutching his neck. I reached to help him and he collapsed in my arms. His throat had been torn out. There was a gaping wound that stretched from his Adam's apple to his collarbone. His eyes danced in their sockets for a few seconds and then they stared lifelessly past me as blood poured out of his jugular vein. I screamed in a futile plea for help.

"There's nothing you can do for him now, David. His time is done." Justice said, forcing me to my feet.

"What did this, Justice? He looks like he's

been bitten!"

"I don't know, but we can't linger on that now! We have to find your daughter!"

We passed an alley where five men were raping a woman. They had her on her hands and knees, with one man in front of her and another behind her. The other three looked as if they were patiently waiting their turns. The look of sheer horror and shock in that woman's face was enough to make my blood run cold. I threw a rock and screamed at them, thinking it would scare them off.

They never even looked my way.

The two men that had her front and back pounded that poor woman as if they were berserk. The salacious, sick look in their eyes made me think of Jamie. These men were mad-totally insane.

No sooner than the two were finished, another two replaced them. I don't know how long they kept on like that, because Justice pulled me away. My heart went out to that woman. There was no doubt in my mind those men killed her when they were finally through.

"We gotta get off the streets!" I said, feeling weak from the sight of such carnage. It was hard for me to get my bearings. I was disoriented and felt as if I was going to pass out. Justice held onto me, keeping me up.

"Hold it together, my brother! Think about your little girl! We gotta find her!"

Help me, Daddy! Help me!

I'm coming, Star! Daddy's coming!

"Yeah, let's head for my house. Follow me," I

said, trying to keep from vomiting. Justice acted as if he had seen this type of thing often-it just didn't faze him. I led him through the streets.

"Jesus is coming back in his silver chariot to take us away!" a derelict shrieked. He was naked from the waist down, holding a piece a sheet metal over his head, dancing in the street. Another man crept up and bashed him in the head with the claw end of a hammer, snatching the worthless sheet metal and running away in triumph.

I remember when the last blackout happened in New York City. It was more of a nuisance to me than anything else. I thought of how relieved I was that it wasn't another terrorist attack and how people stuck together.

Now the streets screamed with a voice of decadence. Now the darkness reigned and the moonlight ruled over lunatics. All because the lights went out. I read somewhere that people get depressed easier in the winter, how there is an increase in murders because of the lack of sunlight. I know now how important light is to people.

I thought the sun would never come up again. It wasn't just the lights being out-people acted as if they were infected by some form of mental corruption. There was a depravity about people now.

"What's wrong with these people?" I gasped. A car ran over a little girl and no one even looked her way more less helped her. I started to go to her, but Justice stopped me. I looked and saw a group of men had picked her up and ran off with her. I still like to think they were trying to help her. Being a father of a young girl, I shudder to think anything else.

"What's wrong with them!" I repeated.

"The darkness does strange things to people. Bad things move in it, things that are burnt by the light...the enemy moves in the dark."

I didn't know what Justice meant by that back then.

I know now...

CHAPTER V:

∞

And the Light Shines in the Darkness...

Somehow, I managed to lead Justice to my apartment. The streets were a cesspool filled with vermin waiting to prey on anything that moved. Justice was able to get a gun; he pried it out of the hand of a dead naked man, and it was a good thing too-he had to shoot at least three people just to get to my block.

A large furry animal ran across our path. I shrieked in shock and horror when I saw it was a cat. A black and gray tabby, but unlike any tabby I'd ever seen before. This cat was as tall as a Great Dane and as thick as a pit-bull. It growled with fangs as long as kitchen knives, and its claws looked as sharp as scalpels.

It hissed, prepared to attack. There was flesh caught in its teeth and its maw was stained and dripping with blood.

"Get back!" Justice screamed, pulling me behind him. He aimed the gun and shot the cat in the head.

"What the fuck was that? How did a house cat get to be that big?" I asked in disbelief.

"I don't know," Justice answered, inspecting

the dead cat's body. "Maybe it's some sort of radia-tion…you know? That's probably what's driving everybody crazy! Like radiation sickness!"

"That's what killed that old man! Let's get the fuck out of here!" I shuddered in revulsion. The image of that cat would become the stuff of many night-mares.

"Justice, something is really wrong! Remember I told you about those giant mosquitoes that looked like small birds on television? Now this cat! Something really fucked up is happening!"

"You have a gift for stating the obvious."

A squirrel ran past us and I gasped at the size of it. It was easily the size of a house cat. In the dis-tance, I heard a maniacal laugh that twisted every nerve in my spine. I'd heard that sound before, but where?

On television…the Discovery Channel!

"That was a hyena!" I screamed in a mixture of fear and awe. We ran and I desperately tried to come up with some sort of plausible explanation for all of this. Maybe the zoo's animals escaped. Maybe some warped scientist was performing genetic experi-ments on animals creating mutations. Maybe people got hold of some new drug that made them halluci-nate.

Or maybe I was really crazy.

We slipped around to the back of my building, climbing over the fence to the backyard and up the fire escape. I opened the window to Star's room. Justice was right behind me.

Just as I figured, my place was still ransacked.

The furniture had been overturned. Star's mattress ripped to shreds, even the walls had been bashed in. It was obvious someone was searching for something.

The heat in the apartment was overwhelming. It was like breathing stale steam. Justice and I searched carefully, not really knowing what we were looking for. A clue- anything that would give some hint as to what happened. I racked my brains trying to think of what they were looking for, but I kept drawing blanks.

My livingroom furniture was hacked to pieces, the television's screen smashed into shards of glass and plastic. The entertainment center overturned and all of Star's pictures were missing from the walls.

I went to my bedroom. It reeked of body waste and the mattress was still there. I stood there-knees weak and stomach threatening to explode again. The sight of that blood soaked mattress was more than I could bear. Justice caught me before I collapsed.

I rushed to the bathroom and splashed water over my face. The water felt good, my stomach calmed down.

"We should get to a hospital! I mean if it's radiation, maybe we're infected! Did you see those animals? This is something out of Food of the Gods!"

"Look, maybe you should try to get some sleep. I'll keep watch until morning. Things always look better in the morning," Justice said. I nodded, feeling like a wuss.

"I found a radio, if you know where some batteries are-"

"Look in what's left of the kitchen cabinet," I

answered. "I always keep a set in there. You should find some candles in there, too-if they haven't melted from the heat."

I continued to splash the water on my face, listening as Justice rummaged through the remains of the kitchen. He yelled back that he found the batteries and soon I heard the static of the radio as he searched for a station.

The Emergency Broadcast System was now in control of the airwaves. Martial Law had been declared and the radio announcer urged everyone to stay indoors for their own safety. The Federal Emergency Management Agency (FEMA) was now in charge of all local government and law enforcement agencies. The National Guard patrolled the streets of Manhattan. Deployment to the outer boroughs was scheduled in a matter of hours. There had been over a thousand casualties reported by the National Guard, mostly looters who thought the blackout would be a good time to raid places like Fifth Avenue.

Con-Edison issued a statement that they were experiencing a total meltdown. Every attempt to restore the power met with failure. Likewise, hospitals and places that had emergency generators were experiencing the same type of malfunctions. The announcer went on to describe how people suddenly stooped to new levels of violence. Reports of rapes, arson and murders kept pouring in.

"It's the darkness. People act weird when it's dark like this," Justice said.

"That's bullshit, Justice! It must be more than that! What about that cat, and that squirrel? This shit is really serious! It's like a war zone out there! How are we going to find Star in all of this!"

"Don't worry. The same power that got you out of that asylum will bring you to your daughter."

"I wish I had your faith!"

"You'd better hurry up and get it! Without it, there is no way you can win. The road is gonna be rough, David, but the prize is at the end! Keep your eyes on the prize!"

"What are you babbling about-"

There was a crash coming from Star's room, glass shattering. Justice pulled the pistol out from his waistband and we rushed to the room. My first thought was those mutated animals had made it inside. The figures were shadows, but I was able to make out a woman with three men behind her. The woman was being chased.

"Freeze, mutha-fucka!" Justice screamed, but the men kept coming. Even though the light was dim, I could see by their eyes that the men were stark raving mad.

Justice took aim and hit the first man in the upper chest area. He fired again and the bullet struck the second man in the head. I couldn't see where the third got shot, but I heard him yell as he fell off the fire-escape. His body landed with a sickening thud.

Justice covered the window with boards using what was once Star's furniture as I helped the woman. "Are you all right?" I asked her. The helicopter flew overhead, its floodlights briefly illuminated the room. The woman was young and beautiful-about twenty-one, twenty-two years old, with long wavy hair and a deep creamy complexion.

"Yeah, they were trying to rape me! Can I stay here until the sun comes up? Please?"

"What's your name?" I asked her, trying to stop her from shivering. There was glass in her hair. I figured she crashed through the window in an attempt to get away from her would be rapists.

"Sandra, but everyone calls me Sandy," she answered trembling. She was terrified, but trying like hell to hold it together. Her eyes had a wide fright-ened look to them, like a doe caught in the headlights.

"Let me show you to the bathroom, Sandy. You have glass in your hair and your forehead is bleeding." I led her gently by the hand. She reluctant-ly followed me. No doubt, the shadowy gloom of my apartment contributed to her fear.

I got a wet rag for her head. The cut wasn't deep, but it bled badly. I found a band-aid in the med-icine cabinet. She was scared and no wonder- the apartment looked as if a demolition team on crack went crazy and she didn't know me from Adam, but given the choices I guess I was the lesser of two evils.

"You don't have to worry about me, Sandy. I'm not going to hurt you. Justice and I will make sure nobody hurts you."

"Justice?" she asked, looking confused. Come to think of it, I had not seen Justice since he shot the three men.

"Yeah, he was the one that chased your friends off. He's probably taking care of the bodies. I never thought I'd see the day when things would get this bad."

"You live here, mister?" she asked, the pain and fear in her eyes evident. The streets had done something to this girl, something I could only guess at.

"I...used to live here. The cleaning lady is off this week. Listen, are you okay? I mean did those guys-"

"No. I managed to get away from them before they did. People just went plain fool since the lights went out. They broke in and began raping and killing everybody. The look in their eyes...like they were crazy! They didn't want money. They just wanted to hurt people. What happened, mister? Why is everyone so mean?"

"David-call me David and I was just wondering the same shit. I've seen some hardcore stuff in the past few hours. Did you see those weird cats? And I could have sworn I heard a hyena cackle! Did you hear it?"

"No. I heard a lot a crazy people laughing, but no hyena."

"What about the giant cats? Did you see any of them?"

"No."

The confused look on her face told me not to press it any further. Maybe I imagined it. Maybe the medicine was still in my system, distorting my perception. My reality.

"The radio said the lights were out in parts of Long Island and even in Westchester. Nobody can explain it," I said, changing the subject.

"This is the scariest thing that's ever happened.

I mean-I can see people trying to rob stores, you know. I mean to get money-food and shit, but they're out there killing each other! For nothing!"

I thought about that little girl, the one hit by the car. The look on the men's faces as they ran off with her...

"Maybe it's the heat. You know, the heat and the darkness. Bad combination."

"Did you know the phones were all out too? Even the cell phones!" she said.

"No. I guess I didn't think about it."

"It's scary...it's like something out of an old science fiction movie! Like we were being invaded or some shit!"

She chuckled, a nervous little titter that served to release some of the fear she felt. It wasn't easy having your whole world turned upside down overnight. We've all grown up believing in certain certainties: the sun rises in the morning, the fire department will come when called and people though sometimes mean acting, were really good at heart. Now I wondered how much of that was really true, especially the part about people.

I lit a candle and we went into the livingroom. I didn't know where Justice went. I figured he was outside looking for clues, or maybe he disappeared figuring I was okay now.

Sandy and I listened to the radio. Fear was evident in the announcer's voice as he read the news. Acts of violence kept pouring in, news helicopters reported gang rapes, random murders and arson on an immeasurable scale. I said a silent prayer that where

ever Star was, she was with someone who was protecting her.

Help me, Daddy! They're hurting me! They're
touching me...down there!

"You have any kids, Sandy?" I asked, staring
into the flame of the candle trying to shake the image
of my only child being molested-or worse out of my
mind.

"One," Sandy sighed. "A little girl, Jaleesa.
Child Welfare took her away last year. I was...well I
was on drugs and they took her. I'll get her back when
this is over. I'm off drugs now. Been clean for six
months. Wouldn't have started with them if it wasn't
for Hector, he's my boyfriend. He got strung out and
then he had me selling myself to support his habit.
And then I got strung out! Well anyway, what about
you? You have any kids?"

"One. A little girl, same as you. I don't know
where she is, but I'm going to find her."

Come get me, Daddy! Come get me!

"I'm real scared," she said, putting her hand on
my shoulder. I held her and we sat on what was left of
the couch, drawing strength and solace from each
other listening to the screams and shrieks of violence
outside. The whirling sound of the helicopter flying
overhead, coupled with the deafening reports of gun-
shots and screams of pain and horror below was
enough to drive anyone insane.

Sandy got up and lit another candle. I helped
light a few, strategically placing them around the
room to get the most light.

"What's in here?" she asked, getting close to

my bedroom.

"No! Don't go in there!" I screamed, but it was too late. I could see the look of horror in her eyes-a look that was now directed toward me. Sandy lumped me with the freaks who tried to rape her.

"No, Sandy! You don't understand! I...I didn't do it!" I pleaded, taking a step toward her. She shrank back with a look of disgust and fear.

"Just let me go! I...I won't tell anyone!"

"There's nothing to tell! Listen to me! I'll tell you everything! Just sit down and I'll tell you what happened!"

She sat, uneasily watching my every move. I searched for the words to convince her that I wasn't like them, that I was like her-confused, lonely and scared out of my mind.

Against my better judgment, I decided to trust her with the truth. I told her everything, from the hot day downtown to the lights going out and Justice helping me escape. I told her it all and when I was through, I cried. I cried because I realized how truly crazy I sounded.

"Do you believe me? Cause if you don't you can go. I won't try to stop you and I won't hurt you," I said to her, hoping like hell that she did believe me.

"I want to believe you, David. I really do. It's just that...everything you've told me sounds so crazy! Why would anyone want to take your daughter?"

"Look at what's happening now, Sandy! Why are people running around killing each other for nothing?" Something that I said must've penetrated. She moved toward me. The hostile glare in her face softened. I opened my arms for her to come to me and she did.

"I'm glad you believe me," I said. "I really need for someone to believe me." It felt good to hold her. The heat made her skin flush and I could feel her body relaxing in my arms. Her hands explored my body, gently massaging my chest and working its way down in circular motions. My manhood grew from her soft touch, but after what happened the last time I made love to a woman my libido quickly dwindled.

Besides, we were sitting on the same couch that Tara and I were on the night we...

"I'm sorry, Sandy. I'm too worked up thinking about my daughter."

She smiled at me, an odd smile that made me feel embarrassed. I'm not use to being with a beautiful girl and not being able to perform, but I figured that given the circumstances she understood.

"You know," she said, her voice was soft and melodic. "My grandmother use to tell me a bedtime story about a tribe of Africans that stole children for a ritual. She said they had the power to make it rain or thunder. They could ruin crops and make people sick and crazy. She said when the slave trade began they were spread all across the Caribbean and America. Legend has it when they are reunited the world will end in fire and darkness. Maybe they all joined up and they're loose in the city."

"Why did...why did they steal the children?" I asked, suddenly feeling a chill go through me. Sandy's expression had changed. She no longer seemed the frightened little damsel in distress.

There was something eerily familiar about her tale-it sounded too much like the strange enemy Justice described. For that matter, where in the hell was Justice?

"They needed their blood to complete the calling."

"What is the calling?" I asked. Sandy went on with her peculiar tale, still massaging me.

"There were twelve in all, just like the Apostles. They were separated for hundreds of years. The elder was a woman. She lived in Haiti. Legend says she will begin the calling when the blood of the last child becomes available. Star's blood. All we wait on is the full moon and then the European and his dog will suffer the final defeat!"

Her voice became demonic and guttural. Her eyes closed to slits-like the eyes of a cat. The pretty features of her face warped and twisted to reveal a hideously deformed caricature of a woman.

"What's wrong, lover boy? Don't want to kiss me now? Aren't I as beautiful as your lover Tara? Come to me, David! Let me feel the warmth of your throat in my hands. Let me feel the beating of your heart as it slowly stops!" Her voice was loud and monstrous. There was something profane and odious about it. It was an abomination to everything decent.

She lunged at me. Her speed defied description. She knocked me over. We tumbled and fell over the broken shards of the entertainment center, knocking over the candles. "Get the fuck off me!" I screamed, trying to muster up some form of courage. I was scared beyond belief. Sandy's strength was enormous! She hit me in the face and I felt dazed-punch drunk. Everything went hazy; I saw her rearing back for another blow. Her hands were giant claws and then I saw Justice standing behind her. He fired twice and Sandy's face exploded into a mass of thick bloody tendrils.

"Get her the fuck off me!" I screamed, struggling to get Sandy's body off me. Her weight belied her small frame. Justice helped me up and I was never so glad to see anyone in my life. I was covered in blood and I vowed never to hold another woman in that damned apartment.

"Where the fuck was you? Who the fuck is she?" I asked hysterically.

"I was hiding, seeing if my suspicions about this bitch was true. This is one of the enemies. I only wish we could've gotten more information out of her before I sent her to hell."

I stood up and wiped my face, lightheaded from hyperventilating. "She told me about an African tribe-"

"I know. Right now we have to get out of here. She was after you and there might be more of them coming. The streets have gotten rougher. Prepare yourself."

"Where's Star? This bitch said something about them using her blood-"

"I don't know where she is, but one of the guys I shot had a tattoo I recognized from the G building; an emblem of twelve circles, interlocking into one ring. All of them had it and I'll bet-" He pulled Sandy's arm, ripping her sleeve. "That this bitch has the same mark!" He exposed the tattoo. "See! Here it is! We find this crew and we find your daughter. I know it!"

"You have any idea where we can find them?"

"No. I've been off the streets too long. We need somebody that knows where scum like this hangs out."

"Shakim," I said confidently. If anyone knew where to find a bunch of freaks like this, it would be Shakim.

The sun's rising didn't do much for the streets of Brooklyn that morning. There were still random acts of violence, only now it was more visible. Justice and I stepped over bodies, garbage and the tangled remains of cats and dogs. There was a fetid, pungent smell about the streets that repulsed and disgusted me. It was a smell no amount of soap and water could wash away.

I thought about the story Sandy told me. The abnormal way her face contorted. What did Sandy mean by the European and his dog? Where was Star? What did her blood and the full moon have to do with it? Was she in the hands of some fanatical cult?

The National Guard arrived. They directed us down the street. Curfew was dusk and anyone out past that time was subject to arrest. They spot-checked people for weapons. Luckily, Justice and I managed to avoid them.

Soot mixed with black and silver ash covered the streets like dirty snow and there were still the screams and shrieks of people in shock and pain.

Brooklyn looked like Europe during World

War II.

    We passed a woman in an abandoned car. She was naked and crying hysterically. Sitting beside her was a man with his throat cut from ear to ear. I wanted to help her. To tell her everything would be all right, but I couldn't bring myself to go near her. I cursed myself for not being stronger. For not being human enough to offer the woman my shirt at least to cover herself. But truthfully, there was little I could have done to help her and I doubt if there was anything I could have said to assuage her pain.

    Justice shook his head and kept walking. I followed behind him. All around us was more of the same: children wandering aimlessly, women screaming and crying, wounded people trying to get anyone to help them.

    "The soldiers will help them," Justice said. "They have the resources to help them. We have to get going!"

    "What is this, Justice? It looks like something out of a horror movie out here!"

    "Just stay focused. Ignore what you see and let's get to your man Shakim's house."

    Shakim lived across town, in Bushwick. Normally it wasn't a long walk, but under these conditions he might as well have lived in Afghanistan. Now that the sun was up I managed to get a good look at people. There was a look of lethargy on most faces, others looked as if they were in shock. Some looked totally detached and devoid of any feeling whatsoever. I half expected the majority of people would have been trying to find stores to stack up on food and candles, but most of the stores had been emptied the night before.

"How long will it take to recuperate from this? I mean how long do you think it will take before things are back to normal?" I asked Justice.

"Things will never be the same. There is a disease in the air, people are really sick this time. I don't think putting the lights back on will cure this."

"A disease? If that's true then maybe this is another attack! I mean-"

"It's an attack alright, but not the one you thinkin about. This ain't from a virus or a germ, David. This type of sickness was already inside these people. This is a sickness of the soul, David."

"Do you know what that crazy bitch was talking about? I mean it stands to reason that she was looking for me-hell, she knew Star's name! That means the three guys you shot were with her!"

"You are gone hafta change the way you look at things, David. You too conservative in your thinkin. You're gonna see things that'll make you wish you were back in the G building."

"Hell! You mean worse than what we've already seen?"

"Yes."

"Just tell me I'm going to see Star again. Just tell me I'm going to see her and that she's still alive and well. I don't care what happens to me, Justice. I need to know my baby is okay."

"You'll see her again. That, I can promise you. Let's find your man Shakim and hope he knows where those bastards hang out."

I wondered how Shakim would react to me. The last time I saw him was at Sharon's funeral. Did he believe I killed Tara? Did he think I was crazy? I imagined the shoe being on the other foot, would I believe him? No, I wouldn't. It would be a lot easier to think he went nuts and keep the glue in my world.

Star, I thought to myself. He'll believe me because of Star. He knew how much I cherished my daughter. Star would be the focal point. Even if he didn't believe me, he would help me for her sake. Shakim was Star's godfather.

The sun baked the streets. It wasn't even noon yet and the day already had the makings of another scorcher. My body was drenched and I felt lightheaded. Inhaling that rancid stench didn't help any.

"We gotta get off the streets! It's too hot!" I told Justice. The heat didn't seem to bother him. Meanwhile, I was a prime candidate for a sunstroke. My hands started shaking badly and I could feel a tingling sensation in my fingers and toes.

"How much farther?" he asked, frowning. "We really ought to keep moving!"

"About sixteen, seventeen blocks. I have to stop and at least get some water. The sun is cooking me!" It was a struggle to stand. I felt so weak and exhausted. I wondered how those soldiers could walk around in all that gear in this heat.

"Alright, we get some water and a half hour of shade. You better toughen up, David. I can't help you if you're going to pussy up on me all the time!"

I wanted so badly to say something to him, but I didn't. He was right. Justice was the one who made every smart move since we left the hospital. He turned the corner and headed toward a building with most of its windows boarded up.

"Keep a look out!" he barked. He pulled one of the thick plywood planks that served as a barrier from a window. I was amazed at his power. Justice had the stamina and strength of an Olympic athlete. He never seemed to tire. I peered up and down the block, looking out for soldiers.

"All good!" I said, hurrying through the window. The air was heavy with dust, but it was cool. We made our way through the semi-dark apartment. I was looking for the kitchen, hoping the water was still on in the building.

There was a smell of rotten sheetrock and mildewed wood. Graffiti covered most of the walls, vile and crude pictures of copulation. Some future Rembrandt spray-painted a picture of a young man with an angry scowl on his face holding a gun in one hand and a fist full of hundred dollar bills in the other.

I saw a group of teenagers huddled in the corner of one of the rooms. Dope fiends from the looks of them. They regarded me impassively. I doubted if they even noticed the lights were off. Judging from the look of them, they didn't regard Con-Edison as a necessity. There was one young girl performing fellatio on a man. She looked willing enough, I thought. None of my business.

"Got any candy, daddy?" one girl asked me. She looked like a zombie-emaciated, her eyes glassy and wide. Her skin was blanched and pallid and she smelled as if she had not washed in months. I looked around and saw other girls with similar looks about them. The place reeked of body odor and sex.

"No, no candy here!" I said, trying not to vomit. "I need water! Where's the sink?"

"No sink here. They took it. Sold it for three Jumbos!" she wiped her nose in her shirt. "Got anything to smoke? I'll take care of you real good, daddy!" she said, "What's your fantasy?" She took off her dirty T-shirt and showed me her breasts. They were badly scarred with thick whip marks. The scars were as thick as rope. Her torso and back were also scarred. Someone had beaten this girl, and judging from the thickness and length of the keloids, they used something like a Cat of Nine Tails.

"Who whipped you like this?" I asked her.

"Daddy beats me when I don't do right. You wanna beat me, daddy? I'll take care of you real good." She grabbed at my crotch and I shoved her hand away. I backed away from her. I could see the leering look of madness in her eyes. She stepped out of her filthy jeans and slowly walked toward me, naked. Her legs and back were just as scarred.

"You're gonna like the way I feel," she moaned as she walked closer, her hand deftly working between her legs. "You gonna really like the way I feel."

The others appeared behind her, all naked and walking slowly. I continued to back up as I noticed that they were all scarred, even the men.

"You wanna play with us, daddy?" another girl asked. She was even more hideous that the first. Her body looked as if someone dipped her in boiling hot oil. I looked up in her face and saw that she was severely burned. "We wanna play with you!"

They shuffled toward me like mindless zombies. I kept backing up until I backed into the wall. The first girl lunged at me and I barely moved out of the way in time. She crashed into the wall and went through the flimsy sheetrock. The girl behind her grabbed me and I flung her into the group. Her skin felt like wet sandpaper. I hurried away from them, shuddering in disgust. The girl I grabbed left a slimy film on my hand where I touched her.

"You sure you don't want us, daddy? You can have all of us! Even the boys!"

"No, nothing. Justice! Where are you? Let's get out of here!" I screamed, feeling dirty and sickened. I punched through a wall of sheetrock and made myself an exit. Running down the hall, I saw the open window I came through. I could hear the girls lumbering behind me. Was Star in a place like this?

They're touching me, Daddy...

The idea of it caused my blood to boil. I rushed back through the opening Justice made in the window. Surprisingly enough, he was outside waiting for me.

"Justice! Did you see that? They're only kids! They couldn't be a day over sixteen! They looked like somebody tortured them! Where were you? How did those kids get like that?" I wiped my hand against the streetlamp, trying to get that slime off.

"Still think we need to stop?" he asked sarcastically.

"No. We have to press on and find her-and

whoever has her is going to get fucked up!" I screamed shaking.

"Now you're talking! Let's get to your man Shakim's house. Then we'll find this group that wears that mark. I'm betting they're the ones that have your daughter and they can solve this shit!"

"The twelve circles," I mumbled. What did it mean? Twelve. What significance did that number have? Sandy compared them to the Apostles. Was this group a bunch of religious fanatics? And what was that bit about the European and a dog? Why Star? What did she have to do with this?

"Justice, when is the full moon?"

"Judging from the moon last night, it should be in about three days."

Three days, I thought. We have three days to save Star.

My pace quickened in spite of the heat. I could picture Star scared to death in the lair of some twisted cult. By now she'd probably given up all hope of my rescuing her. I imagined all the terrible things she'd heard about me, about how I killed her Aunt Tara.

The good news was Star was still alive. Sandy confirmed that. There wasn't a doubt in my mind that I would find her. If God didn't want me to find her, I'd be on my way to the Hawthorne House for the Criminally Insane, or doing life in Sing-Sing or Comstock.

I found myself thinking about after I found her. Where would I go? Unless I could convince the authorities beyond a shadow of a doubt I was innocent of all charges I'd be shipped upstate and I'd never see

Star again. I doubted if my sister Gina or Sharon's family would bring her to see me. And then there was this supposed conspiracy, how deep did it go? Who were these people? Was Star chosen at random, or was she purposely picked out?

And why kill Tara and let me live? Why didn't they just kill us both? Poor Tara. She was so beautiful. So intelligent. Why did she have to die like that?

What her mother must think of me now!

My mind blazed with these questions and I only hoped and prayed that Shakim would aid me in finding the answers. This was all so incredible. Before these terrible events the most exciting thing that happened in my life was going to a strip club with Shakim and getting a VIP lap dance from some voluptuous exotic dancer.

The heat caused the air to shimmer like a fine silk sheet blowing in the wind. I imagined what desert nomads must've felt like, trekking across endless miles of sand dunes. My stomach turned from inhaling the putrescent wind. "Just another six blocks or so," I mumbled to myself, hoping Shakim had put some water away.

"How you holdin' up?" Justice asked.

"I feel like a fried egg, sunny-side up!" I said, trying to make light of it. A man and a woman lay naked on the curb. They were both dead. The man must've been raping the woman when the heat got them both. He must have weighed at least four hundred pounds. I figured his heart gave out.

She was smothered beneath his thick flaccid rolls of flesh. He had a sardonic grin on his face that reminded me of Troy back on the ward. It was a look of sheer hedonistic insanity-what the old people called lap dog horny.

What was it that made everyone so lustful lately? It seemed everyone we passed was in the act of, or had just committed murder or rape. If they didn't fall into those two categories-they were victims of those two categories.

"Heat bring out the dog in a man," Justice said nonchalantly.

That made me think about Sandy, how she said the European and his dog were damned. All this time I thought it was a real dog, like a Pit Bull or a Doberman. Now it made me think, she could've meant a man.

A horny lap dog...

"Then why aren't we affected, Justice? Why aren't the soldiers and police out here doing the same thing?"

"Some of them are. It depends on what was in a man's heart before the lights went out. He feels he can move freely in the dark. He feels no one will see him."

"Who?" I asked.

"The enemy."

"Who? The devil? You're saying these people were possessed?"

"Possessed, yes. But not by a red guy with horns and a pitchfork. The enemy opens doors that were already there inside a man. Most of us keep this type of monster locked away so deep we don't know it's there. Some of us keep the beast closer to the sur-

face. The closer the beast is to the surface, the easier
it is for the enemy to unleash it. You're now seeing the
true nature of these people. So as a man thinketh..."

I looked around, shuddering at the carnage.
Justice was right. Something had released the savage
brute within people. The barbarian that lurks within in
the heart of us all.

Finally, we made it to Shakim's block and not
a minute too soon. I fell to my knees from the heat.
Justice helped me up. I pointed the brownstone out.
"Third floor," I said. My tongue felt as dry as cardboard.

Justice threw me over his shoulder as if I was
a newborn baby about to be burped. I'm about a hundred and seventy pounds soaking wet, but Justice
picked me up as if I weighed an ounce.

He scaled three flights of steps with me on his
shoulders, in heat that would rival the Gobi Desert in
the summer. Shakim's building was unusually desert-
ed. This was usually one of the rowdiest buildings on
the block; the police knew the address by heart.

I knocked on Shakim's door feeling a bit nervous. Suppose he wasn't home? My head ached from
the sun and I badly needed to lie down. There was no
answer. I knocked again, harder this time. "Shakim!" I
called, my throat felt like I'd gargled sand.

"Shakim!" I was on the verge of panicking. I
banged the door so hard I thought I broke my knuckles. Justice stood at my side, looking strangely blasé.

"Who the fuck is it!" Shakim called back. My
heart sang in my chest. We made it! We made it, I
thought.

"Shakim, it's me! David! Davy P! Open the door!" My head really throbbed now and I knew if I didn't get to lie down soon I would pass out, perhaps for good.

I heard the chain-lock slide back and my hands trembled in anticipation of seeing him again. The door opened partway-just enough to show him that it was really me. A flashlight's beam hit me in my eyes, blinding me.

"Shakim! Shakim, it's me! Please, help me, man!" That's when I finally collapsed and passed out.

∞

I woke up on the couch with a wet rag on my head and Shakim standing over me with a glass of water. Justice sat quietly in a chair across from me with an odd look on his face.

"Man, how'd the hell you get out?" Shakim asked, passing me the glass. "They wouldn't tell us nuthin! We went to every precinct and nobody heard a you! Where were you at?"

The water was warm, but to me it was ambrosia. His apartment was clean. The air was hot, but there was no trace of the streets' stench.

"In the G building! It's a long story. I got real problems! Some fuckin' cult has kidnapped Star. Give me a minute and I'll school you. Damned, it's hot!"

I gulped the water feeling the gritty dry tightness leave my throat. I sat up, still feeling weak, but determined to tell Shakim the story. I started with the funeral, which was the last time I saw him. I proceeded to tell him everything, from Justice to Sandy, to the crazy people in the streets to the crack-head building. After the tale, I was exhausted. Shakim just sat and looked at me, never mumbling a word.

"Well?" I asked. If he didn't believe me, I needed to know. I needed to get back on my feet and Justice and I needed to get moving. My baby was somewhere out there and I had to find her. I tried to rise but I fell back to the couch. My strength was sapped.

"Okay, so shit is grimy right now! You know me-I'm your man! I gotcha back, but I got one question…"

"Yeah?"

"Where's your man Justice?" he asked, looking me straight in the eye.

"What are you-fuckin' with me? Justice is sitting right there!" I exclaimed, pointing to the chair that Justice obviously sat in. Justice still had that strange look on his face and he was unusually quiet. Had they somehow gotten to Shakim? Why would he ask me such an asinine question?

"David…listen to me, I'm not the big college graduate you are, but I still got enough sense to know there's nobody in here but me and you!"

I was really scared now. What little strength I thought I gained by lying there went away. I could feel cold chills run through my body. If I weren't so dehydrated, I would have pissed on myself.

"Justice," I said, trying to hold my voice calm and steady. "Is this some sort of a joke?" The expression never changed on Justice's face. It was hard to interpret-it wasn't a smile, but for some reason it made

me think of the look Star would have when she was
embarrassed.

"He can't see or hear me, David," Justice said,
strangely.

"What the fuck is wrong with you people?
You're supposed to be helping me! You're suppose to
be helping me to get Star back!" I screamed, on the
verge of hysterics. I could feel the walls of my psyche
threatening to collapse. Were Justice and Shakim in
this together? Was there anyone I could trust?

"David, calm down! You not makin' no sense!"
Shakim screamed. "There's nobody there! David, lis-
ten to me! I'm your man! If there's trouble, you know
I'll help you, but you gotta get right in the head, man!
There's nobody here but us!"

He held me by my shoulders and shook me.
There was a look of fear in his eyes, as if he were trying to ground me in reality. I looked over at Justice;
my eyes pleaded with him to make things right. But
he just sat there looking at me with a look I couldn't
decipher.

"Shakim, I've been in the nut house for a
minute. I know they gave me a lot of medicine and
shit. I know that sick twisted bitch tortured me with
mind games, but if you're telling me that chair is
empty then we have a problem. Cause' either the guy
that's been helping me is an angel, or a figment of my
imagination!"

"Listen to me! That chair is empty! You came
in here alone. If you see anyone in that chair now, I
want you to take this and put three in his ass!"

Shakim reached into his waistband and pulled

out a .45 automatic. He placed it in my hand and aimed it at Justice. "Blast him!" he said and I understood his logic. To Shakim I needed to dispel any thought of Justice. To him, Justice was a phantom. An imaginary playmate I made up to get me over the rough times. A by-product of a psychosis, or perhaps the result of the medication. I held the gun and wrapped my finger around the trigger. No matter what he was, I could cure myself.

All I had to do was squeeze...

"Nooooo! Justice is real! I couldn't have made it all this way by myself! He carried me up here! He shot that bitch when she was going to kill me, he got me out of the nuthouse!" I screamed, furiously shaking my head back and forth. If I let Justice go I would be in big trouble. I knew that instinctively.

Justice represented the cunning, the planning- the sheer will power that I needed to get me out of the nut house. He gave me strength I needed to get through the streets and most of all he kept me focused on finding Star.

I dropped the gun. My hands were shaking too badly to hold it. Justice stood up and walked over to me. Shakim was still oblivious to his presence. What was going on?

"Justice, please! Please tell him!" I pleaded, feeling the hinges on the door of my sanity buckle.

"I told you, David-he can't see me. No one can. I'm here to help you, but only if you have faith. Faith, David is the only thing that can help you now." He held my hand, and I calmed down. His hand was soothing, reassuring. Like a father talking to his son.

Like the father I never had.

Whatever Justice was, he had helped and for now that would have to suffice. If he was just a figment of my imagination, then so what? I'd successfully done things I would've never dreamt I could do. And if he was an angel sent to help me then what could be better than that?

Either way, I thought, he's help. So don't look a gift horse in the mouth! You don't have to understand everything! That's what faith is, believing when you don't understand!

"Okay, Shakim. I…understand. Justice was something I created. Now…let's talk about this cult that wears a tattoo of twelve circles."

"You okay now? You know there's no Justice?"

"There's no Justice…there's just us!" I said, squeezing Justice's hand to let him know I still believed in him.

Shakim chuckled and from the look in his eyes, I guess he bought it. It felt good to see Shakim again, real good to be amongst a friend in a world that went crazy overnight. I was anxious to get started looking for Star, but I went back to sleep feeling weak and feverish.

When I woke up Shakim was smoking a cigarette and listening to the radio. Justice was gone. My headache had lowered to a dull throb. It felt easier to sit up and my hands stopped tingling. My strength was returning.

"Shit's really bad out there, man. The radio said a lotta soldiers are passing out. They're setting up temporary hospital units. It's like something is sucking the power out of the city and it's spreading. The guy on the radio said Westchester is blacked out, along with Long Island and parts of Jersey. And they said something about giant cats biting people and shit. Ain't that some shit!

"Hey, your sister moved to California with that guy she was dating. Tara's family kept fucking with her about you. We couldn't get any information on where you were. Somebody said they were probably holding you as an enemy combatant. You were quite the talk on the streets for a minute, man."

"Shakim…I need you to help me to find whoever's got Star. You gotta help me, there's this girl that-"

"Yeah, I know-she had a tattoo of twelve circles. You said your man Justice shot her. I've been thinking about that tattoo. I've never seen anyone wearing it, but I have seen it before. In a book maybe, I can't really remember."

He scratched his head and there was an odd look of detachment on his face. Was it something in the air? What was it that was making everyone either homicidal rapists or lethargic zombies?

"Shakim, I need you to focus for me, where did you see the tattoo?"

"In…a book. A book…on African legends…college book."

"Are you all right, Shakim? Are you feeling okay?" I got up and crossed the room to him. I cut off the radio. There was more static than words now. As if the Emergency Broadcast System didn't have enough power to transmit a decent signal.

"I'm good, just that sometimes I get slow. Ever since the lights went out that'll happen every so often. Just shake me to get me back. The book is over here somewhere, I kept my old text books from my minute in high school."

He cut on the flashlight and we searched his bookshelf. There were mostly books by Donald Goines, Stephen King, and Toni Morrison. Odd combination, I thought, but at least he reads. We came across a hardcover book that read, African Legends and Tribes.

"Here it is!" he plucked it off the shelf and we took it to the table, situating the flashlight so that we could read the book together. Shakim thumbed though the pages and I felt my stomach turn from nerves. There was going to be something in this book that scared me. I just knew it.

"This is it, the legend of the Death Tribe!" He pointed to a portrait of a group of Africans, twelve in all. Their eyes all had the same eerie glow to them. At first, I thought it was the way the camera caught them, then I realized that the glow was the actual color of their eyes. They each had a tattoo of a figure eight laid on its side; the symbol of infinity.

I stared at the picture in awe. The Tribe consisted of six men and six women. The youngest stood out for some reason. He seemed to have a confidence that leapt off the page. They stood as regal as any royal family. I had never seen black people so beautiful. The women were built like goddesses. Their breasts high and proud, their waists' pinched, their hips' wide and strong. Their hair hung in long lustrous jet-black locks. They were flawless. Their skin was as black as ebony, with a soft glowing radiance that reminded me of moonlight. The men looked as if every one of their muscles was chiseled from black steel. Strong, proud, resolute. These were not the Africans they showed us in school; cowering savages ripe for soul saving by white Christian missionaries. This was a strong, intelligent, fiercely proud tribe that defied everything I had been taught.

My eyes were glued to the picture, mesmerized by it. This was the type of portrait you would imagine hanging on the wall over the fireplace of an aristocrat's mansion.

"Why did they call them the Death Tribe?" I asked.

"I'm not sure. They was like a gang and shit. They could fuck anybody up by touching them or something like that."

"How come I never heard of this tribe?" I asked, staring at the picture.

"Well, you know what they say," Shakim chuckled, "If you want to keep something from black people, put it in a book." He turned the page and there were about dozen pictures with captions under them. One caught my eye.

"The old woman! Shakim, I saw this old woman downtown! The one with the jewels on! This is her!" I gasped. My fingers traced the picture. It was her! She was standing with a group of about thirty other people in what looked like a field of rotten crops. The same obese woman who collapsed in my arms was in this picture with a grin on her face. She was the only large person in the picture, everyone else looked emaciated. The hair on the back of my neck stood at attention as I realized why she was grinning.

She was the only one eating.

"That's her, Shakim! That's her!" I said, covering my mouth. My headache was back in full bloom now. The woman looked as if she was grinning at me. As if she knew something that I didn't. There was a look of madness in her eyes, a look of sheer anger and hatred.

"That's impossible! This picture is over two-hundred years old!" he said staring at the picture also. "This woman is long dead somewhere in Haiti! She was some sort of Voodoo priestess. They say she could ruin crops and make people sick by touching them." He paraphrased the caption under the picture.

"I don't give a damn! This is the same woman I saw downtown! She had-oh shit!"

Shakim turned the page while I spoke and I saw a man sitting on a porch, wearing a suit that looked as if it were never new. There was a look of extreme sadness in his eyes and I damned near had a heart attack when I realized who he was.

"The man in the sandwich board! That's him! This is the guy that got hit by the car!"

"Yo! You're really buggin' the fuck out now! This guy was worm food before Lincoln wore pampers! This picture was made when slavery started!"

"I don't care! I saw this man downtown the day I bought Star those sneakers! The day you called me during half time at the Knicks and Nets game, remember?"

"I remember the call. I remember the game. I remember you telling me there was a nut in a sandwich board. I don't remember you telling me he was over two-hundred years old!"

I ignored him and just stared at the picture.

"Look," Shakim said, obviously exasperated. "There's an old African guy named Kenyetta who knows all about this kind of shit. He used to be a college professor before he started drinking. If we can find him, he can help us piece together a lot of this. He'll definitely know where this cult hangs out."

"Can we find him with all the shit going on outside?"

"I know where to find him, that's not the problem. The problem is getting to him."

"Why?"

"He lives on the eighteenth floor in the Sumner projects!"

I sighed deeply. The one place that was guaranteed to be a madhouse in this heat and power failure was the projects. I shuddered just thinking about having to climb all those stairs, not to mention what we'd come across.

"Fuck it, let's get it over with!" I said trying to prepare myself to go back out in that heat. The National Guard had us in a catch twenty-two. Either risk a heat stroke by day, or risk getting shot by the U.S. Army at night.

Shakim suggested we travel through the train stations, it would keep the sun off our heads and we should make good time if we didn't get lost in the tunnels. We'd normally be able to get to Kenyetta's house in under a half hour if the power was on, now we'd be lucky if we made the trip in fewer than three.

Sneaking into the train station was no easy feat. The soldiers kept it well guarded. Still, we were able to elude them and enter the tracks. The air was thick and dusty and I wondered if we shouldn't have taken our chances with the sun. I could only imagine what my lungs looked like after inhaling that grime.

I took wide steps, being careful not to trip over the tracks. Power or no power, I was still leery about going near the third rail. Our puny flashlights served more to agitate the rats than light the way.

"I hate rats! I've always hated rats and I will always hate rats!" I mumbled.

"Don't mind them! They won't fuck with you if you don't fuck with them."

"I'm not fucking with them, and I hope they know that!" I retorted. I just hoped we didn't come across any giant rats. Seeing an extra large cat was one thing-a giant rat would've sent me back to the loony bin in a plastic envelope.

"Yo, Dave...there's something I gotta ask you, man. I mean, we'll always be down together, but I gotta know-you know?"

"No, I don't. I forgot you speak your own language. Why don't you translate that into English?"

"I mean when you was in the joint they didn't stuff you, did they? I mean did they put the fruit in your looms?"

"What?"

"You know-did they-" he could barely get the words from laughing so hard.

"Hell, no!" I shouted realizing what he was referring to. "The most that happened was one crazy ass tried to snatch an orange off my tray! What the hell! Am I walking funny or something? Why would you ask me some dumb shit like that?"

"Just had to know that's all. I just had to know," Shakim chuckled. "Just wanted to make sure you wasn't changing your name to Davina or something like that. Just wanna know who I'm walkin' in the dark with! You all pussy over a few rats and shit!"

It felt good to hear him laugh. It reminded me of the good old days, before the madness. Here we were, walking the underground tracks of the subway and he still found time to make jokes. Nothing shook Shakim. Nothing scared him. I gave silent thanks that he was with me. Where Justice was solemn and stoic, Shakim was loose and wore his heart on his sleeve.

"Still the same old Sha!" I mumbled.

The mirth was a welcome break from the horrific reality that surrounded us.

We passed a few people living in the tunnels between stations, drug addicts and a few runaway teenagers, mostly. Like the rats, we ignored them and they ignored us.

There seemed to be an entire sub-culture living underground. I doubted if most of those people even knew there was a blackout. The one good thing was that none of them seemed to be affected by the madness happening on the surface.

"Sha, let me ask you-did the news say anything about this being a possible terrorist attack? I mean, I've seen some people acting as if they got hit with some kind of nerve gas-"

"Nah, they said it ain't terrorists. Just a whole bunch of people who were crazy before the blackout is now a helluva lot crazier. That's all. They said there was a lot of looters and people actin out, but most of the people on my block were pretty cool about it. You know how it is. One or two knuckleheads ruin everything."

"It was a hell of a lot more than one or two! There are some real bizarre things happening out there!"

"Man, listen! They'll have the lights back on in no time. Shit happens. You just concentrate on Star and how you're gonna clear your name afterwards. You thought about that?"

"No. All of that is irrelevant. Once I find Star, everything else will fall into place. I know it will."

Help me, Daddy! Come get me...

I'm coming Star, and not even hell will be able to stop me!

I saw a man heating a can of Campbell's soup with a butane torch. There was a woman behind him lying on a bunch of filthy car seats grouped together as a mattress. The man stared at us. There was a tense moment. He no doubt thought we wanted his woman and soup.

"Take it easy, old timer. We're just passing through. We don't mean you no beef," Shakim said.

"It's my last can, but you're welcome to share it with me," the man said nervously. I'll never forget that; the only thing that man had in the world was a can of soup, yet he was willing to share it.

"That's all right, sir. You keep it," I said, wishing I had something I could give him. We kept on, passing the old man and trying to light the tracks as best as we could.

"Be careful, son. The tracks can be tricky-especially in the dark."

I turned to thank him, but he was gone. The woman, the can of soup, even the bed they were lying on-gone!

"Sha! What happened to the old timer?"

"Huhn? Shit, he probably gated outta side exit. These bums, they know the tracks better than the Transit Authority!"

Yeah, that's probably it! There's a logical answer for everything! Only Carl Lewis couldn't move that fast on his best day! It's impossible for an old man and a woman to have moved that quickly without me hearing them!

Impossible!

We traveled deeper into the blackness of the tunnels. We no longer saw anyone or even detected another human presence. I had no idea where we were, or which way to turn. I had to totally rely on Shakim. I kept hearing a faint banging sound. I dismissed it as just water running through the sewer pipes, but then I realized there was a measure and rhythm to the banging. Shakim seemed oblivious to it and I tried to ignore it, but the banging got louder and louder.

"Sha! What the fuck is that?"

"Fuck is what?"

"You mean you don't hear that? Like somebody banging drums or a pipe or something!"

"No, I don't hear shit. Now shut up and quit tryina scare me!"

The banging continued to grow louder and louder. It was drums, some kind of African dance song. The measure increased in tempo until it doubled and then tripled and just when I thought it couldn't get any faster it sped up again.

"Sha! You gotta hear that! It's like some wild African drummer on speed! Listen! You-"

Just then, something unseen ran into me with the force of a battering ram. I was thrown clear across the tracks and landed in a heap. I hit the back of my head against one of the railings and all I saw was silvery-white light.

"Sha! Something attacked-"

I heard a growl like a lion and I instantly thought of that huge cat Justice killed. My flashlight was about six feet away. It's beam of light pointing toward the wall. The animal prepared to leap again.

"Sha!"

Shakim fired one round. The tunnels amplified the pistol's report as it echoed throughout the station. The animal moaned a low throaty howl of pain, and then it was silent.

"You okay?"

"Yeah," I answered, barely making it to my feet. "Where's the flashlight?" The light went out when Shakim fired the pistol. I wanted to make sure the animal was dead, but I didn't want Shakim firing blindly.

"I don't know, mine's busted. Shit, man! I

think that was a tiger or something!"

"Tiger my ass!" I screamed, feeling around the tracks in pitch-black darkness for the flashlight. If Shakim hadn't been with me, I would have been mental mayonnaise.

"I found it!" I screamed, giving silent thanks to God for small blessings. I shined the flashlight on the dead cat, confirming my suspicions.

"Look! I told you it wasn't a tiger!"

"What the fuck!"

Sha got a good look at the animal, as did I. It was a house cat, but this one was deformed beyond anything I'd ever seen. The animal had no neck; its head was set in its chest. The tail looked more like a monkey's than a cat's and the eyes had the distinct look of human. In it's mouth I saw the label of the old man's soup can.

"God help us! It's the fucking end of the world!" he said, not knowing just how close to the truth he was. Something had perverted nature and although my rationale wanted to contribute the monstrosity in front of me to radiation poisoning, I knew it was something deeper than that. This was something that went against everything I was taught. This was the old fairy tale of Chicken Little come to life.

The sky was falling.

"I heard the radio say there were weird lookin' cats, but GOD-DAMN!"

"That's nothing compared to what me and Juser, what I've seen on the streets! I told you I could've sworn I heard a hyena!" We kept maneuvering the tunnels, using certain markings to guide our way. I wondered how Mr. Levy was making out throughout all of this-poor man, in an old folk's home with no lights and no power. I figured Mrs. Levy was probably out somewhere drunk and looting.

I remembered Shakim saying something about my sister Gina being in California, good! That was one less thing I had to worry about. I didn't know Gina was even dating a guy, and here she was so seriously involved she moved away with him. I guess I was just too wrapped up in Tara to notice.

I wished like hell I had the sense to leave Star with Gina the night of the funeral. Things would have been so different, but then again would they? If it was Star they were after then did it truly matter where she was? I think not; Justice said I had some very powerful enemies and I believed him.

We climbed up the ladder of the subway grate, emerging about a block away from the Sumner projects. It had to be at least one hundred and fifteen degrees outside. The heat and the idea of entering the projects with all the madness chased away the shock of the deformed cat. As soon as I overcame one horrible incident, another one was waiting to take its place.

"It's like fuckin' Death Valley out this muthafucka!" Shakim groaned. Sweat poured off both of us just that quickly. We were drenched, like we had been in a thunderstorm. Shakim pointed to the building and we hurried to it.

The streets were still littered with refuse and the soldiers were holed up in makeshift tents. Someone mentioned the radio had stopped broadcasting, which scared me, because the radio was our only link to the outside world. It was the only way for me to know the outside world knew what was happening.

Most of all, it was the only way I knew the madness hadn't spread.

The hallways of the project building reeked of urine and body odor. People had camped out in the lobby and we had to step over a man to get to the stairs. I didn't know if he was asleep or dead.

The staircase was even worse than the lobby. Every other flight of stairs we saw prostitutes (both male and female) working, rapes (both male and female) in progress, and people doing drugs. The higher we climbed the more outrageous the acts grew.

It was like Jacob's Ladder in reverse. The higher we went the closer to hell we got. Any trace of civilization deteriorated and all semblance of a normal society quickly reverted to the barbaric rituals of the Stone Age. The strong conquered the weak and any hedonistic whim was immediately satisfied with little or no repercussion.

I stayed close to Shakim and tried to keep my eyes off what was happening around me. Every vile and profane lust of the flesh surrounded us. People had no qualms or reservations about what they did or whom they did it in front of. Justice's words echoed in my mind, This sickness was already inside of these people.

We finally reached the eighteenth floor and I couldn't bear to witness anything else. I leaned over the banister and felt my stomach erupt. I vomited and watched as the thick goo fell on a woman giving a derelict head. I don't think either one of them noticed or cared.

"C'mon!" Shakim barked, knocking on a door. "This is his place!"

"Who the fuck is it? Get away from this door!" a voice cried from the apartment.

"It's me, Kenyetta. Shakim. I brought someone to meet you. I need some information on something! Open up!"

"What you want? I ain't got nothing up here! No drugs, no booze and very little food! I-"

"Open the fuckin' door! If I wanted to hurt you I wouldn't have knocked!"

The peephole opened and after a few seconds I heard what sounded like a half dozen locks being unlatched. Shakim entered the apartment. I stayed in the foyer. There were books strewn all around. Photos and newspaper clippings of historic events were pasted to the walls.

"It's just me an my man, baby! Just came to holler at cha for a minute!" Shakim hugged him and motioned for me to come in. I was glad to get away from the stench in the hall. It smelled worse than the abandoned building those young crack-heads propositioned me in.

"Hey, man! It's some really crazy shit going on out there! You should have seen this fucked up cat I killed in the train station! The shit was like somethin' out of a horror book! You seen any funny shit up here?" Shakim asked him.

"Nah, man. Just the usual crack heads and dope fiends, but we had them when the lights were on! Most of the people are holed up in their apartments, scared to go outside. Business as usual," he chuckled, but I didn't think it was funny. A wave of revulsion came over me and I shuddered involuntarily. My body shook with waves of disgust at the vile and inhuman things I'd just witnessed.

"You know the radio's off now. That means shit is about to get real thick and chunky! Who's this?" Kenyetta asked, pointing at me.

"My name is David-David Peters," I held out my hand for him to shake.

"Kenyetta," he answered, shaking my hand and looking at me coldly. His grip was firm for an old man.

Shakim pulled the book we brought from out of the knapsack and passed it to him. Kenyetta's eyes never left me and I felt uncomfortable under his icy stare.

"We need info on that tribe in this book-the one with the funny eyes. My man here is trying to school me to some spooky shit that's happening. Some freaks snatched his daughter, killed his ex-wife and sister-in-law and framed him for it. You know any-thing about a group that wears a tattoo of twelve cir-cles?"

Kenyetta pulled a pair of reading glasses out of a drawer and placed them on his face. He took the book from Shakim and perused the page with the Tribe on it. I watched his every move, his every facial gesture. I was looking for any sign of recognition, any indication he knew this group.

His lips trembled ever so slightly.

My head started throbbing again. My hands

tingled, but I ignored it. I was close to finding my daughter and something told me I was close to finding something else...

Something I didn't want to find.

"Perhaps you'd better sit down. It seems we have a lot to discuss."

CHAPTER VI:

∞

Welcome to the Jungle...

Kenyetta sat on the couch and thumbed the pages of the book. Not once did he look Shakim or me in the face as he spoke. He cleared his throat and began his strange tale. It seemed the entire world grew quiet. His voice was low and unassuming, but it filled the room as if he were on a loud speaker.

"The Tribe you speak of came from many different tribes, some Bantu, some Bambara, the Mende, the Ewe, Shabazz and so forth. They were different. Death-Bringers they were called. The pupils of their eyes' were silver. They had strange powers. Some could make crops wilt. Others infected men with sickness just by a touch. Each had a birthmark that united them in blood-the symbol of infinity. They were shunned and expulsed from their native tribes.

"No one knows how they first came together. Legend says it was a song that one sang the others heard. They traveled for many full moons to an uncharted jungle where they formed their own tribe. They were a family and the jungle belonged to them. They found peace and solace together and they claimed the jungle as the land that the gods ordained for them.

"All entering the jungle must pay them for safe passage. They hunted by night and remained quiet during the day. They were supposedly invisible to any entering the jungle. They traveled by treetops you see, as agile as acrobats.

"There were eleven of them-twelve with the child. They were all brought to the jungle because of their strange eyes and each had a unique way of protecting themselves when threatened.

"The eldest male was named D`ike. He and Nicah, the female were both sixteen. They were the leaders of the group. They had been in the jungles the longest. D`ike was the only surviving member of the original group that lived in the jungles.

"D`ike was the lawgiver. He made sure that the group lived by a strict code of ethics and values. Nicah was the enforcer. She meted out punishment for any infraction.

"After them were K`embe, and D`aim, who came to the group within days of each other. K`embe was the next oldest male and as such naturally assumed that he was next in line to lead. D`aim on the other hand being the second oldest female had no such aspirations.

"Next were the two males, Molo, and Jomo. The three females, Iyanni, T`keya, and Meeka. Followed by Kwame and the youngest female, S`ianna.

"They had more or less come to be in the group the same way. Either their former chieftain or a brave family member brought them. Each one of them found strength in the group. The ties that bound them were much deeper than their eyes or birthmarks. They were a family, with D`ike and Nicah assuming the parental roles. They owned the jungle. They moved through the tops of trees, unseen by anyone wandering far below and because of their powers they had nothing to fear from any beast.

"The twelfth child was by far the mightiest. His powers were said to surpass all the others combined. They called him Malik, meaning King."

"Why was Malik so special?" I asked, riveted by this strange tale. The mention of the jungle brought back that strange dream and the paintings in Tara's apartment. I was sure there was some kind of connection.

"His power was a combination of all the others. He exuded nobility and esteem. Royalty and majesty surrounded him. He wore glory and honor as we wear our skin!"

Kenyetta was very animated now. There was something about this Tribe that held a religious like zeal with this man. The way preachers would rave about the Gospels.

There were twelve in all, just like the Apostles...

"Continue," I said quietly remembering Sandy's words.

"Besides Malik, K`embe's power was the most profound-"

"Oh, yeah? Fuck could he do, fly?" Shakim said sarcastically.

"No. He was impervious to any weapon-"

"Oh, this is such bullshit!" Shakim interrupted.

"Let the man talk!" I said. "Let him finish! Go on, man! Tell me about K`embe."

"K`embe came from a tribe of warriors. His village was notorious for plundering and destroying neighboring tribes. His power had not made itself known until he hit puberty.

"The warriors returned triumphant from battle and the dance was prepared to thank the gods. K`embe had his eye on a young girl, a captive from a neighboring tribe. Because of his silver eyes, he was thought of as a fierce warrior. The sight of him scared most men. It was K`embe's first battle and he felt he deserved his choice of woman.

"The girl was terrified of K`embe. Another young warrior intervened saying K`embe's kind could not be allowed to breed. 'What mean you my kind? I am a warrior! Defend yourself!' K`embe barked as he reached for the young warrior. His intention was to fight hand to hand, but the warrior grabbed a spear and tried to stab him.

"K`embe mocked the young man, 'Yes! I can readily see why such a frail warrior would need such a weapon when facing K`embe! Perhaps you should grab the shield also!' The other warriors offered K`embe a spear, but he declined. It would make his victory that much more succulent to defeat the upstart barehanded.

"The young warrior ordered K`embe to arm himself. It was ignoble to strike an unarmed man. K`embe replied the warrior lacked the skill to use the weapon properly. This was a great insult. The young warrior was furious, outraged that K`embe would slander him in such a fashion. In a fit of rage, he threw the spear with deadly speed. The tip pierced K`embe's chest, embedding itself deep within him. Everyone gasped in horror, even the young warrior seemed shocked. He never meant to kill K`embe, just to frighten him.

"K`embe laughed, pulling the spear from his chest. 'Why does everyone stare with their mouths open? Did K`embe not say he was unable to harm me?' he asked the village. The gaping wound sealed itself shut. The rest of the Tribe looked on in horror. K`embe was not natural-not human. No man could survive such a wound. The young warrior grabbed the spear to inspect it, and when he touched the tip of it K`embe's blood burned through his hand like acid.

"From that day on the rest of the Tribe shunned him. K`embe could not understand such brusque treatment. He decided he was bigger than the Tribe-better than they were and as such, he set out to find a tribe worthy of his special talents. He wandered into the jungles and found the Silver Eyes."

"This is bullshit! Okay, so we have African fairy-tales, too! What the fuck does this shit have to do with Star being missing?"

"Shakim, there is so much more to this world than Brooklyn. There are things that defy description." Kenyetta seethed. "Think about it! We were the first men to walk the earth! Do you think the European's version of Africa is all there is? Do you think National Geographic really depicts where you came from?"

"Fuck National Geographic and fuck the

Europeans! I want to find my goddaughter!"

"Wait, Sha! Let him finish. I have a feeling we're going to need to know this! How did the Tribe get captured, old man?"

"There was a captain of a slave ship, the Good Ship Jesus it was called. He was obsessed with the Tribe. It took him twelve trips to learn their secrets; a year for each member and on the twelfth he captured them. There were three ships that carried the Tribe: the Good Ship Jesus, the Good Ship Kingsley and the Good Ship Sea Master. The captain sent the Sea Master to Portugal, the Kingsley went to the Caribbean, and the Good Ship Jesus went to the newly formed colonies called the United States.

"The twelve were separated. No one knows how the captain captured them, but it was said everyone on board those three ships died a horrible death. The twelve never forgave the neighboring tribes for giving the Europeans access to them. You see they believed the other tribes betrayed them.

"The Tribe set a curse only the youngest could invoke. When he calls them together from the Four Corners of the earth they will be reunited and when that happens…"

"What?" I asked mesmerized. "What will happen?"

"I believe we're seeing the effects of that now."

"Wha-what you mean this blackout and the heatwave are because of some stupid ancient tribe? Look, man-I came to you to find a gang that uses this tattoo. All I wanna do is find my goddaughter! This is bullshit!"

"Keep going," I said, ignoring Shakim. He didn't believe in Justice and he didn't see the way Sandy's face changed. We were dealing with something outside the realm of what can be considered natural. There wasn't a logical or rational answer to these things.

Kenyetta closed his eyes. He looked so tired, like a man who'd been carrying a great weight for a long time. He took a deep breath and continued his strange story.

"The captain went mad, nightmares it was said. He spent the rest of his days trying to find the source of the Tribe's powers. He could not believe that blacks could have such a power. The legends are sketchy, but somehow he discovered a way to bring them back together only something or someone would always stop him.

"The power of the Tribe was promised to anyone who could bring them back together. That's where this group who wears the twelve circles come in. You see…every so many years there is a ritual and on the night of a full moon, they're supposed to bring back the Tribe. I think they're going to do it this time."

"Why? Why this time?" I asked, my mouth went dry with fear thinking about Star in the hands of these lunatics.

"The heat, the blackout, the madness-it's all part of the ritual. They want to bring the jungle back, the dark, and the sickness. I think they're going to do it this time."

"I think they have my daughter. I want you to take a look at these two pictures and tell me who

these people are!" I took the book from him and
flipped to the pages of the sandwich board man and
the big woman. "Them! Who are they?"

Kenyetta looked at the pictures and again I
saw his lips tremble ever so slightly.

"Why do you ask?"

"I saw them downtown Brooklyn the day I
bought my daughter's sneakers. The man was wearing
a sandwich board that read the dead know what the
living are doing. The woman was wearing a fist full of
large jewels. I saw the woman pass out in front of me
and an ambulance came to get her. The man got hit by
a car, he told me the people in the ambulance that
picked up the old lady weren't paramedics."

"Did either of them touch you or your daughter?" he asked with a cool and austere look that was a
little too indifferent for my taste.

"Yes, the woman grabbed my daughter and the
man touched me-so?"

"So, you're both damned."

"What the fuck? Who were they?"

Kenyetta pointed to the portrait of the twelve-
to one young man in particular, the oldest looking
one.

"The man you saw in the sandwich board is
D`ike, the oldest of the Tribe. The woman you claim
you saw is this one here-" He pointed to a beautiful
woman in the portrait. Strong, young, but somehow
motherly. "Nicah, the oldest female. Legend says she
was dropped off in Haiti. D`ike is the only one able to
stop the ritual. It is said when he gives in to Nicah the
curse will come true."

"Man," Shakim jumped up, quaking in anger. "This is such bullshit! Where do these mutha-fuckas hang out at?" He pulled the pistol out of his waistband and took it off safety. "Just tell me where the baby's at!" He placed the gun to Kenyetta's head. "Tell me you sick, twisted mutha-fucka!"

"Shakim, don't kill him! He has info we need! Just hold up! Just hold up!"

"Fuck that! He's got fuckin' fairy-tales and some twisted fuck's got Star!"

"If you kill me you kill the only chance of your friend redeeming his soul and finding his daughter. The anger you feel is because you have now discovered that Santa Clause doesn't exist. The world is not flat and there are powers beyond the scope of what you call the normal world."

If Kenyetta was bluffing, he was doing a damned good job of it. He disregarded the gun at his head as if it were only a finger. I really believed I was looking at a man who didn't fear death.

There are men and there are worms...

"Shakim, Shakim, don't kill him-let me talk to him. Let me talk to him!"

"Talk quick then! This mutha-fucka's got all of about two minutes to tell me where Star is or he's meeting God with a bullet in his cabbage!"

"How can the two be the same as in the picture? What about their eyes?" I asked.

"You saw what your mind allowed you to see. You saw what they projected themselves as being. I'll wager you were the only one who saw them as being as close to what they truly are."

"Which is?" I asked, feeling angry at this man's sudden smugness. I had half a mind to tell Shakim to slap him with the .45 a couple of times.

"Gods, Mister Peters. They were-they are black gods! Their coming will pave the way for a new Africa! Your daughter is an unfortunate casualty. They shall be resurrected and all shall be made whole again!"

"That's it! Your ass has had one too many over the years! You don't know shit from shampoo! I'm gonna put a cap in his ass, help him remember where Star is!" Shakim shouted.

I saw Shakim was serious now-not that I doubted him before, but I really thought we were playing bad cop-good cop. I barely pushed Shakim's arm in time when the gun went off. The bullet lodged in the nearby wall. The recoil was deafening. Had I been a microsecond later Kenyetta would've been dead. The bullet would've ripped into his skull at point blank range.

Yet, the man did not so much as blink.

"If you know," I pleaded. "Please tell me where she is. She's just a little girl-just a scared little girl!"

Help me, Daddy!

"You don't understand, do you? Your daughter is the final piece! There is something special about her! In two nights, we will begin the blood calling. All will be well then! As it was in the beginning so shall it be in the end! Do you think the gods would allow what was done to Mother Africa without retribution? Do you think we have no past? That-"

"Shakim is going to kill you if you don't tell me where she is. We've passed a lot of bodies. One more won't mean anything. Now I'm asking you for the last time to tell me where she's at!"

"Now we're talking!" Shakim screamed, putting the pistol between Kenyetta's legs. "You got three seconds to answer and listen-I count real fast!"

"I'm not afraid to die."

"Oh, I'm not gonna kill you-just yet! I'm gonna let you walk around without nuts! I'm gonna shoot your dick off! You ever see what a bullet does to the balls? It ain't pretty! I saw a guy in the joint once, got shot in the package and had to have his meat rocks removed. Couldn't tell if he was a boy or a girl and guess what? Neither could anybody else! His name was Patty and he wasn't Irish!" Shakim spat. That got Kenyetta's attention. Like most men the thought of dying was acceptable, the thought of pissing through a plastic tube was not.

"Alright-I'll tell you, but it won't do you any good. The people involved are very powerful! Very powerful! You'll need my help if you want any chance of saving her!"

"No!" Shakim said. "I've seen this shit before! He's setting us up! One..."

"Listen to me, David Peters! The Tribe chose your daughter, there is something special about her and about you!"

"Yeah, a minute ago they were cursed! I dropped out of high school-I wasn't kicked out! Two..." Shakim counted, pressing the gun deeper in Kenyetta's crotch.

"Only I can retrieve her. They'll kill her the moment they see you!"

"Three!"

"No! Wait a second!" I said, taking the gun from Shakim. "Who killed Tara? Why was Sharon murdered? Who were the men in the ambulance?"

"I can't tell you that! They'll kill me!"

I fired one round into his kneecap at point blank range. The report of the bullet echoed throughout the cluttered apartment. The bullet tore his knee in half, amputating the thigh from the calf muscle. His lower leg fell to the floor with a thud. Kenyetta howled like a banshee.

"You done did it now, son!" Shakim mocked. "My man David is crazy! You better start talking some real shit, real quick! Or else you'll be shaking hands with Yacub!"

I turned back to Kenyetta. "Now I know you won't run away from us. I'm going to ask you one more time, because you only have one more leg. Answer my questions!"

"You...sonavabitch!" he yelped, holding the bloody stump that was a whole leg moments ago. "Okay! Tara worked for us! She was supposed to get you drunk and bring the child to us. She changed her mind and a few hot headed members went too far. It was an unfortunate tragedy really, but she is just one of many who will be sacrificed for a higher cause."

"Higher cause?" I gasped, my blood boiled with rage. "Do you have a clue what I've been through? What I'm going through looking for my daughter? You fucking freaks ruined my life and

killed Tara!" I slapped him across the face with the
butt of the gun. He spat a clump of blood on the floor
and stared at me defiantly.

"I'm going to shoot you again. This time I
think it'll be in the other leg." I calmly pushed the gun
as deep into his thigh as I could and pulled the trigger.
"Maybe now I have your attention. I want to know
where my daughter is. I don't care how many times I
have to shoot you. I'm an escapee from the psychiatric
ward of Kings County Hospital. Like Shakim said,
I'm crazy."

Kenyetta screamed again. Now both legs were
mangled spreads of crimsoned meat. Blood sprayed
everywhere. The room reeked of gunpowder and
burnt flesh. Kenyetta's face was pale and ashen. His
screams died to low whimpers of pain. He was bleeding to death. I took neckties and made tourniquets for
both of his legs. His femoral artery was ruptured.

Death was imminent.

"You're going to die, but before you see the
devil on your deluxe tour of hell I want you to tell me
where Star is. I can make the pain go away or I can
prolong it for a long time." I put emphasis on the
word long, stretching it out in a sadistic sort of way.

This was my first blow of retaliation at the
bastards who had turned my life upside down. This
was the first strike. The first stand at getting my
daughter back and getting back at those who took her.

"Why did they kill Sharon?" I asked, pushing
the gun deep into his groin.

"To get to Tara," he gasped, his voice barely
audible. "It was the only way to trick her. The men

you saw on the streets that day are members of our movement. Please...I have told you all I can. Don't kill me before I see the fruition of my labors. Your daughter's blood shall herald a new era! Please...let me live and I'll take you to her...let me live!"

"Tell me where she is and I'll let you live."

"She's in Coney Island. They move her daily. The place where the ritual will take place is on the beach. Hundreds, perhaps thousands will gather to witness the miracle! Let me live long enough to see it! Let me-"

He lunged at me. His face had the same horrific glare Sandy's had. I fired the gun again, the bullet struck Kenyetta in the forehead. His head jerked back and when I saw his eyes again they lacked the light of life. He was dead. I killed him.

"I am a man. I am not a worm!" I screamed at Kenyetta's corpse in rage. "A man! Did you hear me, Kenyetta? I am a man!" I fired the gun again, shooting him in the face. The bullet tore into his features and ripped them into an unrecognizable gob of gray and red tissue.

"I understand, David. I know. Give me the gun, okay? What's done is done. Let's get to Coney Island and find her," Shakim said, taking the gun out of my hand. The look on his face was one of awe. He'd never seen me act so violent-so vicious.

I wondered whether it was really Justice that killed Sandy and those men that were chasing her.

Maybe I did it.

I thought about my time on the Psyche Ward. The other inmates gave me respect because of Justice, but I would have to constantly tell them what Justice said. I always thought it was because they were just too dumb or too afraid to ask him to repeat himself. Now I realized they couldn't see him. No wonder they regarded him with reverence and awe. They must have believed I really was crazy.

You can be down with us now!

"Did you hear me? Let's go!"

"No, let's look around first. There might be clues about these mutha-fuckas around here," I said, strangely calm in spite of what'd just happened. "I need to know all about this group. Look for any clues."

"Like what?"

"Pictures of members, names. Journals. That sort of thing. It'll help me to clear my name after we get Star back."

We searched the small apartment, which was full of African literature and artifacts. Many of which I felt belonged in museums. It seemed Kenyetta was an expert on African Folklore; he also dealt heavily in the occult. Shakim came across a collection of Voodoo masks and protective charms.

We found a small opening secreted behind a bookshelf. Shakim made a comment about it leading to the black cave, but I was in no mood for jocularity. I was convinced everything Kenyetta, Justice and Sandy said was in some form true. There were powers beyond the reckoning of logic. The glue that held my world together was a farce, a sham.

I was ready to believe in anything at that point-monsters, vampires, witches, ghouls and goblins. I didn't give a damn so long as it brought my baby and my sanity back. There are some things a man is always ready to kill and die for.

We found a pouch that held about three-dozen portraits. They were so life like they looked like a very early form of photos. I spread them out on the floor, marveling at the detail and crisp lively colors. Together, they seemed to tell a story. I saw the twelve tribal members Kenyetta referred to as the Death Tribe. I touched them, tracing my finger over each member.

It was no sooner than when my fingertip touched the twelfth member that a sharp freezing sensation raced up my arm. I felt myself being pulled, dragged into the engraving as if I was water being sucked into a drain. A complete sense of vertigo came over me. I felt disoriented, spinning wildly and falling…falling…falling…

I land on a tree branch…

I am barefoot and naked except for a small cloth that barely covers my loins. The air is hot and sticky and there is a smell about this place that defies description. There are sounds that blend in harmony making music only the blessed can dance to.

I am perched high in a tree, many-many hundreds of feet above the ground. Birds fly by me impassively. There is a huge snake coiled on the branch beside me and I am not afraid of it.

I am home here.

There are others swinging high above me, in taller trees. They are my family and I am theirs. Sunlight bleeds through the treetops, warming me.

The sun commands the day to begin and my family climbs down. We respect the sun, but we worship the night.

The darkness is the only god we serve. We are blessed to see in the dark. Animals fear and respect us. All of nature is our domain. The jungle is our throne. A woman swings past me, her beauty rivaled only by her agility.

Her body is firm and well built. She wears a cloth that barely covers her large and full breasts and her strong and inviting hips. She smiles at me, flipping through the air with the grace of a butterfly.

My manhood stirs beneath my loincloth.

I race down to her. My feet seem to know every branch, my body every shift of the wind.

I glide.

I glide across the wind as surely as the birds fly. My arms and legs are strong and I am home here, in the treetops with the sun sprinkling the jungle floor like seeds from ripened fruit.

She lay on the branch, her back arched in anticipation of my arrival. My soul hungers for her. Above me, the others are pairing off in the same manner. The sun's rising seems to increase our libido and we ravenously seek our mates.

"Come to me, my love! Shield me from the sun with your body!" she says to me. By now my loincloth is nothing more than a nuisance and I cast it aside as such. "But who shall shield me, my love?" I ask her playfully in a voice that is not my own, but it does not matter-I am home here.

"Since when does the mighty king need a

shield?" she retorts, teasing me by flaunting her legs. I am almost there now. Another level and I will be with her. I am hot with desire. My body burns and my loins ache for her. My breathing is heavy and labored. The sight of her drives me mad with desire. "I fear," I say, my voice husky and thick with carnal want. "The sun holds no heat hot enough to match the fire in my veins!"

"Then let the fire in your blood consume us both, but have a care-I too have a flame!"

I embrace her. Our bodies locked on the thick branch of the tree. I take her. She moans, growls and purrs like a lioness in heat. She is as majestic to me as I am to her. Our bodies writhe and dance, intertwined like the roots of the mighty tree we lay in.

I am home here.

We continue the dance. Our passion swells to a deafening crescendo. I am the wave and she the shore. The jungle is full of the sounds of love and love-play as the birds caw in their nests. I look around and see the rest of my family in similar throes of desire.

She pulls my face close to hers, her eyes bright like the sun itself and I think to myself, life is good. I am content with my woman and my family and my jungle. A feeling of deep reverence and affection overtakes me and soon I explode within her. She gasps, arching her back even further to receive me. I hold her, spent of physical energy, but spiritually refreshed.

"I love you," I whisper to her.

"And I you," she replies.

I settle in her arms, her body my bed and the

shade from the leaves above my blanket. "I am home here," I say drifting off to sleep. "I am home here…"

"Yo, Dave! Dave! You alright?"

It was Shakim, shaking me. The pictures were locked in my hands. I reluctantly woke up. My head ached and the light hurt my eyes.

"Why…did…you wake me?" I asked, suddenly feeling very depressed. Like a junkie coming down off a high. I wanted to get back to that jungle, back to that woman. I was vaguely aware I had a massive erection. "I was home!"

"You can't keep fuckin' flippin' out on me like that! 'Pose we in the middle of a gun fight?" Shakim stammered, terrified. How long had I been out? Was it real? Judging from the bulge in my pants, it certainly seemed real. I told Shakim what happened.

"I can't take this spooky-pookie shit anymore! If a gang's got Star then I can deal with that! But you talkin' some voodoo shit! Some old down home roots shit! I can't deal with that! Man! I thought your ass was gonna die! You kept jerkin' and flippin out! All you kept sayin was you was home like fuckin Dorothy on the fuckin Wizard of Oz!"

"Shakim, listen to me," My head throbbed badly now. My vision was doubling. "These pictures, they somehow took me back to them. I ran with the Tribe. I made love to one of the women! She was so beautiful! The jungle was so beautiful! It had a life all its own! You should have seen the way we moved from tree to tree like acrobats! We-"

"Man, quit this Tarzan shit! Is your ass back to normal or what? I'm tellin you, David! You my man and shit, but keep this up I'm gonna shoot you and take your black ass back to the G building! You heard me?"

"Yeah," I mumbled, holding the portraits tightly, praying that I would be transported back to the jungle. I sat looking at each picture carefully, trying to figure out which was the woman in my vision.

"Look, man! We don't have time for this shit! This is your daughter! You act like you'd rather sit there and remember a wet dream than go find her! You see what's going on out there. The rapes, the murders-well your daughter is somewhere out there!"

His words hit me like a punch in the face. He was right. While I held those portraits I'd forgotten all about Star. Was this the reason Kenyetta was so obsessed with this tribe? Had he ran with them, just as I did? Had he too made love to that woman in the treetops?

"Okay," I said, putting the engravings back in the pouch. "Let's get to Coney Island!"

We headed back down the stairs. I, with the pouch slung over my shoulder and Shakim with the gun in his hand. The madness continued in full bloom. People had no qualms about copulating out in the open. At least now the women seemed more than willing.

Someone told us that all of the batteries had suddenly died. Cars, radios-anything that needed any form of electrical power to run wouldn't work and no one could explain it. The soldiers and government people were totally baffled. We managed to get a bunch of Glow Sticks from one soldier. He said it was the only source of working nightlight other than the moon.

"Don't be out after dark," he said. "If you are this is the only thing that will work. They don't light much, but it's a little better than a cigarette lighter."

We thanked him and kept moving.

The heat was still unbearable. The humidity made the streets as steamy as a sauna. My head was pounding so hard my vision was blurry. There was no way we were going to make it all the way to Coney Island-not in this heat. Even the soldiers were passing out.

"I keep thinking about what Kenyetta said, when he said the blackout and heat were all part of the ritual. Could this group of ancient Africans have the power over the weather and power supplies of entire towns? Just what are we dealing with, Shakim? What about how he said the Tribe chose Star, can you believe this shit? Damn! The sun is cooking me!" I held the pouch over my head to block the heat.

"Look, man! I can't...I can't get into the voodoo shit, but I have to admit there's something really weird happening. Let's just find Star. I know once you see her everything will be okay!"

"I'm thankful she's still alive. Kenyetta said they'll need her for their ritual. Something about the full moon."

"You hear about this kinda shit all the time, and you pray it'll never happen to you, but you gotta be ready for it. Don't worry, David! We'll find her and when we do I'm catching a body over this one!" Shakim said.

"Thanks," I said, thinking about what I did to Kenyetta. "I already caught one."

"I didn't see shit."

We went back down in the train station, the tunnels a welcome shade from the sun. We were both leery about running into another deformed cat, but we had little choice. The sun would have cooked our brains if we stayed out in the street. Even in the train stations, it had to be at least a hundred degrees.

I pulled a bottle of water out of the knapsack on Shakim's back. The water was hot and flat, like it had just been boiled. I drank it thirstily, trying to fight off the symptoms of dehydration and nervous exhaustion.

"You know how to get to Coney Island through the tunnels?" I asked cracking the Glow Sticks. The phosphorus gave off a soft greenish light that barely lit more than three feet around it. If something jumped out at us, we wouldn't see it until it was right in our faces. Still, it was better than total darkness.

"Hell no, but this is the only way we'll have a chance to get there. With all the cars not working we don't really have much say-so. Even if the cars were up and running, the National Guard wouldn't let us drive-traffic control they call it."

"You think it's true about up-state being blacked out?"

"That's what the radio said, right before it went off the air."

"The Emergency Broadcast System. How many times had they interrupted the ball game with that damned irritating high pitched whistle, talking about 'this is a test, this is only a test.' Now, when we need the shit the most it breaks down!" I chuckled.

"Some people on my block thought we were being invaded by aliens. I mean, I never even heard of FEMA before this shit happened!"

FEMA was only used in direst of circumstances, usually to rescue flood and earthquake victims. For the Feds to be involved meant the President had to have declared a State of Emergency and that meant this thing had spread a hell of a lot farther than Brooklyn. Even still, the smattering of agents we saw in the street seemed frustrated and totally ineffective.

"Someone should tell the Feds that it just might be a terrorist attack after all. A bunch of voodoo worshipping freaks with a tattoo of twelve circles!" Shakim joked.

My thoughts turned to the story Kenyetta told us, about how the Tribe placed a curse only the youngest could invoke. Kenyetta believed the heat and the blackout were part of the curse. What would happen if this cult were allowed to complete their strange ritual? Would the Tribe come back to life?

I thought about the vision I had running through the trees with them. They were not evil, that much I knew and neither were they the enemy. The love they felt for each other was genuine and pure.

"Shakim, do you think Kenyetta was the leader of the cult?"

"I don't know. I've been thinking about that myself. That story he told about the Tribe, about the youngest being the strongest. I mean, if this shit is true then we have to find a way to beat this tribe. I-"

"I don't think it's the Tribe we have to beat. Whoever is in charge of the cult is who we have to go after. If Kenyetta was the one in charge then we don't have to worry about this happening again."

"What do you mean?" Shakim asked, leading me though the train stations. Although he swore he had no idea which way he was headed, we were both silently confident he was going the right way.

"Didn't he say every so often they try to reunite the Tribe? They're using Star to get the Tribe's power."

"Can you believe how sick people are? They would hurt a little kid for some whammy shit! I'm really looking forward to busting a cap in somebody's punk ass!"

"People have always done crazy shit for power. The Tribe was a very powerful group. I mean that vision I had was so real-"

"So how did the white man steal them?"

"I don't know. If what Kenyetta said was true, the Tribe had a weakness some slave trader discovered and used. "

"You know, I don't think Kenyetta was the leader. Remember he said the people involved were very powerful. If he had loot like that he wouldn't have been livin in the projects."

"Good point. Here's another thing that's bothering me: I saw the sandwich board man and the big lady downtown. They were real! Other people saw them, too. If they were members of the Tribe then how were they downtown? And why did the lady pass out and where did the fake ambulance drivers take her?"

"Maybe…maybe they're bringing the Tribe back one by one. Maybe you saw them when they tried to escape and the ambulance people came back to get them. Remember he said some shit about when D`ike gives in to Nicah-"

"That's right! He said D`ike was the only one able to stop the ritual! I think you might have hit something with them bringing the Tribe back one by one. Maybe that's why shit is getting crazier and crazier."

"What do you mean?" he asked.

"Think about it! The blackout is spreading, people acting crazy, the heat. I'll bet you the more members they bring back the more hectic shit gets!"

"So what'll happen if they bring back all twelve?"

"Maybe the world will blackout…I don't know! Maybe everybody'll act the way we saw those people in the hallway act. Remember? The heat? The dark? The sickness?"

"The twelfth member was the strongest. That's what he said. He said the Tribe picked Star. I'll bet you Star is the twelfth member."

Silver Eyes, silver sneakers, the silver crayon that Star scribbled the figure eight with. There were too many coincidences for it to be a coincidence.

I was glad Shakim believed this was real. I could only imagine how hard it was for him to accept this. I knew there was a lot more at stake than my daughter and my freedom. It was as if civilization hung in the balance.

"Man, do I wish Justice was back," I thought out loud.

We managed to maneuver through the subway without incident. I was amazed that Shakim led us right to Coney Island without making one error, as if something was guiding our way. I felt it. And although Shakim didn't say anything I knew he felt it also. When we came up out of the train station the sun was just setting. The heat was no less stifling, but at least I didn't have the sun frying me like a bug under a magnifying glass.

We were about a mile away from Coney Island. I could see the top of the Cyclone roller coaster. The National Guard still patrolled the streets, but there were a lot less of them. The people we passed on the streets had now broken out in large running blisters. Their faces looked as if someone scalded them with hot water and their scalps were bald and bleeding. "They remind me of the group back in that abandoned building, only those dope-fiends looked like this had happened to them a long time ago."

"You think the heat did that?" Shakim asked with a look of disgust on his face. "I only hope that shit ain't contagious."

"No," I answered covering my mouth. The fetor of the street was unbearable. "This is the sickness of the Tribe. You were right, Shakim! They're resurrecting them one by one!"

We ran more out of fright than anything. I felt curiously drawn to the amusement park. I thought about the last time I was there, walking with Star and

Sharon on the beach. It brought back the dream I had that night in my apartment when D`ike and Nicah stood on the shore with me. I thought about Gina telling me to stay away from the beach.

The sickness had afflicted everyone we passed. FEMA had set up makeshift hospitals and they were giving out water and flashlights to people.

A young soldier with blisters on his hands and face announced curfew would be in another fifteen minutes through a bullhorn. Some of the soldiers looked as bad as the people they were trying to treat.

"Where are you guys running to?" a soldier asked us. He was wearing Private First Class insignia and didn't look old enough to shave. "We're trying to get home before sundown, sir!" I answered respectfully. We didn't need to be stopped-not now.

"Get goin then!" the soldier answered nastily.

"I could've shoved that M16 up his ass!" Shakim whispered.

"I know, but remember I escaped from the G building. If I'm caught it's over. Besides, we're real close to finding Star!"

"My bad...I forgot."

We kept running, pacing ourselves so we wouldn't collapse. I had no idea how I was going to defeat a cult who were trying to resurrect a dozen members of an ancient tribe who had godlike powers, but I was either going to do it or die trying.

"We better get off the streets! The guards will shoot us if we get caught out here!" Shakim panted.

"We'll stay in the park. There's an old ticket outlet we can hide in."

The ticket outlet was a round gazebo type structure, a little bigger than a photomat. I expected a cool breeze to come off the ocean, but it seemed the closer to the water we came the hotter it got.

As if the heat started on the beach.

I drank my last bottle of water and opened the pouch. I wanted to take another look at the pictures, hoping Shakim wouldn't tease me about it. I spread them out, shining my flashlight over each one. I was looking for the girl I made love to in the treetops.

I came across a portrait of a woman named S`ianna. I recognized her noble stance and the tease in her stare. She was the one. I traced the portrait with my fingertips. My heart raced remembering it. The short time I spent with this goddess was the closest I ever came to bliss.

"S`ianna," I said in awe, reading the caption under her name. Shakim was asleep. "The youngest female of the Tribe." I looked at the other portraits, repeating the strange names. There was D`ike, K`embe, Molo, Jomo, and Kwame, the men. Then there were the women: Nicah (I still found it hard to believe the morbidly obese woman I saw downtown was this buxom beauty), D`aim, Iyanni, T`keya, Meeka, and S`ianna. I pulled the last portrait out of the pouch. It was a young man, no older than about thirteen.

There was an air of nobility about him. An arrogance usually reserved for royalty. I stared, remembering Kenyetta's words, 'the twelfth child was by far the mightiest. His powers were said to surpass all the others combined.' My fingers traced the picture, entranced by the majestic figure.

"Malik," I said out loud. His was without a doubt the most intriguing of all the portraits. The look on his face displayed great power and pride, yet immense sadness.

Tears welled in my eyes. I imagined the joy and beauty this tribe-like so many other African tribes felt. They were home and suddenly they were thrust into a nightmare of unimaginable proportions.

I began to sway. My eyelids fluttered. The small room became a mosaic combination of the jungle and the ticketron. I could see Shakim lying next to me out of one eye and I could see the leaves on the trees of the jungle out of the other.

I tried to pull my hand away-to scream and wake Shakim up. It felt as if I was living in two different worlds. Two different time periods. My hand was glued to the portrait. I could feel Malik's presence invading me.

I kept blinking and soon I couldn't see Shakim anymore.

Only the jungle…

A large bird caws loudly overhead and the myriad life forms all writhe and move with a rhythm and vitality that screams at me. I am in the jungle now, on the warm moist ground.

I am standing over a pond. I see my refection in the stagnant water. My eyes are the color of silver. They glow with an effulgence that radiates power. My sinews ripple and my skin glistens with a slick sheen of sweat. My hair is as long as a lion's mane, my locks thick and full.

There are thousands of different life forms on the jungle floor. I hear the scowl and roar of the black panther, the grunts and laughs of the monkeys, the hiss of giant snakes slithering by my feet.

Mountains and waterfalls hide the jungle. Only the bravest, or the most foolish trespass here. The gods have seen to our every comfort and blessed us with protection. The animals fear and respect us.

Especially me.

High above I see the graceful dance of my tribe as they lithely maneuver the treetops.

I am home here.

"Malik! What is it that enthralls you so?" D`aim asks. She is as beautiful as the moon that shines behind her.

"Perhaps our king is contemplating the meaning of the world?" Meeka teases. My heart leaps in my chest. I am beyond words at the sheer beauty of my sisters. The sight of their bodies fills me with joy and want.

"I am contemplating a game-a contest of sorts!" I answer in a voice that is soaked with desire. "Which of you I can reach first!"

The two girls turn and run playfully through the treetops. I follow, climbing quickly as the fun of the moment overtakes me. It matters not which one I catch. I love them both and as a tribal member, I can make love to any of the women in my tribe.

The joy is in the hunt. I chase them, feeling the stirrings of lust overtake me. Perhaps I will take them both.

I can.

I am exceptionally virile.

The moon looms over me, lighting my way. Not that I need it, for I am as comfortable in the darkness as most are in sunlight. Only…sunlight hurts my eyes and I prefer to move at night.

Meeka and D`aim separate, spoiling any idea of my taking them both this evening. I have to make a choice, the mature D`aim versus the young Meeka. I love them both. I want them both.

I swing and flip, landing on another branch. My muscles ripple with power and my libido increases the closer I come to the women. I can smell their sex. They are getting anxious for me to catch one of them. No doubt, they have laid a wager as to which one I will catch.

I wonder who will win.

The moonlight catches me as I spin high through the air, further empowering me. It adds excitement to the chase. I am invincible here-I am home here. I instinctively reach for a branch, knowing it is there. I somersault and plant my feet firmly. The perfect execution of a nearly impossible maneuver. I hear the giggles and sighs of D`aim and Meeka. The chase has raised their libido also, but now is the time for consummation.

And I'm in the mood to be totally consumed.

I glide toward them, like a hawk's wings resting on the cool wind currents. I catch D`aim and while holding her, I flip over three branches to Meeka. It is the first time I have attempted such an outrageous move and I can feel D`aim's heart race as I swing through the trees with her. One simple misstep from me would have spelled our death. I chuckle at her fright. I was never worried about the move.

I am home here.

They sit, seductively waiting for me together. The choice has been made. I can have both of them now. A smile erupts on my face. Life is good. I am happy.

"I have yet to see any living thing attempt that move. Surely your agility deserves reward!" D`aim says, her chest heaving with excitement.

"What reward would you offer? What can top that move?" I ask, trembling with desire.

"Come to me, my king," Meeka beckons me, her voice thick with tease.

"Come to me, my king," D`aim calls. The both of them are so beautiful. I am so elated the gods have given me my family and my jungle. I am the youngest, but for some reason I have the head of the council. D`ike and K`embe say it is because I complete the circle.

And the circle, once completed, must never be broken...

I take them both, dancing in the treetops searching for the limits of my virility, but it is not a contest, rather an expression of our respect and love for each other. I enjoy the softness of their bodies. The eagerness in their assertion fuels me and I am more than willing to please them.

We collapse in each other's arms, spent and satisfied. Meeka brings an odd sound to my attention. My curiosity is aroused. There is a strange scent in the jungle. Something is happening...

"Get back to the rest of the Tribe!" I order, my senses now on full alert. I quickly discern the sounds and smells belong to a group of hunters. They are afraid and new to the jungle.

My jungle.

I track them. High in the trees I look down upon them like a god spying on his creation. They have no idea I am watching. I count at least three-dozen of them. They shriek and cower at every sound. The jungle is a dangerous place for interlopers- dangerous because I make it so.

I get a good look at this strangely dressed group. Their skin is not like mine. They are white and their hair is straight with no curl or lock. They are clad in garments ill suited for travel in my jungle. One man seems to lead the others. He then, is the head of this tribe. It is he I will watch to determine how strong this tribe is and what their intentions are.

On the East Side of the jungle is a waterfall; the men will more than likely camp there to rest. I turn to inform the rest of my family. D`ike the elder is closest to me. We do not speak-instead I motion to him the number of men and their positions. I frown, not knowing why.

My senses are now on overload. Adrenaline pumps through me. My body trembles involuntarily. I have never felt such strange and awkward sensations. They are foreign to me.

I am afraid.

Suddenly, the sheen of perspiration dries on my skin. An odd feeling grasps me. I no longer trust my sinews to hold me. The limbs of the trees have become giant scary things.

What is happening?

My head pounds. Like hands beating the skin on a drum, I can feel the cadence of pain echoing in my ears. I turn to D`aim, my hands reach out to her. I am in such pain and I am so scared.

I shut my eyes. I hear screams and I realize it is the screams of my family. My legs will not obey me. The arrogance and pride I felt a while ago has dissipated.

I try to scream, but all sound is stuck in my throat. I feel myself falling from the tree limb...

I hit the jungle floor and-

Shakim woke me up. Shaking me vigorously, screaming my name. My eyes slowly focused on him. I was back in the ticketron, sitting on the floor. My face soaked with tears. The vision was still hazy in my mind's eye. Bits and pieces of it floated away from me like vapor.

"Was it these pictures again?" Shakim asked, holding the portraits of the Tribe. His voice was raw and scratchy. He was one step from a total mental meltdown.

"Yeah." I held my head as if it were about to explode. I took the pictures from him, shuffling them in my hand like a deck of cards bringing Malik to the surface.

I didn't know if Malik had somehow possessed me, or if I had imagined it all. The idea of me being the reincarnated version of Malik crossed my mind, that I was actually remembering a past life. The more answers I sought the more questions were raised.

"Look, man-maybe I should hold these things! You don't seem to be able to control yourself! Maybe it's the medicine they gave you in the G building. I mean, that would explain you seeing strange shit."

"Like that weird cat? I'm telling you I was there! I saw what he saw! I felt what he felt! Shakim this is unnatural, but I saw the slave traders that came in the Jungle-"

I shifted through the pictures, looking for the engraving of the slave traders. I came across the one I wanted. The name under it read Captain Luke Bartholomew Pearson, he was in full uniform.

"This is the guy I saw. He was leading about thirty people to capture the Tribe."

"How could he capture them if they had these super powers?"

"That's the mystery!" I said, staring at the pictures. I had the feeling I was holding a large piece of the puzzle in my hands, but I couldn't figure out what piece went where. If Shakim hadn't snapped me out of that strange trance, I could have seen what scared Malik so badly.

"Let's figure out what we know so far," I said, trying to apply logic to what was clearly illogical. "We know somehow this cult is responsible for the mysterious things that are happening. We know that over two hundred years ago a strange tribe was captured in Africa and sent to various places around the world. We know they formed a curse that only the youngest could invoke, but only the eldest male could stop. We know in about two days this cult is going to call the Tribe back together and in order to do this they need Star-"

"Yeah, but remember we figured out they were bringing the twelve back one at the time. So that means there are ten of them now. By tomorrow there'll be eleven then by Thursday there'll be twelve."

"We don't know how many of them there are right now. We're assuming that they're bringing the Tribe back one at a time, but we don't know if they're bringing them back one a day. It doesn't matter though. Once all twelve of them are there-"

"They'll use the youngest to start the curse!" Shakim finished. We were starting to understand what we were up against.

"You think...they'll kill her when they do this ritual?" Shakim asked nervously. This was all having one hell of a strain on his psyche.

"I ain't gonna lie, Sha- the bitch I saw in my apartment looked as crazy as they come. I...yeah, I think they'll try to kill her. That's why we gotta do whatever it takes to get her!" My mouth was as dry as sand. Shakim had pulled the blanket off my worst fear and left it exposed for all to see. If I failed, Star was dead-there were no two ways about it.

"I think they'll stop at nothing to try to get at the power of the Tribe. I don't know if the same thing happened to Kenyetta that happened to me when I touched these pictures, but if it did, I know why he kept them hidden. I've never felt anything like it! It's like every ride you've ever taken at an amusement park as a child, like every good movie, every good story, like every good feeling rolled up into one! Shakim, it was like heaven!"

"What, like the way they tell it in church?"

"No," I answered, searching for the right words. "Not that heaven. Our heaven!"

Shakim just stared at me, confused. I wished there was a way he could've felt what I felt, but part of me wanted to keep the pictures for myself. It probably wouldn't work for him anyway, I thought. Didn't Kenyetta say there was something special about me?

I held the pouch close to my chest, the way a schoolgirl carries her books. The portraits were as addictive as nicotine. The idea of parting with them was inconceivable.

I would have rather died first.

"So what's our next move?" Shakim asked, looking at me strangely.

"I don't know…I wish Justice was here," I mumbled, feeling a little helpless. We were in way over our heads.

"Look, we been through this! There ain't no Justice!" Shakim retorted.

"You got that right, boy! You and that moolie come out of that shithouse real slow or else my M16 is gonna start talking!" a voice barked over my shoulder.

My blood froze and I turned and saw the young Private we came across earlier. I discreetly let the pouch slip to my side. We were surrounded by at least a half dozen soldiers. There was one man in full dress greens, with an assortment of medals and ribbons adorning his chest. It took me a minute, but I recognized him.

He was one of the paramedics who carried the

old lady into the ambulance.

Looks like another heat stroke, Jerry!

"It's them ain't it, sir! Just like I told you, it's them!" the young soldier exclaimed excited.

"Well done, son. Well done! Well! We got ourselves a regular Sher-dread-lock Home-boy, hunh?" the fake paramedic/soldier said. The rest of the group chuckled lightly. They all had their M16's trained on us. One pull of the trigger and they could have puréed us like tomato paste. Most of them were sick and I instantly thought of one of the ten plagues Moses brought down on Egypt.

The plague of boils.

"What you want with us?" Shakim stammered. "We were trying to stay out the streets for the curfew! We can't get back to our neighborhood so we figured we'd stay here! We came to check on my grandma and-"

One of them belted Shakim in the ribs with the butt of the M16. A loud whoomf escape his lips as he sank to his knees. I kept my hands on my head with the pouch secure between my feet. They searched us and took the .45 from Shakim.

"You see, boy," the soldier sneered. "What we have here is mind over matter. I don't mind and you don't matter! We found out what you did to that old nigga Kenyetta. Not that I mind you niggas killin' each other. Hell, saves us the trouble! With all you Bloods and Crips cuttin' and shootin' each other I aint gotta waste a bullet! But now it seems that you niggas was good for somethin' after all! Bunch a you darkies seemed ta tap into the power of the moon. Of course a white man brought you niggas down and tomorrow night we'll get that power. A power that's rightfully ours!"

The rest of the soldiers shouted wildly and waved their weapons above their heads. Apparently this man promised them a piece of the pie if they followed him. I felt disgusted as I remembered the joy and love the Tribe shared in the jungle. Men like this destroyed that. Men like this raided Africa for its gold and light and then had nerve to call it the 'Dark Continent'.

"How do you figure that power is rightfully yours? Captain Luke Bartholomew Pearson stole it and afterwards he was driven mad. Can you survive the jungle? No, I don't think so! Do you realize what's happening? The curse is coming true! You-"

"Shut-up! You ain't got a fuckin clue! We gonna succeed where the others failed! We ain't gonna let the boss down this time-we almost through with calling the Silver-Eyes together! I outta put a bullet in this buck's head right here and make you give me the missing piece!"

Missing piece? What does he mean? I thought to myself. This man was a certifiable nut. Not as crazy as Troy, Jamie or Skippy, but not too far off the mark. I thought about what Kenyetta said, about how every so often someone tries to bring all twelve members of the Tribe back.

And how they might very well succeed this time.

"Don't do this! Please, just think about what you're doing! Look at yourselves! You all need medical attention! Look around you-"

"*Shut the fuck up, nigga!*" He rammed the butt of the M16 into my stomach. All the air flew out of me. I collapsed in a heap next to Shakim.

"You stupid, fuckin nigga! I read all your books on Africa, like you coons were the first civilization! Sum a you even try ta say Jesus was black! Dumb fuckin heathens! Give me a fuckin break! I-"

"Can't take the truth-can you, boy?" I stammered, refusing to give this bigot the satisfaction of scaring me. "Let me ask you, Mr. Idiot, have you even seen the jungle? Have you-"

"You, buck, will learn proper respect! After tonight you darkies will be back where you properly belong-in our service."

"I saw you that day downtown when the old lady passed out from the heat. You were wearing a paramedic's uniform then. Now you're wearing an officer's uniform. Who are you?"

"You may call me Mr. Briggs, boy. That's all the information I'll divulge for now."

"Well, Mr. Briggs-I'm going to kill you. There's nothing that can or will change that! Once I have my daughter back, I'm going to kill you!" I said, gritting through clenched teeth trying to bear the pain.

"Death ain't shit, boy. Life's the bitch you got to ride raw!" Mr. Briggs chuckled. One of the soldiers raised the M16 high over his head, ready to smash me with it again.

"No!" Mr. Briggs grinned. "We need this one. Open that pouch, boy!"

They aimed their weapons at the back of

Shakim's skull. I had no doubt they would've killed him and emptied the clips in his carcass, without so much as blinking.

"Okay," I mumbled, really scared now. My hands trembled as I reached in the pouch and pulled out the pictures. I looked at the faces in the portraits and felt an odd need to apologize to them. I had somehow let them down by letting this madman get his hands on them. "Here they are. Take them and go." I picked the portraits up and handed them to Briggs. Another soldier reached to grab them. Briggs slapped him.

"Boy, maintain discipline!" he barked, snatching the pictures. His hands greedily searched them, making sure he rubbed every inch. It was obscene the way he defiled those portraits.

"Fuck you!" I screamed with everything I had within me. A rage filled my soul. A burning hatred for this man consumed me. I lunged at the pictures. The pain in my neck spread and I knew I had a concussion. My hands swept the portraits before they pulled me away.

Again, I felt the freezing sensation rush my arm. I was being pulled into another world, another time. I welcomed the sensation. My mouth watered at the idea of getting back to the Tribe, back to the jungle.

Only this time it wasn't the jungle I landed in...

CHAPTER VII:

∞

The Middle Passage…

It is dark and hot. Sounds and images flood my senses. I am trying to gain my bearings, to determine where I am. Somewhere in the distance I hear the sound of waves. I am on a ship-no, I am in a ship.

A slave ship.

The legends of the sea demons are true. The strange men who entered my jungle are the sea beasts who steal entire tribes to sacrifice to the gods of the waters. I often thought the tales were just stories to frighten young children, to warn them about venturing too far from the huts.

I know now they are true.

I am cramped, lying in the prone position. My hands and feet bound by thick chains. My mouth is dry and although it is unbearably hot, I cannot sweat anymore. I am weak and feverish. My muscles are flaccid. Gone is the strength that catapulted me through the trees. I am as weak as a newborn.

There is a feeling of dread and trepidation lodged in my stomach. Such feelings are alien to me-I am Malik. I complete the circle. My eyes burn, but my chains are too heavy to lift. Flies and mosquitoes buzz around my head, but I am too weak to shoo them away.

Beside me is a man that has been dead for quite some time. He is decomposing and the stench is overpowering. On the other side of me is a woman who is weeping loudly. She has defecated on herself, as have I.

At my head is a young girl, barely on the fringes of womanhood. She whimpers silently, calling for her parents to come and rescue her. By my feet, another man struggles against his bonds in futility. His hands are raw and blood soaked from where the chains have twist and bit into his flesh. I think he would rather lose his hands than to have gained those chains.

The noise is deafening. I am able to decipher many different dialects and tongues. They all scream the same thing more or less. They are praying to whatever gods there are to free us.

But there is no god here.

Because this is Hell.

"What is your name?" the woman next to me asks. She tries to make conversation. Perhaps to share the nightmare-to dilute it, so that it at least seems more bearable.

"I am called Malik. I complete the circle," I answer, not wishing to continue the senseless prattle at this time. I am a warrior and as such I have to formulate a plan of action.

Only I am too weak to move, let alone plan an escape.

I lay wondering where my beloved tribe is. Surely they will come to rescue me. I have to conserve my strength for their arrival. K`embe and D`ike will lead the charge. Surely they will come for me.

I am Malik. I complete the circle. And the circle once formed must never be broken. I have heard this from our tribal mother, Nicah from the time I was able to take my first steps. It has been ingrained in me since the dawn of my memory. This is the one unbreakable rule of our tribe. Never break the circle. It is our mantra-the secret to our existence.

My wrists ache from the bite of the chains, my feet have become numb. A ray of light seeps through the overhead planks of this wretched vessel. People are stacked like leaves. There is not an area on the floor of the ship that is not covered by flesh. In some areas, the people are piled on top of each other four and five deep.

We are stuffed into an area so small that many die from inhaling the spent breath of those around them. Many pray for death. Many prayers are answered.

I hear the death moans of people in anguish. Even the strongest men of the different tribes weep like women. The chains that bind me bind the woman next to me, and the man next to her. The same chain secures us all.

We are all links in the same chain.

The ship comes across turbulent waters. My back snags and rips on a piece of jagged wood. But physical pain is the least of my concerns at this time; it is the mental anguish that concerns me. I have lost my family, my home, and I fear the better part of my sanity. I have no idea how long I have been in this ship and worse yet-I have no idea where we are going.

"What tribe are you from, Malik?" the woman asks again. I do not wish to speak to her. She is hideous. Her complexion is grayish and her skin pallid. She is emaciated; her breasts shriveled and dried-the complete opposite of my beautiful sisters. She stinks of the dead.

Oh my tribe! Where are you? Save me! Wake me from this cursed dream!

"I am of the Death Tribe, feared by animals and loathed by men. I am Malik. I complete the circle," I reply. My throat burns. My voice crackles with fear and uncertainty. I, who have called my tribe together with one roar throughout the jungle, find it a labor to speak to a woman not even three inches away from me.

The woman hisses as if she were a snake. I will not hear much more from her now, I think. The word soon spreads throughout this inferno. There is a member of the Death Tribe among us they say. Blame him for this. Kill him, they say. Kill him and the gods will forgive us!

I lay quiet. There is nothing they can do to me. We are chained so tightly and bound so close together it is difficult to even wriggle, let alone attack someone. Whatever tribe has captured us has extensive knowledge in hunting.

They are breaking our minds and spirits as well as our bodies.

The man at my feet has succeeded in tearing into his wrists. Blood flows like the mighty waterfall that borders my jungle. He will be dead soon and I hear him praying to the gods, thanking them for sparing him further torment.

The young girl at my head screams in what has to be excruciating pain. She is on her monthly issue of blood and rats have sensed a rich meal. They have invaded her. They will eat her from the inside out. I can scarcely imagine a more grisly death.

More moans and prayers assail my ears. People beg the gods to save them, to deliver them. It is a prayer of futility. There is no god here. I remember a tale that wafted through the jungle on the lips of travelers and old women of a man who was ordered by the gods to preach to the sinners of his day. Terrified of what the sinners would do, the man sought to escape the god's edit by sea. A terrible storm struck and the captain and his crew blamed the man for their misfortune. They cast him overboard and a giant fish swallowed him. He lived in the belly of that fish for three days after which the fish spat him on dry land.

I now know how that man felt, for I am in the belly of the same fish.

The sea yarns and roars, but the vessel holds. The violent swaying of the ship upsets my stomach-no matter, there is nothing for me to expel. I heave and retch, but nothing comes out. My tongue is swollen and I am feverish from the heat and a lack of water.

The hideous woman next to me gasps for air. She is choking on her own vomit. She will be dead soon. Rats have begun to feed on the dead man at my feet, enticed by the smell of blood. The rats will eat well here and I wonder how soon it will be before we eat the rats.

Above me, through the dim light that trickles through the planks I see our captors moving about. I know not how I understand their tongue, but it is unimportant-there is no misunderstanding their intentions.

The wails and shrieks of warriors reverberate in my ears. I have seen many men die before. Death is always a warrior's companion, but this is worse than death. This insidious torture strips away the manhood of the warrior. We are all eunuchs here.

All of my life I have prided myself on my courage and honor. Bravery is the shield of every true warrior, but today it is very hard to be brave. The pain I now feel is nothing compared to the pain that I feel is coming. Instinct tells me I am going to a much worse place than this ship.

My mind can barely begin to understand what is happening to me. And just when I believe my fear can get no greater-another shriek of indescribable horror besets my ears.

My body betrays me by shivering and trembling. Each second in this horrid place becomes harder to abide than the last. The only motion there is to measure time is the length of the screams and the violent swaying of the ship.

Fear is a force. It can be just as powerful as the lightning or thunder and just as difficult to control. I try to escape mentally, but this too is dangerous. The

mind can become a labyrinth that can trap the body.
One wrong mental turn and I may never recover. I
fight to resist creating the illusion of a safe-haven. It
would not do for my tribe to rescue me and I am not
hale in my faculties.

I search deep within myself. I search for the
strength to endure this madness. I strain to remember
the comforts of my home, but the images and memories escape me, replaced by the burning stench of reality.

I hear more howls of suffering. I witness more
deaths. I shut my eyes tightly and I remember
S`ianna. The soft and gentle breeze that always
seemed to surround her. Out of all my sisters, she has
captured a very special chamber of my soul. A chamber that not even this hell can shackle.

How I long for you, S`ianna.

The light grows brighter as a doorway above
us is opened. I shriek from the light. It hurts my eyes.
Men rush down. I hear the rustling of chains being
released from the floor of the ship and now the
screams and cries grow deafening as many of us are
roughly forced up the makeshift steps.

I stand naked on the deck of the ship, chained
to at least a hundred other naked men and woman. We
all look around in horror. The reality of the situation
has impaled us like a javelin.

We are surrounded by water. The land is gone.
Gone!

Water is all the eye can see!

Any notion of escape, any chance of overcom-
ing our captors has now been washed away like the

waves of the mighty sea that surrounds us. Our captors leer at the bodies of the women, some at the bodies of men. A young girl is dragged off by six men. Their intentions are obvious. Her screams echo in my mind as I watch them rape her. It is another form of torture. A man is supposed to protect his women and by raping our sisters in front of us they claim indomitable superiority. This is the ultimate insult. This is unheard of in any tribe I know of.

I have never seen men behave like this.

I have never seen animals behave like this.

For the first time in my twelve summers I feel hate. These men have taken away everything imaginable from me. And the horrifying part is I know the worst is yet to come.

Many despair and opt to jump overboard. The captors try to save some, and chained men pull a few of the gold hairs off the ship. They sink like stones because of the weight.

But I will not jump. I will live to see the necks of my captors broken beneath my heel. I am Malik. I complete the circle. And the circle once completed must never be broken.

Others gasp and move away from me as if I am a pariah. The sun drains what little strength I have. I fall to the deck of the ship. Men move toward me.

"No! Are you fellows mad? Don't touch him barehanded! Look at the darkies that were closest to him!" one of the men shouts. I look around at the faces of those who are the nearest to me. It is true. Many have large gray patches on their flesh, large running sores and blisters that ooze a putrid slime.

I did this.

The men order those struck with this malady overboard. In a way, I envy those who die now. Their ordeal is over. I am unchained and drenched with buckets of cold seawater, prodded by long spears with sponges attached to the ends. I am alone now, the deck cleared of all other 'darkies' as they call us. It is just the captors and I. They stare at me in awe. I feel my strength returning slowly. If only the cursed sun would go down.

I would show these gold hairs just what this darkie could do!

"Where is the rest of my tribe?" I ask, trying to control the rage that threatens to engulf my soul. I have never met men like these. They are as cunning as hyenas, yet lower than the roots of the weeds that choke the soil.

"He speaks English!" one man gasps. A look of sheer amazement cloaks his face. You would have thought he heard a monkey speak.

"Never you mind about them, darkie! It seems I was right about you!" the one who warned the men says to me. I recognize him as the leader I tracked into my jungle. There is a look of pride and arrogance that accompanies him. A look I am all too familiar with. A look I once had. I underestimated this man. I shall not do so again.

"Well, darkie! It took me many trips, but I learned your precious secrets! You are now captive, courtesy of Captain Luke Bartholomew Pearson." He postures and laughs, the rest of the men laugh with him. "You see, I had to prove it to the world. No darkie could ever outsmart any white man. You might have been regarded as something special to the other savages, but to me you are just another darkie. I'm going to break you. I am going to learn all of your precious secrets if it takes me an eternity!"

"Not eternity," I grumble. "Infinity."

"I thought a darkie that called himself a king would be a wee bit tougher to capture! But so that it won't be said I am not a Christian man," he holds a figurine suspended from a chain around his neck and kisses it. "Feed him."

I am given molded bread and spoiled fruit to eat. I devour it hungrily and feel my stomach cramp with pain. I have never been hungry before and it is not a sensation I relish, but something tells me it is a feeling I will become quite familiar with.

"Where are my sisters? Where is the rest of my tribe?" I try to sound as regal and as noble as befits a member of my tribe, but in this godforsaken place, it is very hard.

"Oh they're just fine, boy. Just fine. We separated you darkies on three different ships. You see different countries will pay different amounts for you. You darkies are going to be my legacy! You-"

The ship sways violently on a surge of waves, throwing us around like leaves in the wind. I use the opportunity to reach for them, if I can only touch one of them...

"David! Wake up, man! Wake up!" Shakim screamed, slapping me in the face trying to get me to come out of the trance. My eyes were finally able to focus on him. I was never so happy to see anyone in my life.

"You alright, man? " he asked with fear in his eyes.

"Yeah," I answered, shaking my head. We were in a storage warehouse of some kind. "Where in the fuck are we?"

"In deep do-do! We gotta find a way out of here. They brought us in here right after you started freakin out. "

"Freakin out, how?" I asked, trying to get the horrible feelings out of my mind, but I knew I never would.

My soul was stained with it.

"You touched one of those pictures. The one of the boats and all of a sudden you just went blank! Just blank! Your eyes had this far away look in them. I thought you were in a coma or something! Then you started speakin in tongues like those fat ladies do in Reverend Hickman's church. You been out for about six or seven hours. You gonna hafta do better than this shit if we gonna win this thing! I saw Star they-"

"Where is she?" I stammered at the mention of her name. I grabbed Shakim roughly by his collar.

"Calm down! She's okay! I saw her while they were bringing us in here. They thought I was knocked out, but I was fakin. She was in a room down the hall. We're in some sort of underground hideaway beneath Coney Island. The walls and the doors are like two feet thick. Steel, I think."

"Shakim, this shit is real! I touched that picture and I was back on a slave ship! A slave ship-"

"The Good Ship Jesus. I know. I heard Mr.

Briggs tell the other men the story. They say that
when the last of the Tribe is called together they will
steal their souls and take their powers. Sounds like
some comic book shit. I'd laugh if it wasn't so real."

"It was real! I never want to go back to that
awful place. The way they stacked people in that boat
like they were sardines! Chained like animals! You
can't imagine how horrible it was, man! Little children, women, men all chained together!"

"Calm down, man. Everything's gonna be
alright! We just gotta get outta here!"

"You don't understand! I was there! But not as
me! I saw what Malik saw. I heard what he heard and
felt what he felt! Even my thoughts were his! It was
so strange!" I pressed my fingers against the corners
of my eyes, massaging them gently. "Shakim, I think I
am starting to understand. The Tribe, they're not the
bad ones. It's those bastards out there! They want to
bring them back to use them! The Tribe couldn't take
sunlight. They were nocturnal like bats. I think that's
how they were captured."

"How do you know that?"

"Because I was there! In Malik's body! I
mean-I was him. The sunlight hurt his…my eyes."

Shakim looked confused. He was a man of
deep action, not deep thinking. This was beyond him.
He would rather fight his way out, than figure a way
out.

"So then the Tribe doesn't want to come
back?"

Shakim's question made more sense than even
he realized. According to Kenyetta, D`ike was the

only one that could stop the ritual and that was suppose to be the man I saw in the sandwich board. He said when he gives in to Nicah the curse would come true. If Nicah was the one that placed the curse, suppose that's what she whispered to Star that day downtown?

"Shh! I hear somebody coming! We gotta get out of here!" I whispered, hiding behind the empty crates and steel canisters that were strewn around the room. The room was lit from the battery powered halogen lamps that were placed high above us. The ceiling was at least fifty feet high, about a foot or two beneath that was a ventilation grate.

I heard soldiers talking in the hall and then the door opened. A large man carrying a hook with a rope attached came in. I instantly recognized him as the bus driver that day downtown. The smile on his face sent chills up my spine.

"No use hiding! It'll only prolong the inevitable! I'm here for the darkie named Shakim!" He said Shakim's name as if it were a joke. "The other darkie is to come with me."

"I think I can take him! When I do, you get the fuck out of here and find Star!" Shakim said, and I understood. This was something he could deal with. Kenyetta's macabre story, the Tribe, the portraits and all of the supernatural happenings were beyond his sphere of thinking. By his method of reasoning, the man in the doorway was nothing in comparison to all that occurred.

The bus driver swung the rope as if it was a lasso and he was a cowboy looking to rustle steer.

"It won't do to hide. I'll only get madder and then I'll make it hurt more!" he quipped.

"Sha, this is the bus driver I told you about! The whole thing is a setup!"

"Fuck that! I can take him! I'm gonna knock fat boy out and you go get Star!"

"Wait! Let's do it together!" I said, but it was too late. Shakim had leaped into the fray. Before I could blink, the man swung the rope and in that split second I saw Shakim impaled on the hook. The expression on his face was an odd mix of pain and disbelief. The hook disemboweled him. His intestines draped the floor in a bloody curtain.

"Sha!" I screamed, wet with fear and panic. I lifted a crate and hurled it at the man, stunning him. I stumbled, falling all over the barrels and boxes. The man came at me, swinging the hook and laughing maniacally. It grazed my head as I barely managed to move out of the way in time. I held the hook with one hand, trying to keep him from stabbing me with it. The tip of the hook was smeared in a thick gel that smelled like sulfuric acid.

"You'll come with me, or I'll hurt you real bad. I'm not supposed to kill you, yet! See how he hurts! See what my hook can do!" he spat with one of his hands crushing my face.

"That day on the bus," he whispered. "I want-ed to fuck your little girl up the ass, I think she would've liked it." He snickered and sneered at me. Slob dribbled out of his mouth on my cheek. The drool burned. It smelled like rancid meat.

"Fuck you!" I screamed, soaked in hatred. The

mere idea of this animal touching Star had me blind with wrath. His words brought back to mind Star's screams of someone touching her.

I wrapped one end of the heavy rope around his neck and pulled with everything I had inside. His eyes bulged and he gasped for air. His grip on the hook loosened.

"Fuck you!" I swung the hook. The sharp end of it bit deep into his skull, freezing that shit-eating grin across his face for all eternity. I could hear his blood sizzle. The hook left a cigar sized burn ring in his head. "Stick this up your ass!" I pulled the hook out and ripped it across his ass until I hit bone.

I ran over to Shakim. He was pale and in shock from the loss of so much blood.

"Hold on, man! You're gonna be all right! It looks a lot worse that it is!" I wrapped his shirt tightly around the wound, trying to stop the bleeding.

"Did you get him?" Shakim asked me.

"Yeah!" I said, looking back at that huge bag of walking pus. "I got him!" The acid ate away at Shakim's shirt. I could smell his wound burning.

"Good! David, I have to tell you something…you gonna think it's crazy, but just listen to me! That day…when Star was born and you asked me to be her godfather…that day when you put her in my arms for the first time…I prayed, David. I prayed that God would let me be the type of man that would be worthy to be her godfather. I made God a promise that I would die for her-remember? We both said that nothing would ever happen to her-"

"Yeah! But don't talk like that, man! It's not

that bad! You're not going to be able to down any forty ounces for a while, but you'll be okay! We're both going to see her again!" I said, rocking him in my arms.

"I knew when I saw her that my time was done. You go on, David. You get Star and you go on! Tell me again...tell me how pretty it was...when you touched that picture. Man, you should have seen the look on your face! You really looked like a man in heaven! You...think...you think I could get there, even without the picture?"

I tried my best to keep the wound closed, but blood seeped through the cloth and my fists. I knew he was dying and there was nothing I could do about it. "Just stay calm! Everything is going to be alright." I said, trying to choke back tears.

"I never...I never really ever went in for ole Reverend Hickman's version of heaven. Yours sounded much better. Tell me again!"

"The trees...were taller than buildings. The sun...barely breaks through the thick leaves. The jungle pulses with a breath...a life all of its own. The Tribe...they are so beautiful. Black and strong...just like you, Sha! Just like you. Can you see them?"

"I don't know. Hey...your man Justice...does he have dreads?"

"Yeah! How did you know- Sha? Sha? Shakim!"

Shakim was dead.

CHAPTER VIII:

∞

The Substance Of Things Hoped For...

I didn't want to be in that storage room with the dead bus driver when the other soldiers came. The door was locked and there was no key on the man. I had to escape and the only exit was the ventilation grate near the ceiling.

I threaded the rope through the hook and tied it tightly. It took me over a dozen tries, but I managed to snag the grate. One strong yank pulled it down. It took another few dozen tries, but the hook found purchase in the hole and I only hoped whatever the hook had latched on to was strong enough to support my weight.

Slowly I climbed, using my feet to brace against the wall. I didn't dare look down for fear of getting dizzy. My hands burned from the bite of the rope and I was worried about my muscles giving out on me. Every nerve in my body screamed for me to let go before I climbed too high, but I kept going. Justice once told me I had to have faith. Faith was the only thing that could help me now.

I kept climbing, trying to keep my mind occupied. I thought about the captain, how he wasn't afraid of the Tribe. He found a way to cancel their powers, but how? Maybe it was Malik's temporary lapse of concentration that allowed him to capitalize. Maybe it was something else-something I'd yet to see.

I remembered the vision I had of Malik being on the Good Ship Jesus. He was about to attack the captain when I was snatched out of the vision. What happened? Why didn't Malik win? Kenyetta said he was the strongest of the lot, so how did the captain defeat him?

I continued climbing, ignoring the pain in my hands. The ropes were wrapped around my knuckles so tightly I was losing feeling in my fingertips, but I dared not pay attention to that now. I was at the halfway point. I still had just as much to climb as I had climbed.

All sorts of thoughts ran through my mind. I worried about the vent being too small for me to climb through. What if the vent was blocked or if it came to a dead end? I tried to dislodge these thoughts, but with every step, the doubt became more real.

I kept my mind on Star, concentrating on putting one foot in front of the other. My back ached and my arms felt as if they would give out at any time, but I kept going.

I was about twelve feet from the vent when I felt the hook had begun to give way. Fear simmered in my throat like hot bile. I climbed quicker, praying the hook held on to whatever was holding it. My hands were slick from sweat, the rope bit deeper and muscle fatigue set in. I couldn't climb another inch, my limbs just wouldn't move.

The feeling of falling came over me-an indescribable pull on not only my body, but also my soul.
I was falling through time-through worlds.

When I finally landed, I was in the jungle with
Malik. A strange mist covered the ground and the
trees were all enveloped in a silver fog.

"Are you well, David?" he asked me.

"How...how do you know my name?"

"Don't be absurd, of course I know you! After
all, it was I who called you!"

I stood and looked at him. His eyes really
were silver. The pupils looked like miniature full
moons. Luminous. Cool and soothing. The whites of
his eyes were blinding. There was an incredible aura
of intelligence about him. I should have been terrified
out of my wits, but a calm came over me. There was
something noble and blessed about Malik, and something serene and tranquil about the silver jungle.

"Am I...am I dead?"

"No, David. But you would be had I not pulled
you here when I did. That fall would have surely
killed you."

"What do you want of me?" I asked.

"I want you to understand what has happened.
The pain and destruction that is taking place now is
not our doing. We are not evil, David. We only wanted to be able to exist in peace. The Europeans disrupt-
ed that peace. We want it back."

"How can I help you?" I asked, feeling as if I
was caught in an ethereal dream. Kenyetta was right;
Malik radiated with authority and power. I kneeled
before him without thinking. It just seemed the right

and natural thing to do.

"By getting those portraits; they are a psychic link to us," he said, raising me to my feet. "It is how they began the ritual."

"The portraits! Where did they come from? Who sketched them?"

"You will know that in the proper time."

"Where are we?" I asked, looking around in awe. Everything was silver. The trees, the grass, the sky, everything.

"We are in what I like to refer to as my home. This is the world I created after I escaped the talons of the European. I escaped by dying. Death, my dear son is nothing to fear; for as beautiful as life is, we will all enter death's realm one day."

"Is this where people go when they die? Is this...heaven?"

"I built this jungle out of the love and gifts the gods have blessed me with. Here I remain the age I was before we were captured. Free from the memory of slavery. Once, my entire tribe inhabited this sacred place and we wished to spend eternity here. Then they were called away one by one. I am the last. I do not wish to leave."

It was as if a veil had suddenly been lifted from my mind. I was standing in the equivalent of Malik's afterlife-his heaven. All of them were there and the ritual called them away. If I didn't stop the ritual, this place would soon be empty.

"I need to know how they captured you. I mean-how did they manage to get you twelve out of the jungle?" I tried to phrase that question as humbly as possible. I sensed a great reluctance for Malik to speak about it.

"Yes…I guess it is only fitting that you know. It was not one of my more shining moments I assure you. Come, peer into the pool of truth. All will be shown to you."

He pointed to a pond of what looked like mercury. I walked over and stared into it. A picture started to form. The fog that covered the jungle grew thicker. The mist enveloped me. The picture grew wider and sharper.

"Forgive me, my tribe…" Malik said. His voice grew fainter. I was standing with the twelve now. T`keya lay on the jungle floor, her abdomen bleeding, but already the wound was healing. D`ike was set to attack Captain Pearson. The rest of the Tribe had taken up battle stations around him. I was watching this, not as if it was a television show, but like one of those virtual reality games. I could smell, hear, and sense what was happening. Only this time I was still myself. I still had my own thoughts.

Just then, the moon changed colors. It went from its usual silvery white to a coppery orange and then disappeared all together. A total lunar eclipse! The moon is caught in the earth's shadow!

"Steady, men! On my signal!" the captain ordered. "Now!" he screamed, then it happened; the men pulled some sort of pouch out of their vests. The pouches exploded simultaneously, creating a terrific blinding flash of light. The air was thick with the sharp acrid smell of phosphorus, magnesium and gunpowder.

The flash blinded the Tribe and I understood. Light hurts their eyes. Their senses have been over- whelmed. The sensory nerves have shut down. They are now catatonic. The bright flash coupled with the moon disappearing defeated them!

Captain Pearson's plan was simple, but devil- ishly brilliant. If only such a mind had been put to the use of good, diseases could have been cured.

The Tribe howled and writhed in pain. D`ike and K`embe were the closest to the flash and were instantly rendered unconscious. The rest passed out also, but Malik! Malik was in the rear! The flash did not affect him as badly-he will continue the fight!

Only Malik didn't fight. He feigned sleep. Seeing the moon disappear must have frightened the wits out of him.

Captain Pearson's men threw a net over the twelve and while wearing thick cotton padding pro- ceeded to drag the Tribe to the three slave ships that would take them deep into the heart of the worst nightmare known to man.

I felt myself being pulled out of the vision, back into the foggy jungle with Malik.

"Now you know my shame. In the heat of bat- tle seeing my beloved tribe fall, I panicked. And because of my weakness we were captured. Fear is both the warrior's friend and enemy, David. That night it was my enemy. It paralyzed me. I-"

He burst into tears and my heart went out to him. I saw in him centuries of guilt and remorse. If this jungle was Malik's heaven then that silver pool showed me his hell. I could not imagine having to relive this nightmare over and over.

"How could I have let them take us? Where was the strong, virile young man that ruled the jungle? Where was the Malik that completed the circle? How could I have sat idly by while they defiled our women? While they destroyed our home?"

"Malik, you can't blame yourself! It wasn't your fault! You would've only gotten yourself killed! You need to let go of this and realize the fault lies with those sadistic bastards that stole your tribe-not with you!"

"No! Malik is a warrior! A protector of his tribe! Lions and rhinos have felt my strength! I have run with the cheetah and swam with the hippo! The jungle was our home! And I let them take us away from it! I let them destroy it!"

"Don't," I said, hot tears stung my eyes. "Malik, listen to me... I know you're like a king or something, but please just listen to me. You were only what-twelve? Thirteen when this happened? You had no preparation for this type of attack! None of us did! It's easy to see how you would have been afraid seeing the moon disappear like that. It's called a Lunar Eclipse. I'm surprised that was the first time you saw it happen."

"Our power peaks at the full moon and during those moments when the moon hides its face from us we are at our most vulnerable. Still, I should have fought to the death. I should have-"

"Don't berate yourself over it, Malik. It happened. Learn to forgive yourself."

"Do you forgive me, David?" he asked, staring

hard into my eyes.

"Do I? Malik there is nothing to forgive! It's those sick twisted fuckers that stole us who need to ask forgiveness!"

"Knowing what you know. Seeing what you saw. Do you forgive me?"

"Yes, Malik. If that's what you need to hear me say then fine, I forgive you. Is this why the curse was created?"

"Curse? It was they who placed the curse on us! I created this place for my tribe. Here they are eternally young and beautiful. Here D`ike and Nicah remain in the full blossom of their glory, not the faded and wretched creatures you saw in the cursed heat. I only wanted this much, to atone to my beloved family for failing them when they needed me most!

"The European wishes to take even this from me. He haunts my every moment, because of my weakness. For centuries, I've had to contend with the captain wanting to revive the Tribe for his own gain. No one has ever called all eleven away from me. The most was four and that was many summers ago. If you do not stop him we are doomed!"

"But how did they get K`embe when he was supposed to be impervious-"

"K`embe is impervious to any enemies weapon, providing that he sees the attack coming. For every strength there is a weakness."

"Wha-what happened to the rest of the Tribe? I saw D`ike and Nicah, I know they didn't have an easy time of it, but what about the women? What happened to Jomo and Molo? K`embe and Kwame?"

"Go back to the pool. Learn the truth about us and about yourself, but beware; truth is a strange thing. Once learned, it can not be unlearned."

I leaned over the strange pool, allowing the mist to envelop me again. The silver water swirled and bubbled until another picture appeared. I saw the twelve by the shore. The three ships were docked and manned by at least a hundred pirates. These were not the same men who followed Captain Pearson into the forbidden jungle. These were mercenaries, men with no discipline. The men leered at the women, but none touched them.

I wanted to turn and throw up in disgust, but I couldn't make myself look away.

"Look deeper, David. Learn the truth about us and about yourself. We are all links in the same chain..." Malik said. I could hear his voice getting faint. The fog of the jungle grew thicker. I was being drawn into the silver pool. The vision would now take on a horrifying 3D effect.

I felt myself being pulled from the inside, like the Hellhole ride at Coney Island, where you're whipped around so fast you can't move and you're stuck to the wall. When the pulling finally stopped, I am on the beach with the strange tribe instead of just watching them...

There are at least three hundred other Africans here, all chained like animals. Some of the men try to fight and are shot in the genitals to dispel any thoughts of an uprising. The air is thick with the taste of gunpowder and singed flesh, mixed with the salt of the sea. It is a taste I will never forget. It is the taste of fear and conquest.

The taste of slavery.

"You bastards!" I shriek, seething with anger. My hands and feet are bound together. I am hog-tied. A pirate kicks me over and I lay face down in the sand. My eyes burn from the grit, but I cannot even so much as wipe my face. I look up at the sun and wonder where is God on such a day as this.

Women from other tribes are raped right out in the open. The pirates taunt the men, daring them to react. A young girl, no older than eleven or twelve is being sodomized right in front of me. I see the veins bulging in her head from screaming so hard.

"That's enough, men! Get the darkies on the ships now! Don't damage all of them! They'll fetch a good price I reckon! Good day's work this was! Damned good day's work!" a man laughs. It is not the captain, but obviously someone in charge of the pirates.

Mr. Briggs!

Captain Pearson views this with disdain, but a sort of indifference. All he cares about is the twelve. The other Africans are merely payment to the pirates for their assistance. His eyes meet mine and I have never wanted to kill anyone as badly as I want to kill this man.

The pirates are now hoisting people up, roughly forcing them on the ships. Children are torn away from their mothers, wives from their husbands. Tribes are separated. The soldiers are strategically placed, aiming their rifles at them. The bodies of those shot lay strewn across the beach. A constant reminder of what the strange weapons can do to the human body.

"God, please, take me away from this awful place. Take me away from this awful place," the girl whimpers. She looks up at me with eyes that hold fear, shock and a twinge of disgust.

An epiphany overtakes me and I understand. She sees me as one of the Tribe.

She sees me as Malik.

"Keep away, cursed one!" she gasps. I think she would rather go with the pirate that defiled her than to stay on the sand with me.

"Look I so hideous to you?" I ask her. The words come out of my mouth without me willing them to. I am no longer in control of what I say or do. I make the same exact moves Malik made. I think the same thoughts he thought.

I am just along for the ride.

"You are of the forbidden tribe! It is death to be near you, Silver Eyes!"

"Would death be such a bad thing in comparison to what is happening now?"

She hesitates. Her manner wavers. She desperately needs someone to hold her and tell her the world is still a good place to live. Even after being abused by that animal. I shift next to her and allow her to lean her head on my shoulder. Her touch is soothing and we manage to console each other, but I wish it were one of my tribal sisters near me.

"I think," she cries, her voice thick with grief, "that death would be a most welcome option right now. Most welcome indeed." I see the look of anguish on her face. She is bleeding from her rectum. I cannot imagine the pain she is in. Her tribe will shun her.

If she ever returns to them.

"What kind of men are these…to do this thing they have done to me?" she asks, trying to reason the unreasonable.

"They are not men," I reply. My voice drips with hatred. "They are the lowest form of life. Lower than the slugs of the jungle floor."

"Then I am less than they now, for no man will take me for wife after this," she sobs. She is right.

"Get away from that darkie, wench!" the man that raped her barks. He points his rifle at her head. "Shit! This one's infected! Gotta put her down!" He squeezes the trigger and the air shatters from the deafening recoil. I watch in horror as that young girl's face explodes into a thousand bloody pieces of sharp bone fragments and mangled flesh.

Death was a welcomed option.

"Get on, darkie and don't try anyer ya tricks here! I'll put you down, too!" They use long sticks to prod and poke me along. I stumble through the sand, falling and struggling to stay on my feet. The pirates laugh and poke me harder. My body is covered in hot rough sand and the sun blazes down on my back.

I am placed in a cage with the rest of my tribe. Once inside my bonds are loosed. Iyanni is crying hysterically. I run to console her. D`aim and S`ianna are holding each other tightly. The wound T`keyah sustained is almost completely healed.

"Malik! You are alive!" Nicah exclaims, hugging me tightly. Forever the mother, I think to myself. They are all weeping over me and it becomes hard for me to hold back my tears. "When we did not see you we thought the worst! Bless the moon you are alive!" she cries and I too weep, despite myself.

"What are we going to do? What do these men want of us?" I cry sounding weak and afraid. I clear my throat to dislodge the grit that has settled in it. Hopefully the sound of fear can be spat out as easily.

"Join hands!" Nicah orders and we readily obey. "No matter what happens, no matter where we are taken our circle shall never be broken! Our strength is not only in our silver! We are a tribe. The jungle shall always be ours!"

I listen to the power in her voice. To the adamant sedulous authority that she projects, but there is something else in her voice-there is hope! Nicah has somehow injected dignity and honor into a situation that is as surreal as it is nightmarish. I stare at her with eyes that hold love and respect. She is the tribal mother.

She is our rock.

We are joined in a circle. I can feel the softness of Iyanni's and D`aim's palms. My heart longs to be back in my beloved jungle, racing through the treetops and enjoying life as it should be enjoyed. I look at them and my soul aches for I know this is the last time we shall all be together.

"Nothing shall break our circle! Not these men. Not these ships. Not even death!" Nicah yells, the emotion in her voice strong and unmistakable. "I place a curse on all those who would try to separate us! They shall know why we are called the Death Tribe! They shall see why the other tribes fear us!

Why the lions and apes worship us! Why our eyes reflect the moon's silver!"

The beach becomes very quiet-even the pirates ceased their bragging to hear Nicah. I see a chill go through them. Their eyes give away their fear. They heard her curse and it shook even the bravest of them.

"How can this wench speak English?" one pirate asks. The look on his face is one of shock and awe. We ignore him. Our circle is growing stronger. I can feel the strength returning to my limbs.

My fear is evaporating.

"Complete our circle, Malik! Complete my curse! You shall be the final piece! Death to those that have done this!" Nicah screams and the wind howls in answer to her. My hands grow hot as if a fire has been lit in my palms. I feel my birthmark tingle and as I look at the rest of my tribe; their birthmarks are glowing.

"Wish us home, Nicah! Forget the curse and wish us home!" D`ike screams. I have never heard such sheer terror in his voice. He is afraid, not of the men so much as the curse Nicah has just uttered.

"We can not return home! Our fate has been sealed. Our lot in life lies aboard those wretched vessels, but the men who take us shall never know peace! I know not, devils how you negated our powers, but it will avail you naught!" Nicah gasps. I have never seen her so angry, so dangerous. Even K`embe trembles at her rage. She has seen something, I think to myself. She has seen what will befall us.

"Our circle will never be broken! I shall call the curse and even in death we shall be together!" I say, feeling my fear return, but I am determined not to show it.

"Death can not hold us!" Kwame screams. "It is the living that should beware!"

"The dead know what the living are doing!" I retort and we all join in chanting the sentence repeatedly. "The dead know what the living are doing! The dead know what the living are doing!"

D`aim screams and a fire starts in the center of our circle. Fire is her gift and my heart races in my chest. We are going to win! I think. We are going to sing praises of this moment forever! Soon, I will be back in my jungle! Soon I will be back with my sisters, loving them by the light of the moon, with the music of the waterfall serenading us.

"Concentrate on the flame! Feed it with your wrath, D`aim!" K`embe orders. I see the muscles in D`aim's neck about to pop from the strain. Normally D`aim is the meekest among us, but this day she is a force to be reckoned with. The fire grows high now and we all try to direct it at the white men.

"Captain! Captain, what do we do?" one yells. Suddenly the beach is a haven of chaos as blacks and whites run amok trying to get as far away from us as possible.

"Stand your ground, men! The first man that abandons his post will be shot!" Captain Pearson barks. "Their fire can not hurt you!"

I am confused by his confidence. Surely D`aim's fire is no illusion. Surely it is as real as it is dangerous. So why is Captain Pearson not afraid? Does he possess some intuitive knowledge about us?

He must! The fact that we are here proves that! A bubble of dread rises in me. The seeds of doubt threaten to take root. The fire seems to be dying, its heat growing less intense.

The captain is right! Our powers cannot harm him!

Fear pulls me. I let go of Iyanni's and D`aim's hands and as I turn I see the captain running toward us with his men...

"The dead know what the living are doing..." I said. I was back at the silver pool, back in my body. The connection between Malik and myself broken.

"Do you see now, David? Do you understand?"

"Why do you keep doing that?" I asked bewildered. "Why do you keep pulling me out right before the battle?"

"More to my shame! There was no battle, David. I broke the circle. Nicah was taken along with K`embe, Molo and D`aim on the Good Ship Kingsley. Nicah was taken to Haiti where her grief and anger consumed her. Molo was taken to Cuba. D`aim was dropped off in Jamaica, where she died with the hope that one day the rest of us would come and rescue her. K`embe fought to be free all of his days, before he died in Guyana. D`ike, Kwame, S`ianna and myself were taken to America, where we were split up and sold. T`keya, Meeka, Jomo and Iyanni were taken to Portugal and Spain. They spent the remainder of their days as freaks in traveling carnivals, mocked and teased like animals. I broke the circle. I...broke...the...circle."

"But on the ship-you fought them on the ship! What happened then?"

Again, there was the sensation of being pulled out of my body. Malik was still speaking to me, but his words sounded far away. The light around me became so bright I had to shut my eyes. When I open them, I am once again face to face with the captain.

"-You darkies are going to be my legacy! You-"

The ship sways and one of the men comes in contact with me. I reach and in one fluid motion snap his neck like a twig. I am still weak, but determined to fight my way to freedom or die in the attempt. Another rushes toward his strange weapon and I duck and roll out of the way. The report of the weapon is as deafening as thunder and I remember what the strange open spear did to my sister, T`keyah. In the time it takes to breathe, I cross the distance between us. He will not have time to use his weapon. One solid blow to the throat takes the light out of his eyes.

"Stand fast, men! Don't go near him!" the captain orders. I feed off the fear in his voice. I can take them.

I am Malik! I will avenge my Tribe and regain my self-respect.

"Where will you go without us, darkie?" the captain barks. "There is no way off this ship!"

He is trying to distract me, using words instead of blows to fight his battle. He motions to his men and in that split second I am surrounded.

"You will have to kill me! Only in death will Malik surrender!" I say, sounding much braver than I

truly feel. Exhaustion sets in. My flaccid sinews barely respond to my commands.

"No, boy! We don't have to do any such
thing!"

There is a brilliant flash of light and then there
is nothing but the cloying hand of darkness.

I was back in the misty jungle, staring at
Malik. My head hurt like hell and I couldn't stop
shaking.

"At least you got two of those bastards! Good
for you! You showed courage that would have made
anyone proud! What…what happened to the rest of
them?"

"Close your eyes."

I saw the Tribe again, but this time it was like
watching a DVD on high speed. I saw D`ike grow old
and frail. His body and wit destroyed by the ravages
of bondage. He lived his entire life searching for
something to justify his existence. Slavery shattered
his faith in man, God, and nature. It broke him; taking
away all hope from his soul. He was a walking
corpse-dead many years before the body stopped
moving. I saw him walk the fields of Virginia mumbling, 'The dead know what the living are doing,' and
I understood what that phrase meant. The Tribe was
dead. Not physically dead, but spiritually dead. And
they knew. They knew what the living were doing.

I saw Kwame's back, scarred and blistered
from the master's whip. His spirit unbroken, but his
strength sapped and wilted like a rose left in the sun.
Kwame would attempt to escape many times, never
relinquishing his thirst for freedom-until it finally

came in the form of death.

S`ianna was sold to a plantation owner in another town. She gave birth to Malik's son. I watched as the infant was ripped from her breast. Sold to satisfy one of the owner's debts. S`ianna never recovered from that. Her fragile psyche irreversibly shattered. She was reduced to a vegetable. Never seeing Malik, D`ike, Kwame or her son again.

I watched in disgust as the plantation owner repeatedly raped her catatonic body. Slavery negated their powers. Their eyes no longer held the silver hue. Their strength came from each other and from their jungle. Once the slave traders separated them, their strange powers lost all potency.

I watched as Nicah lost her mind in the plantations of Haiti. Her beautiful body become obese and flaccid. The idea of revenge drained her. She died with hatred and bitterness in her heart.

I saw K`embe in the sugar plantations of Guyana, struggling to be free everyday of his life. He was still shunned by the other slaves, as his eyes retained just the barest trace of silver. His freakish power of rejuvenation reduced to nothing, but his pride and spirit would not be broken. I watched as his one prayer-his most secret wish came true.

He died while trying to escape.

K`embe organized a group of six slaves he'd taught to read and write. They plotted to murder the slave master and escape in the dark of night on a ship carrying sugar bound for Canada. K`embe's strategy was brilliant. Every detail was worked out to the minute. He would have definitely succeeded if not for two blacks in his party who opted to betray him.

Molo went insane. His mind would not allow him to accept his fate. His precarious psyche collapsed. He constantly hallucinated, seeing his jungle instead of reality. Like a man stranded in the desert, he constantly saw the mirage of home. He eventually was put out of his misery when he was shot to death in Cuba for a crime he did not commit.

D`aim died on a Jamaican plantation of a broken heart. Her loneliness and grief killed her long before her body stopped moving. She searched for the same love and kindness she had in her tribe. Shunned by the superstitious slaves who would not accept the fact that she was no longer a threat, she gave herself to anyone who would have her. The British soldiers used and abused her body. She became the concubine to any soldier with rank.

T`keya, Meeka, Jomo, and Iyanni performed acrobatics and tricks before the royal court of Spain and Portugal for a year and after the novelty of their eyes wore off they were forced to travel with carnivals and sideshows. They were regarded as freaks and outcasts. The four of them were killed by Spanish soldiers, unjustly accused of witchcraft by a drunken magistrate, who practiced witchcraft himself.

I watched this vision in horror. Shook to the depths of my soul. A rage filled me, an all consuming fire that wanted to burn everything to a cinder. How could anyone in their right mind believe in an omniscient and omnipresent just and merciful God? I remembered Malik's thoughts: There is no God here.

This beautiful, nature loving, black tribe was

destroyed for the slave traders' pleasure. But until death, they believed they would be reunited. Their faith in that one thing enabled Malik to build the silver jungle I now stood in. But even in death they could find no peace. That sadistic bastard would bring them back-exploit them again and again for their powers. My heart ached for them. They represented the total spectrum of the evil, ruthless, blasphemous slave trade.

One chain, many links...

The vision ended. I looked Malik in his eyes and I couldn't stop the tears from streaming down my face.

"Do you now see, David? Do you see what they did to my beloved tribe?" his lips quivered with anger. "Will you help us, David?"

"Malik, listen to me! Anything I can do to help you I will. I mean there's things I don't really understand, but as long as you don't mean Star any harm I will help you."

"I would never harm Star. You really don't understand, do you?"

"No, I guess I don't."

"David, listen to me. Did it ever occur to you why you see what I saw? Hear what I heard?"

"I...I-"

"I am your ancestor, David. You and Star are my descendents, the result of the union of S`ianna and I. It is our blood that flows in your veins. It is the reason I asked for your forgiveness. We are links in the same chain."

His words hit me like a ton of bricks. I suddenly felt lightheaded. The air had become too thin to breathe. What Malik told me made perfect sense. It explained why they wanted Star to complete the ritual.

"Did…did they use Star to-"

"Yes, David. They used Star to call the Tribe. They thought it was my voice they heard and they followed. Nicah and D`ike were called by her the nights before you saw them."

"But how-how?"

"Sharon's sister, Tara. Remember?"

I reached for something to hold on to. Malik grabbed me and kept me from falling. I felt weak and faint. Suddenly it all made sense; Tara's enthusiasm to help me take care of Star, the way she would always volunteer to watch her whenever Sharon and I went out, her obsession with African history.

Aunt Tara had me play a game I didn't like…

"Tara, what have you done?" I gasped. "What have you done? But why-why would Tara or Kenyetta, or any other black person help that racist piece of shit captain?"

"Have not blacks often killed and betrayed each other for the white man's promise of power? Even in your generation this is true. Is this truly so difficult to believe?"

"Yeah, but Tara was different! She studied African culture! She knew all of these things about Africa-she would've never, I mean-this guy is a fuckin slave trader!"

"Who do you think led him into the jungle? The European would have never discovered us if not for the neighboring tribes. I told you-once learned the truth cannot be unlearned. Tara is only a pawn in this; she is no more to blame than Star is. Like others, she thought she was helping us to gain revenge."

The European and his dog...

Pearson and Briggs!

"Malik, what will happen if the twelve of you are called back together? I mean, what is the curse really?"

"If I am ever called from this place I will be forced to complete Nicah's circle. D`ike will give in to her and her wrath will feed D`aim's fire. Nicah's anger is like the lightning. Her hatred is so strong that it absorbs all energy. The recent changes to your cities attests to this. Once she adds my power to the rest there will be nothing to check her. The world will fall in fire and wrath. You see the violence and sickness that has afflicted everyone lately. It is not without reason my tribe was shunned and it is not without reason it is said that my power towers over the others."

That explained the heat, the sickness, the carnal lust that overtook people in a heartbeat, those mutated cats. Those scarred drug addicts. Not to mention the darkness...

Captain Pearson was rebuilding a perverted version of Malik's jungle!

"But...that girl Sandy...the way she made it sound as if she wanted to help you twelve return to get back at the white man! I thought you wanted to come back...to take revenge!"

"Revenge is a double-edge blade, David. The wise warrior never fights for revenge. The people you refer to are either misled or lying to cover a sinister agenda. I have no wish to return to your reality. My tribe and I were happy here. The one place we believed we were safe, until those whose thirst for power called us away.

"Your duty lies before you and you must not fail. The anger and hatred in Nicah's heart is enough to obliterate everything you know. Beware of Captain Pearson, and his lackey, Briggs. Pearson is very shrewd. He will never let you know his true thoughts. He has lived a dozen lifetimes, returning and feeding on the prejudice and hatred of petty men. His followers all believe he will share the power with them. The blacks that follow think they will outsmart him when the time comes. He will kill them all."

"But…how could he still be alive? I mean after all of this time?"

"The hatred and evil that beats in the chest of men like Pearson is not as easily destroyed as flesh. He resurrects Briggs to help him. It was not enough that Pearson captured and separated us, sold us into slavery and destroyed our way of life; he will not rest until our souls are his. Until he owns our powers. Twelve trips he made into Africa and each time he learned more and more about us, but he never learned our origin or the origin of our power. It is this that drives him mad with obsession. It is this that he must never know."

"Can you tell me?"

"I will say no more, David. Prepare yourself to go back to your reality. Time grows short, David. Free Star, restore my tribe back to me and defeat the captain."

"Malik! Wait! Tell me how to beat them! I mean, they defeated you guys-how in the hell am I suppose to beat them?"

"By using the one thing that I lacked in my last battle with him."

"What was that?"

"Faith."

He touched my forehead and all of the rage and fear within me dissipated. It lasted only as long as his hand held me, but in that moment I glimpsed the design of life. In that instant I understood the meaning of Malik's suffering, the purpose of Star's abduction-the reason for mankind's universal woe and agony. It was all so wonderfully plain. Every machination, no matter how complex or simple served a higher cause. We are all fingers on the hand of life.

"There is a God. There is a plan!" I gasped. The moment Malik pulled his hand away from my forehead I'd completely forgotten the specifics, but I remembered that one line.

There is a God!

Malik looked at me and smiled. His eyes pierced me like skewer. My life would never be the same. Prior to this, I thought I was somewhat successful. I had a good job, paid taxes and enjoyed a certain lifestyle. Like most young black men, I didn't really ignore our history, but I didn't make a point to go out of my way to dwell on it either. I refused to wear slavery as a reason or an excuse for failure. Now came the time to prove the mettle of my convictions.

I now know the old adage is true: Those who

ignore history are doomed to repeat it.

I had been assigned an inviolate duty. The captain had to be defeated. These wrongs had to be made right. I had been given a sacred task and even if it cost my life, I would not shirk this charge.

Malik turned and walked into the thick fog surrounding the jungle. He left me standing by that pool of silvery water totally overwhelmed. I shut my eyes and felt myself being pulled back to the storage room's vent.

How long I lay unconscious in that vent is anyone's guess. I do know that I didn't feel as scared. I really felt everything would be all right. I would find Star and defeat the slaver.

A metallic hum steadily grew louder. I figured I was getting closer to the generator. Far in the distance, I saw a pinprick of light and suddenly the air carried a very familiar scent.

Incense!

"Justice?" I asked. I could feel the hair on the back of my neck stand at attention.

"I'm here!" he said. He was crouched holding a lit match. The match went out when I got up to him.

"Follow me, I'm here to take you to Star."

I followed, thinking about the last time that I saw him. The way I was the only one that could see him. Was he real or did I create him to get me through the difficult times?

"Did Shakim see you before he died? Did you know he was going to die?"

"Shakim is beyond this sphere of pain and suffering. He's gone on to his reward. You don't have to worry about him anymore, although he worries about you. The dead know what the living are doing."

"Did Malik send you to help me?" I asked.

"In a way, yes and in a way no, David."

"Why didn't you tell me all of this back in the G building? Why didn't you tell me that I was the only one who could see you?"

"Would you have believed me? No, you wouldn't have. You would have thought that I was a nut. Everything that's happened to you has happened for a reason and it's happened in its own good time. I am here to help Star. The only way to do that is to help you. Star is very important. You know that now, don't you?"

"Of course! A father always-"

"No, David. Star is more important than you can imagine. I'm going to take you to her, but you will have to get her yourself."

We maneuvered the dark tunnel, just like we did back in the G building. He seemed to move effort-lessly in the darkness. Who was he-a member of the Tribe, another one of Malik's descendents? My mind blazed with questions, but I remained silent. There would be time enough for answers. I trembled with anticipation of getting my daughter back.

"How much farther?" I asked. "It seems we've been traveling through these vents for an awful long time."

"A little ways more, they have her in the bay area."

"Where in the hell are we?"

"The government built this complex during

World War II, right after Pearl Harbor. Eisenhower wanted the coasts of Los Angeles and New York City secured just in case Japan tried to get funny and hit the mainland. It was updated and modernized during the Cold War. The amusement park is about a mile straight up, bet you didn't think there was a military presence beneath you all those times you rode the Cyclone! This is the only place in the tri-state area that has power."

"How do you know all of this?"

"To defeat an enemy you learn to know the enemy."

"So the government is the enemy?"

"Not exactly. The enemy has infiltrated many stations. It wears many hats and many faces. Part of the government, part of high society, part of the poor. It's hard to explain."

"Imagine how hard it is to understand!"

"I know, but soon I think you will understand, David. Star will teach you."

I noticed Justice never referred to the captain by name. He always spoke of the enemy, but was it Captain Luke Pearson, or was it someone-or something I'd yet to meet?

I thought about Shakim, lying dead on the floor of the storage room. I thought of all of the things we'd survived together. Helping each other, being there for each other when it counted the most. He'd given his life to save mine and if needed I would give my life to save Star and to return the Tribe to their home.

I hated leaving Shakim like that. I just hoped I

would at least get the chance to come back and properly bury my best friend. I wondered then where the souls of people like Shakim and Sharon went. Did Malik look after them in his silvery jungle?

I prayed that wherever their souls were, they were at peace.

The shaft came to an end and Justice kicked open a grate. He jumped down to the floor. I was amazed at the way he seemed to float to the floor like a feather. Then I remembered I was the only one who could see him.

"Jump!" he said.

"Are you insane! It's at least a fifty-foot drop! I'll-"

"Trust me! Just jump!"

I looked into his pleading eyes and figured what the hell. I leapt out of the vent and was surprised to see that it was only a few feet above the floor. The height of the vent was an illusion.

"Remember this, David. Most of your fears are just like that grate."

We were in some kind of oval shaped foyer. The walls and floors were made of marble. I expected an industrial complex-machines and computers, not this type of palatial splendor.

"You said the government built this?"

"Never mind that. There's not much time. Your daughter and your destiny lie through that door," Justice said pointing to a door across the hall.

"I'll need weapons! They got M16s-"

"No weapon formed against you shall prosper, David. You already have everything you need."

This was it. Although I was terrified at the task at hand, I couldn't let fear deter me. Justice all but told me I had to go up against an entire platoon of armed soldiers with nothing more than faith.

The stuff that moves mountains.

"Are you going to come with me? Are you going to help me?" I asked. The fear in my voice dripped heavily.

"David, you don't need me anymore. You don't need anyone to help you! Malik tried to tell you that! They're waiting on you, David. The Tribe is waiting on you to save them and make things right."

I was more afraid of failing than dying. I searched deep within myself for the strength to walk through that door. I looked at the door, trembling as I slowly walked toward it. My footsteps echoed like drums.

"May the power that blessed you to escape the asylum, survive the madness of the streets and bring you to this point, watch over you now. May it give you the strength to accomplish the duty that has been thrust upon you. May it bless you to hold your daughter once more. May it bless you to right these wrongs. I leave you now, David. My work is complete."

I turned to thank Justice for his prayers, but he was gone. I was on my own now. All of the studying was done. It was now time for the final exam.

CHAPTER IX:

The Evidence of things not seen

I opened the door not knowing what to expect. I came out in a large hall. Halogen lamps placed high on the walls had the place well lit. The ceiling was domed shaped with gold designs engraved in it. The floor was made of marble and there were twelve perfect circles engraved in silver.

"This is where the ritual will take place!" I said in awe. My voice echoed powerfully. The acoustics were amazing. "Star! Star, are you in here?" I screamed. The sound of my voice was so loud it threatened to shatter my eardrums.

There was no answer other than the sound of my voice echoing back to me. In the center of the floor was a platform. I counted twelve steps to the top of it. The twelve circles all had perfect lines drawn from them to the platform and the platform was situated directly under the center of the dome.

I was busy puzzling the meaning of this and why the room was empty when I felt a cool breeze pass me, as if someone had walked by in a hurry. I turned looking back and forth but there was no one there.

"Star, can you hear me? I'm here, baby! Can you hear me?"

Still no answer, although now I began to suspect I was not alone in this room. Call it instinct or radar, I felt there were many other people in that gigantic hall with me.

Laughing at me.

I spun wildly, trying to catch them. But try as I might there was nothing to see. To the naked eye, the hall was empty. But I knew there were people in that room with me. I felt their presence. The way you know someone is staring at you.

I walked around the hall, arms outstretched clutching and grabbing empty air. I kept feeling they were avoiding me-that they would move the second I approached. I couldn't shake the feeling they were mocking me. That they were holding Star and taunting me with her.

"Where are you bastards hiding her?" I screamed, ignoring the echoes that vibrated my head like a tuning fork. "Your mind games won't work on me! You won't be able to trick me like you did Malik! Where are you? Star, if you're in here I'm coming, baby! I'm coming!"

Use your wits, David. Use your intelligence. Malik said the captain was as shrewd as they come. He wants you to run around in a blind panic. He wants you flustered and baffled!

I calmed down and studied the room carefully. I'm a Credit Risk Analyst. It's my job to analyze things and draw logical conclusions from that analysis. Twelve circles on the ceiling, twelve circles on the floor, twelve steps to the top; twelve members of the tribe-then who was the platform for?

There were twelve of them, just like the Apostles!

I walked toward the steps of the platform. The air became thicker as I went. Something was trying to block me from reaching the top. I felt like I was trying to run through quicksand. There was a great weight pushing against my chest, trying to hold me back.

"It won't work! I'm coming! Give. Me. My. Daughter!"

I was more confident now. Soon they would have to reveal themselves. They couldn't hold me from that platform forever. Just then, a breeze blew behind me. I turned and found myself face to face with a familiar face.

Dr. Jasmine Walters walked toward me. Her lab coat floated around her as if a wind blew up from her feet. I backed away from her, terrified beyond words. This woman scared me the way monsters scare children. It was as if a mental dam burst, releasing all of my worst fears. Ice water flooded my veins as every step she took toward me rumbled throughout the hall.

"There are men and there are worms, Mr. Peters." Suddenly I was standing in a pool of worms, but not just the small skinny ones used as fish bait-these worms were as thick as my wrist and as long as my arms. They writhed and coiled around my legs, squeezing, cutting off all circulation. I could feel the weight of them, threatening to drag me down.

"It's not real," I whispered. "It's all in my mind and it's not real."

"I tried to help you, Mr. Peters. I tried to make you a man, but it seems you are wholly content on being a worm."

The worms rose higher, coiling around my thighs. They made a sucking sound, and I immediately thought, that's my soul they're sapping!

"It's not real!" I repeated. To prove it I swiped at one of the worms and it bit me. I could see two small puncture wounds in the web of skin between my thumb and pointer.

Do worms have teeth?

"Let us dispense with this charade, Mr. Peters. You obviously are a lot sicker than I first diagnosed. I have special medicine for you."

My mouth burned, as if I'd just eaten a thousand fiery hot peppers. The back of my throat felt as if it would burst into flames. My eyes watered and ran with sticky, blinding tears. I hacked and coughed up thick clumps of blood.

It's not real! It's not real! Worms don't have teeth!

"You fucked up, doctor!" I wheezed. "Worms don't have teeth!"

Just then, the worms disappeared, along with the burning sensation in my throat. A look of disbelief covered Dr. Walters' face. I took a step toward her and she retreated.

"You fucked up big time, bitch. There are men and there are worms and I am a man. A man that's about to kick a pound of shit out of you if you don't give me my daughter!" I lunged and went right through her as if she was vapor. I landed on my knees.

"Still clinging to that ever elusive thing called sanity, Mr. Peters?" she mocked, standing behind me now. "Such a waste."

"No, bitch! I'm clinging to faith! You're playing with my head, but it won't work! Give me back my daughter!" I ran at her again, only to run through her as if she was only air.

I suddenly found myself surrounded by hundreds of people. The soldiers that captured Shakim and I were there along with the man that called himself Mr. Briggs: the same pirate master from all those years ago. The European's dog.

The two cops who told me Sharon was dead were there. And there were others. People I've passed many times on the streets, orderlies from the G building, a few people from Sharon's job, the limo driver from the funeral home, Cleophus the funeral director and the man who took the picture of Sharon, Star and I on Coney Island beach.

Justice was right! It was a conspiracy, and judging from the familiar faces in the crowd, they must have had this planned for a while.

"Well done, David! Well done!" a man said, clapping his hands walking down off the platform. "I see you've learned a thing or two since meeting Mr. Briggs!"

It was Pearson-the same man who captured the Tribe over two-hundred years ago! He looked as if he hadn't aged a day. He was dressed in the same uniform he wore that day in the jungle. There was a strong smell about him, like seawater mixed with rotten wood.

The man before me was not a man at all. He was the apotheosis of all human fear. He was the wretched and worst part of mankind, the Slave Trader, the Nazi, the nasty man in the raincoat who hung around the schoolyard. He was all of these things and more. It sickened me to imagine Star was prey to this man. His skin was sallow and paper thin, pulled taut over hard sharp features. His cheeks were sunken and his eyes were cold and evil.

I would have sworn I was looking at the devil.

"Where is my daughter? Give Star to me now and leave the Tribe alone, before I fuck all of you up!"

"Before you-Boy, you are funny! Don't let this little charade go to your head, darkie! Everything that has occurred has done so as I've foreseen!" he screamed.

"Where is my daughter? I don't know how you escaped hell, but I'm here to send you back! I'm here to stop you from using the Tribe and to take my daughter back with me. Give me my daughter!"

"You want her? Come take her!"

He stepped aside and I saw Star standing behind him. She was dressed in a flowing silver gown and her hair was wrapped in a translucent silver headdress. She looked like an African princess. The light that poured off the platform was blinding and I had to squint to see her. There was something funny about her eyes. It took me a minute to figure it out, and then

I realized what it was.

Her eyes glowed like silver dollars. Deep rich silver, like the water in the pool Malik had me stare into. The twinkle in them was mesmerizing.

"That's right! Come and get her! You've seen what happens to people who get too close to the Silver Eyes! Come get her, boy!"

"Come here, Star! Come here, baby! Daddy's here!" I said. My mouth was as dry as cotton. I was petrified with fear. Star's eyes stared right through me as if I was glass. They had bewitched her. She looked comatose.

"Why don't you come and get her, boy! Come on up here!" the captain teased. I wanted to run up there and bash that smug face of his in. I tried to step closer to her, but there was some sort of barrier around her. It felt as thin and as fragile as a soap bubble, yet I couldn't penetrate it.

I was on the verge of panic. My mind kept going back to what Justice said about my already having everything I needed to free Star, but I had no clue what he was talking about.

The people around me all stood at attention, rigid and stiff. They just stood there, staring at the platform as if they were in a daze.

"Listen to me! You people think that he'll share the power with you, but he won't! Think about it! This guy is a slaver trader! Wake the fuck up, you fucking retards! Cleophus! Even you can't be this stupid! Help me now! Help me, please!"

"You don't understand, David! He's found a way to cheat death! Think of what this power can do!

Think of all that I can accomplish with the power of the Silver Eyes at my command!" The look on his face was one of madness. There was no reasoning with any of them. The thought of having the Tribe's power had them drunk with desire. The way they stared at Star, like junkies preparing for a fix.

Then all of them ripped their left sleeves off at the shoulders to reveal the tattoo. Twelve interlocking silver circles. The circles began to pulsate and glow. They were one step closer to the power.

"Star! Listen to me, baby! Listen to my voice! I need you to wake up!"

"She can't hear you, David! She is mine now! They are all mine now! Just as the crew of the three ships were mine! I own her, David. I own them and soon I'll own you! You can't defeat me, David. I am beyond anything your feeble mind can imagine. Come on up here, boy! Don't be shy!"

His body shimmered and throbbed with a deep crimson aura. The air around him flared and warped. There was a sharp, acrid nauseating odor that turned my stomach. It was the smell of defamed flesh. The smell traduced murder and execration.

It was the smell of the slave ship.

The circles in the domed shaped ceiling spun open, letting in pinpoint beams of moonlight. The gems Nicah wore dangled from the ceiling catching the light, breaking the beams into twelve lasers.

The ritual was starting.

The bubble like substance that protected the platform enveloped me. I was trapped in its soft, pliable grasp. My air was being cut short; I would soon asphyxiate.

I panicked. My heart pounded and all I could hear was the beating of it drowning out all other sound. I saw how beautiful Star looked in that silver gown. How radiant her complexion was. I thought of how much I missed her and here she was, so close and yet so far away from me.

I fell to my knees and curled up in the fetal position, choking from a lack of air. People around me stared and pointed, laughing along with the captain. I had failed in the most important mission of my life.

The more I struggled against the unseen barrier the quicker I used what little air it held. Images flashed in my mind, scattered fragments of pictures. I remembered watching Star take her first steps. Her first day of school. Priceless memories that shaped and molded me into the man I am.

"I love you, Star," I said, about to pass out again. This time there was no Justice to save me. I'd proven myself unworthy of Malik's trust. This time it would be me asking for his forgiveness.

"I love you, Star," I said again, my voice was stronger. If I was going to die, I wanted those words to be my last.

Star turned and looked at me. The silver light from her eyes bathed me in its glow. I struggled to rise, feeling the thin force field pressing down on me, but there was something else-there was air now. I breathed deeply and fought to stand up. There was a look of fear and shock in the captain's eyes. He had no idea I'd be so hard to kill.

The force field pushed me down again, suddenly doubling in strength. The captain laughed again. They were all laughing now. Just as they'd laughed at Malik so long ago.

I could see silver mist rising out of the twelve circles. The Tribe was appearing. "Star, no! Don't call them!" I screamed.

"It's too late, boy! Meet the Tribe! There's Nicah! There's D`ike!" he screamed excited and it was true. I saw them materialize in the vapor- tortured shrouded figures, silhouetted by the laser beams of moonlight.

"Here's K`embe, and Jomo!" He pointed to the circles across from me. The silver smoke rose from them, revealing two more figures. I felt my heart drop to my knees. I was running out of air and my mind was drenched with fear. The crowd chanted an all too familiar phrase, "The dead know what the living are doing! The dead know what the living are doing!"

I was terrified. I understood what Malik meant when he said fear was a force. I stood rooted, unable to move. Literally petrified with fright. How am I supposed to defeat this evil?

By using faith…

The Tribe was materializing all around me as I listened to the captain announce them one by one. I saw the thick scars across their backs from the master's whip. He wasn't bringing them back as they were in the forbidden jungle, in all their glory and splendor, but as they were after the capture.

"No, Star! Don't call them! Leave them where they are!" I shrieked, but she was oblivious to my presence. The thin bubble grew tighter, threatening to crush me. My eyesight was blurry, but I saw him-the same old man that carried the sandwich board.

"D`ike! Stop this! You're the only one who can stop this!" I stammered, growing weaker by the second.

"No," he said. His voice traveled over the chants of the people. "You are the only one who can stop it."

The bubble was now totally devoid of air. I could hear Justice and Malik telling me faith was the only weapon I needed.

I struggled to get to my feet. My heart raced, pounding in my ears. Every muscle in my body cracked from the strain, but I was determined to stand. I would not give this devil the joy of watching me die on my knees. He would not break me as he did my ancestors.

"I love you, Star. Your daddy loves you so much. No matter what happens, you have to know that. Your daddy loves you, Star." My voice was thick with emotion, but it took every vestige of strength to get the words out. After I spoke those words, the bubble loosened as if my voice poked holes in it. I could breathe a little easier. I felt my strength return.

The enemy has infiltrated many stations. It wears many hats and many faces. Part of the government, part of high society, part of the poor...

Hate! Hate is the enemy! It was hate that allowed Pearson to keep returning!

I found the key to freeing myself! Somehow, my telling Star I loved her loosened the vise-like stranglehold the bubble had on me. "I love you, Star!"

I kept repeating. Slowly the chants of the crowd grew silent, until there was only my voice, booming across the massive hall. My words were reaching her. I could see the faintest glimmer of recognition in her eyes.

"Shut up! Shut your filthy mouth! Don't listen to him, Star! Continue the call!" Pearson screamed. Terror and alarm were in his eyes.

I was on to something!

I closed my eyes and pictured Star as a baby. I remembered the joy and excitement I felt when we first brought her home. I thought of her opening Christmas presents. I thought of the magic of seeing life through her eyes. Eyes that saw the world as a place of joy and wonder. A world where nothing could harm her, because I would always be there to protect her.

I stood, slowly and painfully, feeling every muscle in my body strain to the point of failure. I kept thinking about Star. Her first birthday party. The time she peed on my shirt when I tried to change her diaper and made me late for work. The pride she felt at being potty-trained. The indescribable joy I felt when she first called me daddy.

I remembered a wonderfully silly thing that happened when she was three years old. Sharon had cooked Thanksgiving dinner and invited her parents and Tara. Mrs. Levy got drunk off malt liquor and passed gas. We all tried to politely ignore it, but Star crinkled her nose and said, "Grandma smell like doo-doo!" I laughed so hard that day I had a stomachache.

I walked to her, feeling invisible fingers wrap around my throat trying to push me back. Captain

Pearson was screaming now, his voice hoarse and raw with anger and fear.

"Stop him!" he ordered. I continued pushing to get to Star. Something heavy but unseen pressed against my chest.

"Star!" I screamed, trying to keep her attention. There was a strange detached look about her. When she looked at me I swore she was trying to tell me something without anyone else seeing, but try as I did, I could not read the expression on her face.

All eleven members of the Tribe were circled around me. Only Malik was missing. Captain Pearson's hollering died down. All eyes were on me now. The sharp beams of moonlight crisscrossed the room until each member had a beam of light shining into their chest. The eerie silver color returned to their eyes. It was like watching a baby being born; it was as if they were slowly leaving the womb of the spirit world into this reality.

I stood dumbfounded-like an animal caught in the middle of the road just waiting to become road kill. The one thing I had been charged to keep from happening, and all I could do was watch it happen. I had let everyone down, Malik, Justice, Shakim, and especially Star.

"Star! You can't call him! Leave Malik there! You can't call him!" I cried. I took two more steps toward her, straining against the invisible barrier that tried to keep me from reaching her. I was on the steps, just a few feet away from her when I noticed a look of fear in Star's eyes.

She was afraid of me coming near her!

"Star! What's wrong? Don't you recognize me?" I asked her. She was terrified of something, but it wasn't something that was done to her...it was-

Aunt Tara had me play a game I didn't like...

Something that was about to be done to her!

I stopped in my tracks. I could feel my pulse pound in my ears and the sound of my heartbeat was all I could hear. I was about to make a monumental mistake.

Beware of Captain Pearson, he is very shrewd, he will never let you know his true thoughts.

I turned and looked in the eyes of the captain's followers. Cleophus stared at me as if he were anticipating something. They wanted me to reach Star. If I had touched her, it would have completed the ritual.

"Pretty slick there, cap old boy! But, unfortunately for you my mother didn't birth a fool!" I turned and walked down the steps. Fear and disappointment fell across the face of the crowd. The tattoos stopped glowing. I looked up at Star and saw there was a flash, the faintest hint in her eyes I had done the right thing.

"You're a lot tougher than I thought. I'll give you that, but it won't help you, boy. In fact," he motioned behind him. "You've forced me to play my trump card!"

He clapped his hands twice and a partition in the floor opened. There was a rumbling sound of metal gears shifting. Slowly, a platform rose out of the floor. I saw hands tied to a wooden beam and I wondered who the captain would send against me. I was in a battle of wits. The dullard would die.

The expression on Star's face changed from one of hope to despair in the instant the person tied to the beams was made known.

"You get it now, boy? You see why you can't win now? I am in charge, David! Everything happens as I demand!"

A single tear rolled down Star's cheek.

I turned to see who was attached to those beams and a little whiney gasp escaped my lips as I came eye to eye with the one person I never expected to see again. If I thought I was scared before, I was really scared now.

"Tara!"

My mind went blank. I tried to rationalize what I was seeing, but there was no way I could justify the person in front of me. Tara was dead. There was no way around that.

I saw her.

I saw her body spread open as if someone performed an autopsy. Her face was a bloodied mask of tangled tissue...

Autopsy!

Cleophus! Sharon!

"It was Sharon in my bed, wasn't it! You let them drug me and drag your dead sister out of the grave! You bitch! How could you?" I groaned. My voice strained and cracked in horror. Although I heard those words escape my lips, I really didn't believe them. I couldn't believe that this intelligent, sensitive woman before me could do something so grisly. Part of me was ecstatic she was still alive and another part wanted to climb up there and kill her again. I fell to my knees in a mixture of confusion and disgust.

"No, my love," she winced. Her face covered in a mask of pain. "I am just as much a victim in this as you. I made a big mistake! I-"

"Shut up, bitch! I'll tell you when to speak! Now, David you've got a choice. You either get up there and hug your little girl or I'll kill the bitch and the baby!" Captain Pearson screamed.

The platform kept rising and Tara was suspended high above me. Whip marks covered her abdomen and I noticed how badly she'd been beaten.

I was so confused. Was she a part of this, or a victim of it? It certainly seemed so-after all Malik said she was tricked, and Kenyetta said she changed her mind. Maybe she didn't know how far the cult would go. Maybe when she found out she told them to go to hell and that's when they beat her and-

I looked in Star's eyes for some clue as to what I should do next. I needed to know if I could still trust Tara, or if I was being played for a fool. Star just stared back at me with a look that told me I wasn't getting it. There was something big that I was missing, something I just wasn't catching on to.

"What, baby? What am I suppose to do?" I asked her pleading-begging for a hint as to how to proceed. Where was Justice now that I really needed him?

"I've already told you what to do, boy! Get up there and hug your little girl! Get up there on top of those steps and hug her, or I'll kill all three of you!" the captain barked.

The maniacal look in his eyes told me he wasn't bluffing. They needed me to complete the ritual. If I went to the top of those steps and held Star, the calling would be complete. Malik would appear and take the twelve steps down the platform to the only empty circle. The captain would then take his place at the top of the platform, capturing all twelve again.

I looked in the faces of Captain Pearson's followers. Their eyes were wide in anticipation of seeing the entire tribe reunited. The other eleven members were frozen in their respective circles. They looked like 3D TV images. They kept blinking in and out of sight like a strobe light, as if they were half in this world and half in the next.

Anger swelled within me. I could not believe the overwhelming stupidity of the captain's followers. After all that had happened, they would still follow him. Blacks and whites alike made up the crowd. Each one of them was convinced they would receive a portion of the Tribe's power.

Have not blacks often killed and betrayed each other for the white man's promise of power?

Cleophus stared at me with that conniving, devious grin stamped across his face. My original assessment of this man was correct-he was a fucking weirdo. I was infuriated thinking of this fiend entering my home after desecrating Sharon's grave. I had been played for a sap long enough. I was unsure as to whether or not my next move would be the right move, but something told me it couldn't hurt.

I punched Cleophus in the face as hard as I could. "That's for Malik and Shakim, you gimp creepy mutha-fucka!" I watched him fall to his knees as blood spurted from his nose. The rest of them backed away from me with an odd look of awe on their faces.

Suddenly, I felt strong.

Powerful.

"Don't…let him make the call…you call them! You take con-" Tara muttered right before Pearson poked her with some kind of cattle prod. He wanted to keep her from telling me, but it was too late.

I understood.

I finally understood!

I ran over to the circles that held the semi-transparent tribe. The captain could call eleven, but he couldn't call the twelfth. Only Star or I could do that, and Star refused. Star must have called Nicah and D`ike while playing with Tara, but she refused to keep them in their wretched forms. The captain must have kept them from returning back to the silvery jungle, stuck in stasis between this world and the next.

I stood in the circle of K`embe, feeling his essence dance through me. I came to know him-his wants and needs. His fears and desires. I allowed him to purge himself. Through me, he obtained the absolution he so desperately craved. I saw what he saw that day on the beach. I felt his rage and anger.

Next came Nicah, T`keya, Kwame, Iyanni, D`ike, Jomo, Molo, D`aim, Meeka, and lastly my maternal ancestor S`ianna.

My trip around the circles was complete. I felt the eleven of them dancing within me. They wanted revenge. They wanted the captain dead so that no one could ever tear them away from their precious home again. They wanted to be a complete tribe again.

Captain Pearson was scared shitless. His plan had backfired. He had banked on the fact that I wouldn't catch on to his scheme. He figured I would grab Star at the appropriate moment and complete the ritual. They only needed to hold me back long enough for the other eleven to arrive.

The rest of his followers stood watching me with a look of sheer amazement on their faces. I looked at my reflection in the shiny marble floor and I understood why.

My eyes glowed with the silver fire.

The power of Malik's jungle pulsed within me.

"The Tribe has a message they wish to share with you, Captain! Remember how you extinguished D`aim's fire that cursed day on the beach? Try it now! There's no one here to break MY circle!"

A column of silver fire rose out of me. It splintered and broke off into thick beams, burning the captain's followers. I stood in awe as their fury manifest itself through me. I was nothing more than a vessel for their vengeance.

"You still don't get it do you, boy? Every time one of you darkies kill each other, every time you blacks betray each other you show me the way into Malik's jungle! You can't win, boy! You can't win! Get him! Kill him now!"

Cleophus ran at me, wild eyed with an M16 in his hand. He fired rapidly, on auto. I felt the bullets whiz past me, but not one hit me.

"K`embe," I said to myself, astonished. "K`embe's power was he was impervious to any enemy's offense!" I grabbed Cleophus by the throat and felt it snap in my hand. His body fell with a dry hard thud at my feet. I had no idea as to my own strength. The power of the Tribe rippled through me in great waves. It was an enticing, intoxicating energy and if I didn't maintain some sort of control, it could overpower me.

This is what the captain wanted. This is what Dr. Walters wanted. This is what they all wanted and I had it!

Waves of heat poured off me as I watched the captain's followers burn. I gazed up through the skylight. The moon shone high and full in sky, empowering me even further. There was nothing beyond my power to perform. All that was left for me to do was to complete the circle, to add Malik's power on to theirs and I would be invincible.

Gods, Mister Peters! They are black gods...

I could feel Nicah ordering the Tribe to destroy everything around them. Her hatred and anger had her insane with revenge. D`ike was urging her to maintain control, and I could feel all of them looking for Malik. They were inside me, as real but as intangible as a thought.

I ran up the steps to Star. I could hold her now. Malik could join his tribe now. I was able to control them. Their powers were subject to my will. I looked in Star's eyes and there was no mistaking the message in them this time.

Pride.

She was proud of me and I blushed as I held her. Thousands of images and memories flooded my mind: the craziness on the streets, being locked up in the Psyche Ward, Justice, Shakim, Kenyetta, the train stations. All of that just to get to this moment. Just to get to hold my baby again.

"Never too hot to hold my baby! Never gonna be that hot," I said crying from a mixture of joy and sheer exhaustion.

"I knew you would figure it out, Daddy! I knew you would come back for me!" she said, tears streaming down her face. "You can't keep it, Daddy; it belongs to them!" Her face was firm and stern. I understood what she meant.

I had become drunk with a power that wasn't rightfully mine. It belonged to the Tribe and I had to let it go. I concentrated on freeing them. I thought about the misty silver colored jungle I met Malik in. I thought of the women who danced through the tops of trees that were taller than buildings with an agility that defied human capabilities and I wished them back there.

I wished them home.

I could feel the power leaving me. Like the memory of a dream, it faded.

Star's eyes regained their normal color and as I held her, I could feel Malik's presence joining the rest. D`aim's fire died, leaving a silver colored ash on everything it touched.

I looked up and saw Tara still suspended high above us, unconscious. My heart ached for her. Even whipped and scarred, she was beautiful. I hoped she was just as much a victim in all of this as Star and I was, but I just wasn't sure. The only thing I was sure of was how much I loved her.

"Do you love her, Daddy?" Star asked me.

"Yes...but I-"

"Don't think you can trust her," Star said.

"Right."

"Come here, let me show you. Then you can make up your own mind."

She reached and held me by both ears. A shock went through me. My body went limp and in that second I saw everything that happened the night of the funeral.

CHAPTER X:

The Road to Hell is Paved with Good Intentions...

I had fallen into a deep sleep, exhausted from sex and drinking. Tara sat and stroked my face. I could see the look of love in her eyes. I could see every detail of my bedroom. It was like an incredibly vivid memory playing in my mind's eye. Tara looked up and saw Star standing there, quietly staring at us. Tara grabbed the sheet to cover us.

"Why did you want me to do this, Star? Why did you order me to do this on the day of my sister's-your mother's burial?" Tara asked.

"You should not question me, Tara. I know that which you do not. The dead know what the living are doing, Tara. Besides, I didn't ask you to do anything you didn't want to. You've always wanted my daddy."

"Yes! I wanted your daddy, Star! But I would have never done this without you ordering me to! Sharon was my sister and I loved her, Star! Tell me why it was so important that this happened today of all days!"

"There's no time for regrets, Tara. I see what's

coming. Do you think it was easy for me to have seen my mother in a coffin and had to act like a complete fool?" Star spoke with a quiet serene wisdom. She filled the room with her presence.

"Shhh! You'll wake him!" Tara whispered.

"He won't wake up now. I'll let him sleep through everything that's coming."

"What is coming, Star? Tell me what's going to happen."

"You cannot plant anger and expect happiness. You wanted to play the game, Tara. Now you have to finish it. You had me unlock doors that are still swinging on evil, slippery hinges. You have to see this through. You will reap a bitter harvest from this, but because you truly love my daddy it will be worth it."

The two of them stared hard at each other. Neither blinked, until Tara said:

"I'm sorry I had you play that game, Star. I really didn't know, but I do love your father. And I love you, Star. I don't know what vision you've seen, but I trust you."

"I love you too, Tara. Let's just hope that our love is enough to endure what's coming."

"What's coming?" Tara pleaded.

"The bad times," Star said sadly.

And that was when the bedroom door opened. Cleophus and Kenyetta walked into my bedroom. Tara scrambled to cover herself, pulling the sheet off me, wrapping it tightly around her body.

"What are you doing in here! Get the fuck out of here!" Tara pulled Star close and held her. The look on Star's face was one of vast sadness, yet expectation.

"It's time, Tara! The legend of the Silver Eyes is real! Give us the child so we can finish the ritual!" Kenyetta said.

"I'll give you ten seconds to get the fuck out of here before I call the cops!" Tara reached for the phone and Kenyetta grabbed her roughly by the hair.

"We got somebody we want you to meet!" he seethed, tearing the sheet off her breasts. The captain and Mr. Briggs walked in. A look of soaked raw panic covered Tara's face.

"You've sold us out!" she screamed at Kenyetta and Cleophus. "You've sold us out! Judas! Judas!"

They beat her until she passed out. One of the blows struck me in the head. That's why I woke up with such a headache.

"Leave them alone!" Star ordered and the two of them shrank back from her. Her voice boomed like thunder. Cleophus and Kenyetta ran behind the captain.

"Do you know who I am?" the captain asked Star.

"I know who you think you are." Star replied.

"I am not a man to bandy words or threats. Come with me."

"On two conditions. My father is to remain here, alive and Tara is not to be molested."

The captain stared at her with a hard inhuman glare that Star returned and doubled. Cleophus and Kenyetta trembled in their presence.

"Agreed," the captain said.

"I am so sorry, Star!" Tara whispered, half dazed. Her face swollen and bruised. "You have to believe me! I am so sorry! God knows I never meant for any of this to happen! He knows my intentions were good."

"The road to hell," Star said-

"Is paved with good intentions," I finished, coming out of the trance. Star let go of my ears and I held her tightly. "Star, why did you manipulate-why did you?-"

"She loves you, Daddy. That much I can tell you. She loves you," Star answered.

CHAPTER XI:

∞

Stars Never Eclipse!

Tara was still unconscious when I got her off that brace. I held her tightly and then I kissed her. I don't know why, it just sort of happened. One second I was staring at her, and the next my lips were pressed firmly against hers. Her eyes fluttered, as she woke up and said, "I guess we won after all!"

"Yes. I think we did," I said smiling. Somewhere in the deep recesses of my mind, I could see Malik running with his tribe in that beautiful misty jungle. "Let me take care of you," I said to her. "I think it's what Sharon would've wanted."

Star ran over and held us. I squeezed the both of them tightly, whispering a simple prayer of thanks.

"Where's the captain?" Tara asked crying. "Is he gone?"

"I…think so," I said looking around at the dead bodies that surrounded us. I naturally assumed the captain was among them.

"Good!" she gasped. "If he's really gone then all of this was worth it. They killed Sharon, David! It wasn't an accident! They killed her! They wanted me to give them Star, but I refused! I'm so sorry, David. I never meant for any of this to happen! They tricked me; I thought I was doing something good-"

"Shh! It's okay. I know what happened that night. It's all okay now." She settled in my arms and I held her and Star.

"Kenyetta and Cleophus tricked me, David. I thought I was doing something good. I thought I was helping the Tribe get revenge-"

"Revenge is a double edged sword. The wise warrior never fights for revenge," I said, remembering Malik's words.

When we finally emerged from that underground hellhole, it was daylight and the heatwave had broken. We stood on the beach and felt the cool, clean breeze caress us. The sun had just risen and the sky was a beautiful reddish-orange color. I held Star in my arm and clutched Tara's hand. I thought about the sacrifice Shakim made. He gave his life to help me rescue my daughter. His goddaughter. I would never forget that.

This would become one of my most treasured memories. My daughter, Tara and I watching the majestic splendor of God's sun rising.

"We did it, baby! We won!" I said to Star.

"Not yet, Daddy. We didn't win yet. The captain isn't dead. He can't be killed like that. He's not a real man, but a mixture of all the bad things people think and do to each other. Malik will be okay for a while, but the captain will be back. Next time he won't be able to trick me again!"

"What happened, baby? What did they do to you?" I asked, not sure I really wanted to hear. I wanted to believe the screams I heard in the G Building were just a result of Dr. Walter's mind games.

She shut her eyes and told me.

"Tara didn't know what doors she was opening, Daddy. She and some of the others thought they were doing good, but I knew better. The old lady told me the bad times were coming. She taught me how to use the Silver. I've seen so many bad times, Daddy. So many bad people, but there were good people too! People that helped me. People that-"

"Who, precious? Who are you talking about?" I asked. Tara wrapped her arms around herself and wept silently.

"You saw how they left the jungle-I saw what happened to them when they landed here! The captain took me back to slavery! Remember when you let me watch Roots and I had bad dreams? They weren't dreams, Daddy. They were memories! I was there! I walked with D`ike in Virginia, trying to give him a reason not to take his own life. I tried to help K`embe escape. I helped deliver S`ianna's baby. I held Molo's hands as he died, giving him faith there was something better waiting for him on the other side. I tried to give strength to T`keya, Meeka, Jomo and Iyanni as they were forced to act like circus clowns for food. I have seen these things. I was a part of these things. I know these things."

"Angel! No, don't tell me anymore! Don't say anything else! Let it stay in the past!" I pleaded, but Star was not finished recounting what happened to her.

"I taught some of the slaves how to read and

write. I forged passes for some, helping them get to the Underground Railroad. I climbed trees to cut down the bodies of the lynched. I held the heads of men who sat helplessly by and watched their wives, mothers, and daughters raped. I held the hands of mothers who prayed for the souls of their children as they watched them gasp for air, swinging from a rope while the Paddy Rollers drank and laughed. I helped dig the graves to bury the dead. I looked in the eyes of the elderly, wiped away their tears and swore to them things would get better. He sent me there to scare me, but I wouldn't let him. My Silver is strong and the captain couldn't tarnish it."

There was no sadness in her voice as she said these things. Her small chest filled with pride and respect. Her jaw set and locked. There was a fierce control about her. She was almost a stranger to me now. It was as if I was seeing her for the first time.

"Time is a funny thing, Daddy; the more of it that passes the more of it there is to pass. Malik is safe now, but for how long? There'll be others. They'll read about the power of the Silver Eyes and someone will figure out a way to bring them back. That's when the captain will return. He preys on the fears and greed of men. He believes he is right and he'll return because of his belief!

"The old lady, Nicah she made me see. She made me see what blacks did to each other and what they're doing to each other now. I tried to tell her not to hate, because hate only makes more hate. But I understood why she hated, Daddy. I understood why, because of all the things she'd been through. She was the Tribe's mother and a mother has to protect her children. It's hard for her to forgive; I don't think she ever will. That's why it will keep happening. Nicah's anger and the captain's will are two bad circles locked together: The symbol of infinity.

"So much pain...so many bad feelings. The captain will be back. I only hope that when he comes back I'm strong enough to finish him off for good!"

As the waves rolled onto the beach, I understood. So long as blacks betrayed each other as they did in Tribal Africa, the captain would find a way to return. It would start again and again.

"How did you escape? I mean, from the past?"

"Justice rescued me, and after he did I sent him to you."

I held Tara tightly, pressing her head in my chest.

"Did you meet him? Can you tell me what happened after they took you?" I asked Tara, but she was in no mood to relive the horrors she'd gone through.

"Time is a funny thing, Daddy." Star repeated this with a wisdom that far belied her years. "We came close a lot of times. We almost beat the captain a lot of times and not just Blacks. There were a lot of good white people who fought him, too. There were white men who hid me from him; some hid me in the room with their own children. A lot of people met him and recognized him for who he was. So much pain...he killed so many good men.

"I was in yesterday, waiting for a tomorrow that never came. I sent Justice to you, to help you."

"But why did you send him to me, baby? Why didn't you just have him rescue you?" I asked her, confused and a bit scared.

"You needed him more. Tara had me to protect her, but you were by yourself. The captain tried to scare me by saying his people would kill you if I didn't call all twelve, but I knew Justice was with you. I knew you'd be okay.

"We have to find those pictures, Daddy. All of them!" She added somberly. "I'm going to need them for the next time. Next time it will be different. Next time I'll win!"

"Star, what else do you know about Justice? Where did he come from?"

"I sent him to you, Daddy. I sent him to help you, but you don't need him anymore. You have to find those pictures. You have to find them and we have to make sure the captain never finds Malik's jungle again!"

"Who was he, baby? How did you send him to me?"

"I made him out of the Silver of different people I met. He had Dexter's strength and kind eyes, Shakim's toughness and he had your brains."

"Dexter?"

"The Rasta who sold us the sneakers, remember?"

That's why Justice always smelled like incense!

"Malik broke the circle because he had to, Daddy. That day on the beach when Nicah said the curse Malik knew if he didn't break the circle her anger could have destroyed everything. Hate only makes more hate. Fire burns everything it touches. Malik had to break the circle, Daddy. The captain knew this. He used Malik's integrity and his honor against him. That's how the captain won that day on the beach. But it's also how he lost today, because you have the same honor and integrity Malik had. Malik knew the only way to truly defeat the captain was to wait. The circle will be complete again, Daddy. The circle will be complete again."

A chill went through me when she said that. It made me think of all the sacrifices our forefathers made in anticipation of future generations having a better life. If Malik willingly put himself through that hell so that Star and I-his descendents-would have the opportunity to defeat Captain Pearson then he was one hundred times the man I am.

"An old man once told me," Star said, "the ways of the righteous sometimes seem foolish to the wicked. And that good wins, because it stands firm where evil bends."

There was something different about her, something grown-up and more than a bit sad. This ordeal had taken her childhood away. It had shown her things no child should see. Star went through ten times the hell I went through. She had changed. Her demeanor. Her vocabulary. The grim and brooding way she now spoke. I wondered when I would hear Star laugh again.

It would be a long, long, long time.

There was an aura about her now. The same aura that surrounded the Silver Eyes. She had their nobility. In that silver dress and head wrap the presence of royalty surrounded her. I began to understand what Mr. Levy and my sister meant about protecting Star at all cost. It was as if the future of mankind depended on this small prodigy in front of me. There was something wonderful, yet peculiarly scary about her.

Something I was barely beginning to comprehend.

"And a little child shall lead them," Tara hinted with awe and reverence in her voice. "David, don't ask anymore. Just be thankful that for now it's over. If it takes me a lifetime to make this up to you and Star, I will. I promise you, I will."

I nodded ever so slightly, staring at the little woman in front of me who before this dreadful trial was just a little girl excited over a new pair of sneakers. Tara kneeled and held Star, gently kissing her hands. Star stroked her head as if she were the elder and Tara the child.

I helped deliver S`ianna's baby...

She's not a child anymore! I thought to myself. She'll never be the same after this! What type of therapy are we all going to need now! Maybe once she's back in school, with normal kids-kids her own age-her own age? This child has lived a dozen life times! She's seen things that would destroy the above-average human being!

I looked at both of them, marveling. There was so much they weren't telling me, and I felt it was for my own good. Waves of disgust went through me just thinking about what could have happened to Star and yet somehow I knew as horrible as my imaginings were, they were nothing in comparison to the reality of what happened to her.

Yet, she sent Justice to help me. She was stronger than I was and for the rest of my life she would be a source of strength and inspiration to me. A constant reminder of the decent and good in the world.

Tara and I went back and found Shakim's body. We buried him on the beach. I said a simple prayer asking that his soul find rest and comfort. Tara wept silently by my side. I prayed to be worthy of Shakim's sacrifice.

"This was my godfather, Shakim." Star raised her hands and the wind picked up considerably. Her eyes glowed with a deep silver fire and it seemed the tide spoke with her. "He wasn't a wealthy man. He wasn't famous. He wasn't scholarly. He wasn't pious. But what he was is greater than all of those things. Wealth can be lost. Fame forgotten. Scholars can be challenged. Even the pious may fall. But Shakim had honor, decency and love. For in the end he gave his life for another. I ask that the Source of my Silver watch over him. Bless him to see the fruit of his sacrifice. Amen."

Energy crackled around her. I stood speechless watching. The power radiating off Star dwarfed even that of the Tribe.

"Star! How can you do this?" I screamed into the increasing wind. "The Tribe has their power back! How can you do this?"

"The moon can eclipse," Star answered, staring up into the sky. "The sun can eclipse…but stars never eclipse." Thunder cracked the sky like a steel whip and the wind blew stronger. Lightning danced in jagged streaks. Rain fell in huge sheets from a cloudless sky.

"God chose my name!" Star proclaimed proudly. Her small fists thrust skyward and the sky seemed to explode in agreement with her. The sand under her feet warped and melted into clear crystal. The air around her was thick with ozone and static energy.

Stars never eclipse.

The road ahead of us would be a long and dangerous one. Malik charged me to find and recover those portraits and I have yet to do that. I know I will never have peace of mind until I do find them.

Whenever there's a full moon, I can't sleep. I keep hearing the call of the jungle, and somewhere in the distance, I hear Malik telling me to find those portraits…

Before the nightmare happens again.

EPILOGUE:

The Alpha and the Omega…

Captain Luke Bartholomew Pearson got up out of the debris and regained his bearings. He had lost again, but it was of little consequence. Time is a funny thing, and it is as unending as it is unforgiving. He looked around at the charred remains of his followers, so many sacrificed in vain. He was so close to gaining the Tribe's powers; he actually managed to get eleven of them this time.

His cardinal mistake was underestimating the little girl, Star. That lapse in judgement proved to be his sole undoing. Manipulating the others was easy. Blacks were so predictable. Even David and Tara were typical darkies. He had them pegged correctly from the beginning.

But Star…

She was the culmination of every good trait in the Silver Eyes. She had the grace of D`aim and the persistence of K`embe. She had Nicah's fiery resolve and D`ike's patience. Most of all she had their strengths and none of their weaknesses.

She was content and at peace with herself. There was no desire or want in her heart. Most people, even children wanted something, but Star was happy. Not happy because of anything material, she was happy because of something she had on the inside-something even he could not take from her. He could not snare her with false promises and he could not trick her with lies. His threats were as futile as cotton attempting to smash steel.

There was something else that was terrifyingly different about her. Something he could not control-there was a part of her soul he couldn't see into. This worried him more than anything else.

He beat and yelled at her, but he couldn't scare her. He made her watch as he tortured and killed help-less innocents because she would not obey him, and even then she refused to submit to him. There was a quiet serenity about her, which he found repulsive and dangerous, because others drew strength from her.

His power rested in his faith. Since that first fateful day in the forbidden jungle, he proved to be the Silver Eyes' master because he believed harder. Now here was this child-this black child who chal-lenged his faith and shook his resolve.

Never in the centuries he had played the game of hunt and capture had he encountered such a spirit.

She had absolutely no fear of death. The cap-tain had never heard of such a thing, not even from the strongest of his warriors, let alone a child-a darkie child at that!

She has been here before, he thought to him-self, amused by this turn of events. He was more than a bit intrigued by this child. No matter what he threw at her, he could not shatter her spirit.

He could not break her circle.

Suppose there were others with this… gift?

He wondered how he would defeat this upstart the next time they met.

And, oh-would there be a next time!

The woman screamed from the pains of labor. The midwives held her, ordering her to push. She sat up, straining with all her might to force the child out. It would be her first and she prayed to the gods for a son.

By her side in the birthing room, her husband nervously held her hands, praying for a strong, healthy baby- one that would bring joy, honor and prosperity to the family.

His beloved wife screamed again and he felt a dagger of fear pierce his soul.

"Push! Come on, mommy! One big push should do it! Push hard, now!" the mid-wife urged. The woman bore down and pushed with all of her strength. The pain was excruciating as she felt the child slip from her womb into the world.

She screamed again, but this time there was the distinct scream of another. The child was born. A rush of exhilaration filled the room as all heard the child cry.

"Congratulations, Mr. and Mrs. Peters! You have a healthy newborn son!" the mid-wife smiled, placing the infant in Tara's arms. "Have you thought of a name for the little prince?" she asked, as she took notice of the time and recorded the birth accordingly.

"Malik," Star said proudly. "It means king."

"Yes. Malik. King. Of course!" the midwife answered.

"He's beautiful!" Tara cried. "He's so perfect!" Tears of joy and pride streamed down her face. The pain of childbirth was quickly replaced by love for the bundle in her arms. She looked up into the eyes of her husband, David and saw the love and adoration in his face. He leaned down and gently kissed her forehead.

The past few months went by in a blur and everyone was anxious to put the events of the black-out behind them. The governor set up a special restoration fund, giving out low-cost loans, enabling business and homeowners in the hardest hit areas to rebuild. The ensuing construction provided jobs for many, causing the local economy to boom.

The official explanation was a hallucinogenic drug that somehow made it into the water supply and severe sunspots that played havoc with the electro-magnetic field surrounding the eastern seaboard caus-ing the blackout. People bought it, if only because they were anxious for an explanation so they could forget.

Star looked at her new baby brother for the first time. When she first insisted on being there when the baby was born David and Tara put up little argu-ment. She chuckled at that-since her time with the captain she had seen many births, even helped in the delivery of a few. Each one was just as special; each newborn child represented the hope and future of all mankind. Of course most of the babies she saw come into the world have gone on to their final reward by now.

Time is a funny thing.

Many times David would ask her about those dark days, but she knew it would be a long time before he was ready to accept the total truth. She had lived a hundred lifetimes, experiencing every imaginable facet of the Black-American Diaspora. From the slave auctions to the narrow thorn and bristled laced path of freedom. From the dismantling of the black family, to the restoration and renaissance of the black soul. Knowing David's frail psyche, they would have to readmit him to the psychiatric ward if he knew even half of the things she witnessed and lived through.

There are some things better left in the past.

Tara's pregnancy helped to quiet the nightmares. The birth of a newborn is the herald of growth and a renewal of spirit. A new child was just what was needed to chase away the gloom and bring sunshine into the family. Joy reigned as the anticipation of the new arrival filled the home with gladness. The miracle of life was celebrated with great esteem as Star watched Tara's womb swell with the promise of hope. The excitement of her pregnancy helped them to forget the evil that ruled the streets when the lights were out.

But Star would never forget. Although the excessive rapes and murders ceased, there was still enough hate and evil thoughts for the captain to feed off-enough to sustain him for the next millenium. She would forever remain vigil in her watch for him. He would never again be able to take her unawares.

David and Tara continually showered her with affection, constantly reminding her that although she would no longer be the baby she was still cherished and loved. Secretly she wished they didn't dote on her so much, it would only make it harder to leave when the time came. She didn't mind the new arrival; she was more than happy to have a baby brother.

Besides, she would need someone strong to help her when the captain returned. She was aware of his plots and machinations. He would apply every cunning and deceitful trick imaginable next time they met, but she'd be ready.

She couldn't wait until her brother was old enough to begin training with her. She would show him how to use his Silver.

"He has the mark, Daddy!" Star exclaimed with glee, pointing to the birthmark on the infant's arm. "Now the circle is complete."

∞   ∞   ∞